Studies in the History of
Economic Theory before 1870

By the same author

Nassau Senior and Classical Economics
Housing and the State, 1919–1944
Innovations in Building Materials – An Economic Study
The British Building Industry – Four Studies of Response
   and Resistance to Change

Studies in the History of Economic Theory before 1870

MARIAN BOWLEY
Professor of Political Economy
in the University of London

HUMANITIES PRESS
New York 1973

© Marian Bowley 1973

First published in the United States of America 1973 by
HUMANITIES PRESS INC.
450 Park Avenue South New York NY 10016

Library of Congress Cataloging in Publication Data
Bowley, Marian, 1911–
    Studies in the history of economic theory before 1870.
    1.   Economics — History. I.   Title.
HB75.B777   1973   330.1'09   73–12761
ISBN 0–391–00321–6

Printed in Great Britain

Contents

Preface

Histories of economic theory offer a fascinating subject for study and a history of histories would throw a good deal of light on the history of economic theory itself. No such study is included in this book and this preface is only intended to indicate the nature of the studies included.

Some histories are essays, often brief, appended to a new work in order to show its relation to the work of predecessors. Naturally such essays are apt to illuminate the views of the author rather than those of his predecessors, for the object is usually either to show the originality or superiority of the new work or to find support for it by appeal to past authorities. Such history is liable to be highly selective, if not obviously biased, nevertheless it can be stimulating and important to contemporaries as a guide to the understanding of the new work. It provides incidentally material for later historians. Other types of histories which are intended to be more general surveys of the development of economic theory also involuntarily provide material for later historians. It is not only that the actual choice of periods and theories for study inevitably reflects the influence of interests prevailing at the time when the historian is writing, but the judgements passed on the theories included provide information also as to the current state of economic theory and the outlook of the historian himself. These influences cannot I think be eliminated and it does mean that the history of theory has to be continually rewritten, since the usual purpose of histories is to consider the extent to which earlier economists have contributed to the solution of problems with which later economists happen to be concerned at any particular moment. In some ways this is the type of history which is of most interest to economists and may be of most value to them by suggesting the need for new developments, either to complete or to generalise earlier theories or to modify them to make them relevant to current problems. Unfortunately this approach can obscure the reasons why earlier writers tackled particular problems, and even the nature of the actual questions they were trying to answer and the meaning which they attached to particular words. Not unnaturally this quite often results in misunderstanding of the answers as well as the neglect of some of the relevant discussions. This must detract from any value the study of history of theory may have.

The studies in this book deal with a few of the problems which seem to me to need reconsideration for these reasons. I have attempted therefore to adopt an approach which I think is not used as often as it profitably could be. This involves trying to discover some of the actual questions that some of the economists of the pre-classical and the classical periods were asking, why they formulated them in the way they did and how this influenced their answers and, also, what assumptions they made implicitly as well as explicitly. In brief I have attempted to look at the treatment of various problems by a number of writers in their own analytical setting rather than from the point of view of modern economic theory. I hope that in consequence I have avoided writing of them as though I were correcting students' essays pointing out with regret that they had not read an important article in a recent issue of some modern journal. The results of adopting this approach has surprised me and I am convinced that its neglect led me to misinterpret certain aspects of the theory of value and wages in my *Nassau Senior and Classical Economics.*[1]

The first study in this new book is a re-examination of the theories of interest developed by seventeenth-century English writers. This demonstrates that at least two theories of interest were developed, a monetary *and* a non-monetary one; the differing relations of these theories to the theories of money, the balance of trade and economic activity of the period are also discussed. The later studies in the book deal with various problems in the developement of the theories of value, wages and profit. A study of the theory of value in the seventeenth century is included: this is a revision and extension of my 1963 *Economica*

---

[1] This was recently reprinted. Unfortunately I was not consulted about the reprint so I was unable to indicate in any way that I had revised some of the views that I had held when I first wrote the book more than thirty years ago.

article on this subject in the light of the realisation that the development of the theory of value in the seventeenth century was to a large extent a by-product of the work on money, trade and interest. This is followed by a comparative study of the development of the analysis of the price mechanism in the eighteenth century with particular reference to Cantillon and Adam Smith. It is much influenced by my investigation of seventeenth-century developments and their effect on later writers, since this convinced me that, in common with many others, I had hitherto failed to appreciate fully the nature of some of the questions Adam Smith tried to deal with and the interest of his discussion of them. This leads to what I believe is a new explanation of why the labour theory of value appears in the *Wealth of Nations* and why it occupies only a few short paragraphs.

The fourth study, 'Utility, the Paradox of Value and "all that" and Classical Economics', is the natural outcome of my modified interpretation of Adam Smith. It seems to me that the significance of the work of Adam Smith and the classical economists on the relation of utility to value has been misunderstood in some respects by other people, as well as by me, as a result of the enthusiasm for the marginal school. A revised view is put forward. The fifth study, 'Market Structures and the Theory of Value in Classical Economics', deals with problems of the analysis of market structures in relation to the break-up of the classical theory of value; this was touched upon only in my old book on Senior.

While the second, third, fourth and fifth studies are all directly concerned with problems of the history of value theory and the price mechanism, the sixth study deals with some of the aspects of wages and profit theory which of necessity emerged with the development of the theory of the price mechanism. Recognition of the need for theories of wages and profits at all is a specific contribution of eighteenth-century economists, for whereas they inherited a substantial contribution to value theory from their predecessors, they inherited little but opinions, policies and prejudices about the determination of wages and profits. The sixth study examines the influence of this situation, combined with particular approaches to wages and profits arising from the price mechanism analyses of Cantillon and Adam Smith, on the development of wages and profit theory; it includes consideration of attempts at emancipation from these influences. The study seems to me to demonstrate once again the importance of considering the growth of classical political economy in relation to its eighteenth-century roots if its peculiar achievements and failures are to be understood.

University College London   Marian Bowley

I English Theories of Interest in the Seventeenth Century reconsidered

PART 1   PROBLEMS OF CONTROL OF THE SUPPLY OF MONEY

> Money is but the Fat of the Body-politick, whereof too much doth as often hinder its Agility, as too little makes it sick.
> PETTY[1]

(i) Introduction

During the two centuries since Adam Smith launched his attack on the Mercantile system, outstanding contributions to our knowledge of seventeenth-century thought on problems of money, trade and interest, have been made by historians of economic thought of the neo-classical school, for instance Viner and Heckscher. Explicitly or implicitly they have considered the work of the seventeenth century in the light of their correctness according to classical and neo-classical theory. The Keynesian revolution neessarily required a re-assessment in the light of new criteria and Keynes himself provided an initial and highly controversial essay in re-assessment in Chapter 23 of *The General Theory of Employment, Interest and Money*. I am not concerned in this study directly with these questions; rather it is a tentative attempt to look at English seventeenth-century theories of interest, for there were more than one, in the light of two facts. The first is that discussions of problems both of money and foreign trade had been going on intermittently over some centuries without reference to the possible role of the rate of interest as an economic phenomenon, except to a limited extent in connection with the concealed interest-payments on loans made through foreign exchange

---

[1] *Verbum Sapienti*, Hull's edition, 1899, Vol. I, p. 113. All page references to Petty's work apply to Hull's edition.

bills, the so-called 'dry exchange'. This was the natural consequence of the legal ban on interest on money loans, lifted finally
in England only in 1571. The second fact I am concerned with is
that in seventeenth-century England and Scotland there were a
multitude of projects for establishing banks, but, not only no
banking system but no banks except of ephemeral character until
the establishment of the Banks of England and Scotland at the end
of the century. Similarly there was no paper money, in the ordinary sense; there were only coins and the precious metals and various credit instruments such as trade bills and goldsmiths notes.

It is the problem of the influence and interaction of these
circumstances on the English seventeenth-century discussions of
the rate of interest as an economic phenomenon that this study is
concerned with. The question of arrangement is complicated by
the fact that there were at least two theories of the role and determination of the rate of interest with variants. To avoid confusion
I have started by indicating briefly what seem to me the relevant
aspects of the heritage of the seventeenth century in the fields of
money and trade theory and the actual seventeenth-century developments of them. The discussion of actual theories of interest put
forward follows in the second part of this study, with some brief
reflections on their relation to certain aspects of the projects for
banks.

(ii) *The Necessary Stock of Money and the Balance of Trade before 1600*

The great seventeenth-century discussions of money, foreign trade
and the exchanges were continuations of earlier discussions which
had occurred intermittently from early in the middle ages. R. de
Roover in his book, *Gresham and the Foreign Exchanges*, and
R. G. Hawtrey in his essay, 'The Silver Recoinages in England',
in his *Currency and Credit* make this clear. From different angles
they demonstrate the belief in the existence from the middle ages
to the late seventeenth century of an endemic problem, that of
maintaining the supply of metallic money so as to preserve what
Petty described as the quantity of money 'necessary to drive the
Trade of the Nation'. For brevity I shall call this 'the necessary
stock of money' following the page heading of Chapter V of
Petty's *Verbum Sapienti* in Hull's edition. The course of these
earlier discussions shows that in England consideration of foreign

trade and the exchanges was from time to time linked with the early attempts to solve the problem of maintaining an adequate supply of a means of payment in the form of metallic money.

It so happens that the discussions occurred after the attitude of the church to trade had passed through a period of slow modification. The authority of the church might still be invoked on the one hand to support the traditional view that since profitable trade involved buying cheap and selling dear, traders inevitably broke the rule of the just price. This contributed to the popular belief that in trade one man's gain was another man's loss so that there was no mutual gain from trade. On the other hand there had been learned churchmen from the time of St Augustine who attempted a more fundamental analysis of the nature of trade. Considerable progress had been made with this inquiry by the thirteenth century, and late in that century a particularly complete justification of trade had been put forward by the schoolman, Ricardus of Media Villa. It is convenient to quote Beer's version of his reasoning:

Let us envisage two countries, A and B, unequally endowed by nature. A produces corn in abundance, but little wine, while country B has an abundance of wine and a deficiency of corn. We know that the market price or the just price of a commodity varies with its plentifulness or scarcity. The same commodity when plentiful is less appreciated than when it is scarce. In this manner a sextarium of corn in country A will be cheaper than in country B, while conversely a dolium of wine in country A will be dearer than in country B. Now, it is natural for the business of trade and commerce to equalise supply. The merchant, then, buys corn cheap in country A and sells it at the higher market price that is ruling in country B, or he buys wine cheap in country B and sells it at the higher market price that is ruling in country A, so that in reality the consumer is not in the least overcharged, for he pays for each commodity the normal price, the just price, which is ruling in his respective country. The exchanges are equal, yet the merchant earns his profit, and he does so rightfully, for, far from having injured either country, he brought benefit to both. His profit is therefore neither usury nor *turpe lucrum*. The same rule of equality of exchanges which we find in international trade applies also to the business transactions of individuals in their own country. The commodity which the consumer receives is of more immediate utility to him than the money he gives for it, while to the merchant the money he receives for his commodity is of greater immediate utility than the commodity which he surrenders, so both draw equal benefits from the exchange.[2]

Despite Ricardus the traditional belief that trade involved no mutual gain did not disappear, and discussions of the monetary problems connected with foreign trade were frequently entangled with the implications of the doctrine of the just price and the nature of trade. It is, I think, partly at least owing to the existence of these diverse opinions about the nature of trade that so many inconsistent statements were made even in what may be called 'high level' discussions, as distinct from popular ones; sometimes they appear to be introduced disingenuously when they can be used to strengthen an argument.[3]

It is not necessary to elaborate on this matter further before looking quickly at some of the problems connected with money, and the contributions made to their solution before the seventeenth century. Since paper money was not available the supply of means of payment depended on the supply of the precious metals, particularly silver which was more plentiful than gold. Before the inflows from the New World increases in supply depended on the limited output of the mines in the old world. Increases in the volume of transactions for any reason must therefore have tended to exert a downward pressure on prices unless counteracted by increases in velocity of circulation or dishoarding or debasement. With many prices fixed by law or custom any such downward pressure would presumably be impeded and checks to growth and unemployment of resources may have occurred from time to time. For those countries which had no gold or silver mines, or inadequate ones, the supply of the means of payment depended on the extent to which the precious metals were imported from, or exported to, other countries apart from internal hoarding or dishoarding. In this general *Konjunktur*, if any country lost silver (or gold) through international trade or financial transactions a

[2] Quoted from M. Beer, *Early British Economics*, Ch. III, pp. 42–3.
[3] See on this Viner, *Studies in the Theory of International Trade*, Ch. I.

local crisis might develop; complaints of shortage of circulating medium might be made and associated with the depression of trade and employment. The difficulties were enhanced by deterioration of the coinage from wear and tear and stripping of coins and culling of heavy coins for export. The needs of governments for actual cash for their own transactions varied of course with their activities; wars in particular increased their needs. They had a special interest in net inflows for this facilitated the collection of dues at the ports payable in the precious metals while seignorage on the metal taken to the mints for coinage increased their cash revenues.

Quite apart from the special requirements of governments the problems of preventing the disappearance of money from the circulation stimulated discussion of what determined the inflows and outflows of the precious metals. The simple theorem that if the balance of trade was favourable the precious metals would tend to enter the country, and vice versa was early recognised. For instance in 1381, a time of mounting anxiety about the state of the coinage in England and the adequacy of its supply and the level of employment, an official of the Mint, Richard Leicester, pointed out that:

> as to this that no gold and silver comes into England, but that which is in England is carried beyond the sea, I maintain that it is because the land spends too much in merchandise, as in grocery, mercery and peltry, or wines, red, white and sweet, and also in exchanges made to the court of Rome in divers ways. Wherefore the remedy seems to me to be that each merchant bringing merchandise into England take out of the commodities of the land as much as his merchandise aforesaid shall amount to; and that none carry gold or silver beyond the sea.

His colleague Richard Aylesbury made a similar statement.[4]

The principle was restated at fairly frequent intervals with

[4] *English Economic History: Selected Documents*, ed. Bland, Brown and Tawney, pp. 220–2.

It will be noticed that Leicester makes no distinction between visible and invisible items, and after the term 'balance of trade' was introduced in the seventeenth century it was used in the sense of the balance of payments as well as in the more limited sense of the balance of visible trade.

varying degrees of sophistication during the sixteenth century. For instance Clement Armstrong expounded it about 1535; it was included in the *Discourse of the Common Weal of this Realm of England* probably written in 1549 by John Hales; it was expounded by Sir William Cholmeley about 1553, by Sir Thomas Gresham and Sir William Cecil in 1559 and 1564 respectively, by a Mr Lewis, M.P. in 1593 as well as by a number of other writers, some anonymous.[5]

The nature of the specie points and of the terms of trade and the effects of the exchange rates on the latter were also recognised. It was argued that unfavourable terms of trade made it more difficult to balance payments for imports and exports. (The traditional view that gain from trade depended on buying cheap and selling dear naturally predisposed some writers to attach importance to favourable terms of trade.) Gresham and Cholmeley among others elucidated all these matters. It was also realised that the rates of foreign exchange contained an element of interest. This was admitted in the report of the Royal Commission on the Exchanges in 1564.[6]

The development in Europe from the fourteenth to the sixteenth century of international money markets and banks had facilitated not only the financing of trade through foreign exchange bills but, also, short-term international borrowing and lending by means of foreign exchange bills unconnected with trade transactions. As there was no organised market either for foreign exchange bills or for capital, and there were no banks in England, English borrowers and lenders who had the necessary expertise used the foreign financial centres by using foreign exchange bills.[7] In this way movements of short-term funds

[5] R. R. de Roover gives a most interesting account of these discussions in his *Gresham and the Foreign Exchanges*, Ch. 2, and a useful list of statements on the balance of trade theorem on p. 260, Table 4. On the *Discourse of the Common Weal* see n. 11, p. 8 below.

[6] E.g. by Cholmeley and Gresham. The *Report* is reprinted in *Tudor Economic Documents*, ed. Tawney and Power, Vol. III. See also de Roover, pp. 184 et seq.

[7] This practice was sometimes attacked with great vigour, for instance by Thomas Wilson in his *Discourse upon Usury* of 1572. Tawney's introduction to the 1925 reprint which he edited contains a great deal of useful information on the whole problem of the attitudes towards foreign exchange transactions.

could influence the sterling exchanges and at the same time the interest element in the loan transactions affected the spread of the exchange rates. For these reasons the foreign exchange markets were of peculiar importance to the economy of this country which in many respects could have been justly described then by a de Gaulle as 'a backward offshore island'. The concern caused by movements of the foreign exchanges against sterling was reflected in the setting up of four Royal Commissions on the exchanges to consider successive crises and outflows of the precious metals in the twenty years after the great Elizabethan revaluation of 1560.

The individual factors or combination of factors to which any particular occurrence of unfavourable exchanges or balance of payments was attributed varied. They included failure or dislocation of foreign markets, excess of luxury imports, speculation and unfavourable terms of trade, culling and export of the heavier coins. Whether or not the crisis was directly reflected in unemployment, or with the failure of a particular market, unemployment was associated with crises and thus there was anxiety lest a shortage of money should lead to a slowing down of economic activity.[8] The question of practical interest was thus naturally *not* whether it was desirable to prevent unfavourable exchanges and outflows of the precious metals, *but* how to do it. One of the favoured methods was to try to control the exchanges, and Gresham's abortive attempt to establish an exchange equalisation account is a well-known illustration of the seriousness with which the problem was regarded. It was reflected also in contemporary pamphlet literature.

De Roover[9] shows that it was early recognised that deliberate debasement of the coinage provided an immediate answer to shortages of the circulating medium, the precious metals. It was apparently realised also that when the coinage had deteriorated by wear and tear so far that a general re-coinage was necessary, there would be less disturbance to economic life if the new coinage was based on the general level of the existing metallic content of the worn coinage. (This method was of course also cheaper.) In these cases the supply of money was maintained by official recognition of a *de facto* lower metallic standard of the coinage.

---

[8] See for instance de Roover, Ch. 2, and Charles Wilson, *Mercantilism*, pp. 17 et seq.

[9] Ch. 2. See also Hawtrey, op. cit.

Many of the medieval debasements were of this type. The fact that different countries pursued such policies in complete independence of each other added to the monetary disturbances.

Deliberate debasements had of course a certain popularity with impecunious governments as one of the easiest ways of increasing revenue. After debasements of this type however it was not unusual for attempts to be made to raise the metallic content of the coinage again towards the old standard. One of the most famous revaluations of this type in England was that of Elizabeth Tudor's reign when the coinage was restored after the prolonged debasement of the three previous reigns.

There was indeed ample practical experience of debasements and revaluations to stimulate attempts to analyse their consequences. A condemnation based on something like a scientific analysis of the evils of deliberate debasements and of deteriorating metallic currencies was provided about the middle of the fourteenth century by the French churchman Nicholas Oresme.[10] He showed that such debasements impoverished the people in general to the benefit of the King and dealers in money. His conclusions about the tendency of worn and debased money to drive good money out of circulation is recognised as an early statement of the so-called Gresham's Law.

The *Discourse of the Common Weal of this Realm of England*, provided a particularly able analysis of the effects of debasement on prices and on transferring wealth from those with fixed money incomes to those with flexible incomes; it attributed much of the contemporary distress among workmen to this.[11] Official recognition of the effects of debasement on prices and the dislocation caused by revaluations appeared in Elizabeth Tudor's proclamation of 27 September 1560 preceding the great revaluation. It states that owing to the debasement prices have increased 'to the lamentable and manifeste hurte and oppression of the state' and goes on to explain that the people who have suffered most are 'Pensioners, souldyers, and all hyred servantes, and other

---

[10] Nicholas Oresme 1320–82. *Tractatus de Origine, Natura, Jure et Mutationibus Monetarium.*

[11] Although written about 1549, the *Discourse* was first published in 1581 with a dedication by W.S. See Lamond's edn of 1893, pp. 17–21, 67–69, 104 particularly. W.S. added that now it was not debasement but the inflow of the precious metals keeping prices high. pp. xxxiii and 185–8.

meane people that lyve by any kynde of wages, and not by rentes of landes, or trade of marchandise'.[12]

Appreciation of the effects of changes in the supply of money on prices did not perhaps require a major analytical effort in relation to debasements and revaluations of the coinage. In England alone there were plenty of examples even if the changes were modest by modern standards. There had been seven debasements in England from 1299 to 1526 and during these two and a quarter centuries the weight of the silver penny had been reduced from $22\frac{1}{2}$ grains to $10\frac{2}{3}$ grains. These debasements were followed by those of Henry VIII, Edward VI, and Mary Tudor and the Elizabethan revaluation already mentioned.[13] Between the latter and the controversy over the re-coinage at the end of the seventeenth century, however, there was only one quite small debasement (1601); discussions in England became concerned with the effects of changes in supplies of the precious metals on prices with unchanged metallic contents of the coinage. A distinction was recognised between the familiar case in which the value of the coin changed in relation both to the value of goods and to the precious metals, and the new case in which the value of the coin fell only in relation to goods. This distinction appeared in a later version (1581) of the *Discourse of the Common Weal* already mentioned. It had been made even earlier by Bodin in France.[14]

This section has, I hope, served to demonstrate that English seventeenth-century writers on interest started out with a considerable heritage of tenets and theories about money. The belief in the need to maintain a supply of circulating medium appropriate to the needs of the economy was firmly imbedded and, also, that changes in the supply of money affected employment. There was also a considerable body of ideas about the effects of change in the supply of money on prices and the distribution of income. Moreover the terms of trade and the relation of the balance of payments and foreign exchange rates to inflows and outflows of

---

[12] *Tudor Economic Documents*, Vol. II, p. 196. The Proclamation goes on to set out the measures intended to ease the transition to the new coinage to avoid loss to holders of the old coins, etc.

[13] See de Roover, Ch. 2.

[14] See n. 11 above. Jean Bodin 1520–1596. Bodin's contributions to the problem are contained in his *Résponse aux Paradoxes de M. de Malestroit touchant l'enchérissement de toutes les choses et des monnaies . . . etc.* 1568 and *Discours sur le rehaussement et diminution des monnaies . . . etc.* 1578.

the precious metals had been the subject of prolonged and well-known discussions.

Such a heritage of ideas is not easily or quickly discarded; their influence continued and many were developed further throughout the seventeenth century. Owing to the legal bans on interest before 1571, however, these ideas had been developed without regard to the possible role of the rate of interest or the factors determining its level. Hence anyone who advanced a theory of interest inconsistent with the traditional ideas of the importance of the supply of money was faced with the problem of showing them to be unsound or irrelevant, and was moreover necessarily involved with questioning the importance of the theories concerned with the balance of trade.

The next section is devoted to indicating the seventeenth-century analytical background to the discussion of the rate of interest.

(iii) The Necessary Stock of Money and the Balance of Trade in the Seventeenth Century

The great controversy over the foreign exchange early in the seventeenth century naturally emphasised the importance of a connection between economic activity and outflows of the precious metals. It is of particular concern to us that discussions of the economic desirability of lowering the legal rate of interest took place at the same time.

In 1600 yet another Royal Commission had been set up to consider the familiar problems – decline in sales abroad, unfavourable exchanges, outflows of the precious metals and depression at home. The famous, or notorious, Gerhard de Malynes was a member of this Commission and published his views on causes and cures of the troubles in 1601 in his *Treatise of the Canker of England's Commonwealth*. It is this pamphlet which provides the literary beginning of the discussion to be considered in this section.

Malynes was in complete agreement with the general opinion that the outflow of the precious metals had depressing effects on activity at home and that it occurred when expenditure abroad exceed earnings abroad. In his view it was necessary to prevent the outflow and also desirable to have an inflow. An inflow would, he claimed, mean favourable exchange rates which would improve the terms of trade, make it easier for exports to pay for imports, increase the yield of customs and increase the amount of bullion taken to the Mint for coining and therefore the revenue of the Crown. It would also, he claimed, increase employment at home.[15] In a later pamphlet Malynes argued that the export of capital had disadvantages in addition to its effect on the exchanges. By diverting capital abroad it prevented investment in the provision of the equipment, ships and gear which was so badly needed by the fishing industry which was considered at this period to be of much public importance.[16]

Malynes, for all the abuse hurled at him by some of his contemporaries who disagreed with his policy, had a subtle intellect. He proceeded to consider whether the quantity theory of money in the simple form then usually accepted had any relevance to the problems of inflows and outflows. He pointed out that while individually goods are cheap or dear according to the demand for and supply of them, plenty of money made things in general dear, and vice versa:

> plentie of money maketh generally things deare, and scarcitie of money maketh likewise generally things good cheape . . . Whereas thinges particularly are also deare or good cheape, according to plentie or scarcitie of the thinges themselves, or the use of them.[17]

We are not concerned here with Malynes's contribution to the theory of the foreign exchanges as such. However, his conclusion that control of the foreign exchanges was the correct policy is historically important in connection with this study,[18] for his proposals for rigid exchange control were naturally highly unpopular with, and alarming to, the merchant and financial community.

---

[15] Malynes, pp. 15 and 94; pp. 2–3; pp. 76 et seq. All page references are to the 1601 edition.

[16] *The Maintenance of Free Trade*, 1622, p. 42.

[17] *Treatise*, p. 10. Malynes was familiar with Bodin's economic writings and wrote a commentary on them in *England's view the unmasking of Two Paradoxes: With a Replication unto the Answer of Maester John Bodine*, in 1603. On the use of a simple quantity theory in the early seventeenth century see J. D. Gould, 'The Trade Crisis of the early 1620s and English Economic Thought', *Journal of Economic History*, XV, No. 2, 1955, 125–6.

[18] *Treatise*, part III.

In the two decades following the publication of Malynes's pamphlet the country was afflicted by a multitude of economic and financial problems. There were, for instance, problems of the expenditure of the Crown, of the rights and privileges of the trading companies, of the difficulties of maintaining the appropriate ratios between the Mint prices of gold and silver; there were difficulties also in the wool and cloth trade and the fishing industry. In speeches and in print these problems were discussed with vigour, particularly by those whose interests were most closely affected. The events which led directly up to the famous controversy between Malynes, Misselden and Mun over the control of the exchanges may for our purposes be considered as starting in 1618. In this year there were complaints of a scarcity of coin. The Privy Council became concerned and an attempt was made to enforce the Statutes of Employment. This year also marks the beginning of the Thirty Years War and disruption of continental markets. Under the pressures of war and rumours of war an acute crisis developed. By 1620 repercussions were serious in England. Demand for cloth dwindled abroad and with it exports and employment at home; at the same time the exchanges became unfavourable and bullion left the country. How far subsidies paid by England to her allies abroad aggravated the outflow during these years is not clear. Following tradition a Commission on the Exchanges was set up in 1621; Malynes was a member.[19]

In the same year Sir Thomas Mun as a leading member of the East India Company felt it necessary to answer attacks on that company's privilege of exporting bullion. In the critical situation of the time this privilege was an obvious target for attack by other companies and merchants jealous of the special rights of the company. Mun's *Discourse of Trade from England unto the East Indies* was primarily a pamphlet defending the East India Company. He was naturally concerned to show the East India Company's export of bullion could lead to a net inflow of bullion,

---

[19] See E. Lipson, *The Economic History of England*, Vol. III, pp. 305 et seq. Charles Wilson, op. cit. Gould, op. cit. For further information about the problems of the cloth trade and Malynes's connection with it see Friis, *Alderman Cockayne's Project and the Cloth Trade* and generally on English public finance of the period see Dietz, *English Public Finance 1558–1641*.

rather than to consider whether a net inflow was always desir-able.[20]

Both Mun and Misselden were members of the Committee of Inquiry on the Depression of Trade set up by the Privy Council the next year. The Committee paid considerable attention to the problems of the quality of England's chief export, cloth, the desirability of preventing the export of wool as raw material, the need to increase consumption of cloth at home and the desira-bility of encouraging the fishing industry and shipping. Various proposals to improve the English currency and relate it more accurately to continental currencies were also made but 'the most important remedy (as we conceive) is to provide against the over-balance of trade'.[21] In effect this conclusion meant that it was officially accepted that direct attempts to control the exchanges were futile, and that if the unfavourable balance of trade could be prevented the exchanges would look after themselves. It meant abandonment of the attempts to control the foreign exchange mar-ket and reliance on efforts to prevent the balance of trade becom-ing unfavourable. Discussions of the rate of interest would in future have to take into account possible effects of changes in the rate on the balance of payments as such.

Misselden was not content to leave the Committee's conclusions unsupported by further propaganda. His two pamphlets – *Free Trade or the Means to Make Trade Flourish* and *the Circle of Commerce; or, the Balance of Trade* – published in 1622 and 1623, respectively – were largely directed against Malynes as the most dangerous propagandist of the old view. Misselden empha-sised the *real* as distinct from the monetary factors, such as exchange speculation, as the chief causes of the unfavourable balance of payments. Equally important, he argued that the cur-rently accepted explanation of the determination of the prices of individual goods by supply and demand was applicable to the prices of currencies and therefore to the foreign exchange rates.

[20] *Discourse of Trade from England unto the East Indies*, p. 22. In this pamphlet Mun favoured the enforcement of the Statutes of Employment (p. 44) as a means of checking the export of bullion but in his second pamphlet, *England's Treasure by Forraign Trade*, Ch. X, he argued strongly that the Statutes were extremely damaging. All page references to these tracts are to the reprints in *Early Tracts on Commerce*, ed. J. R. McCulloch (1856), 1952 reprint.

[21] Quoted in Lipson, p. 309.

The supply and demand for currencies depended, he asserted, directly on the balance of trade, and he supported the various proposals for improving the demand for exports put forward by the Committee.[22]

Nevertheless like Malynes he attached great importance to the supply of money and like Malynes favoured continuous mild inflation. He advocated debasement of the coinage as a means of bringing about an inflow of the precious metals and incidentally discouraging hoarding. This would, he believed, stimulate economic activity at home 'For [he said] money is the *vitall spirit* of *trade* and if the spirits faile needes must the body faint'.[23] The blessings of inflation are described with enthusiasm:

> And for the dearnesse of things, which the *Raising of Money* bringeth with it, that will be abundantly recompensed unto all in the plenty of *Money*, and quick'ning of trade in everyman's hand. And that which is equale to all, when hee that buyes deare shall sell deare, cannot bee said to be injurious unto any. And it is much better for the *Kingdome* to have things deare with plenty of *Money*, whereby all men may live in their severall callings: than to have things cheape with want of *Money*, which now makes every man complaine.[24]

As we shall see later, Misselden like Malynes considered that a low rate of interest was one of the advantages of plentiful supplies of money. Misselden did not pursue the analysis of inflation in any depth and his analytical acumen was perhaps not very great. In particular he did not discuss the limits to price rises that might be created by the existence of unemployed resources which, not unnaturally at that time, was assumed by all writers. He also assumed like many of his contemporaries that the precious metals could be retained in a country by means of enforcement of the Statutes of Employment.[25]

The pamphlet war between Misselden and Malynes which started immediately after Misselden's first pamphlet was notable chiefly for the picturesqueness of its language and the increasing

---

[22] Misselden in *Free Trade*, Chs. 1 and 2. The discussion of the exchanges is particularly clear in his second pamphlet *The Circle of Commerce*, pp. 21, 69 and 97–8. References are to the original editions.

[23] *Free Trade*, p. 28.   [24] Ibid., Ch. 7, pp. 106–7.

[25] Ibid.

violence of mutual abuse, rather than for any further analytical insights.

It is not improbable that the importance Misselden attached to debasement as a means to achieving inflation was due to the fact that he was a member of the Merchant Adventurers, and thus had a direct interest in any method of stimulating exports. On these matters of inflation and debasement Mun was in sharp disagreement with Misselden; indeed Mun might well have been called 'a sound money man' if he had lived in the 1920s instead of the 1620s.[26]

It is Mun's second and most brilliant pamphlet '*England's Treasure by Forraign Trade*' that is of particular interest here. It was probably written between 1622 and 28, after the main Misselden/Malynes dispute. It is evident that for some reason he felt his son John should be given a treatise of advice containing the petition to the House of Commons which he had drafted for the East India Company in 1628, and his more fully developed thoughts on money, trade and the exchanges. Its posthumous publication in 1664 seems to have been intended to support the Restoration policy of freeing the export of bullion.[27]

The brilliance of his exposition of the thesis that, if the balance of trade was looked after, the foreign exchanges would take care of themselves has tended to overshadow the more original discussions in the pamphlet of greater interest to us. At the very time that the practical issue of policy had been settled on the lines favoured by Mun, Mun himself raised the question of whether the maintenance of a favourable balance of payments (as distinct from avoiding an unfavourable one) was either practicable or desirable. Mun seems to have stumbled on these doubts by accident as a result of his consideration of the advantages of being able to use the precious metals as trading commodities, and the credit arrangements of the Italians. He declared:

it is in the stock of the Kingdom as in the estates of private men, who having store of wares, doe not therefore say that they

[26] See for example *England's Treasure*, Ch. VIII.

[27] On this point see ibid. Ch. X. The Act of Parliament which finally freed the import and export of gold and silver bullion and foreign coins from all restriction had been passed in 1663, the year before publication of Mun's pamphlet. Ch. IV–VII contain the substance of the petition.

will not venture out or trade with their mony (for this were ridiculous) but do also turn that into wares, whereby they multiply their Mony, and so by a continual and orderly change of one into the other grow rich, and when they please turn all their estates into Treasure; for they that have wares cannot want mony.

Neither is it said that Mony is the Life of Trade, as if it could not subsist without the same; for we know that there was great trading by way of commutation or barter when there was little mony stirring in the world.[28]

It is interesting to notice that Adam Smith made a somewhat similar point in the *Wealth of Nations*, explaining that if bank money were used instead of metallic money the latter could be exported as a commodity.[29]

It is, Mun said 'the necessity and use of our wares in forraign Countries, and our want of their commodities that causeth the vent and consumption on all sides, which makes a quick and ample Trade'. It was not the amount of money in the Kingdom. At this point Mun seems to have perceived that the connection between the quantity of money and the general level of prices had a bearing on the desirability and practicability of maintaining a favourable balance of payments. He noted 'for all men do consent that plenty of mony in a Kingdom doth make the native commodities dearer', hence it would diminish the volume of trade for 'dear wares decline their use and consumption'. It follows, he claims, that if treasure is imported and prices rise, then trade will be lost and the money will disappear again so that nothing is gained by the favourable balance of payment.[30] Unlike Misselden, Mun was therefore opposed to inflation. The validity of his argument is not affected of course by the fact that it enabled Mun to point out that it would be better to use the imported treasure to buy foreign commodities to trade with, as the East India Company wished to do. The attempt to reconcile the implications of the quantity theory with the national policy of trying to maintain a net inflow, led in effect to the implicit conclusion

[28] Ch. IV, pp. 137 et seq.
[29] *Wealth of Nations*, Bk. II, Ch. II, Vol. I, 276 et seq., ed. Cannan (1950). All page refs. are to this edition.
[30] *England's Treasure*, p. 138.

that net inflows of the precious metals would do no harm, *provided* that their influence in prices was neutralised by their re-export by the East India Company![31]

A practical obstacle to maintaining indefinitely a favourable balance of payments was pointed out later on in an attack on extreme policies designed to restrict luxury spending on foreign goods. He asks

> if we should become so frugal, that we would use few or no Forraign wares, how shall we then vent our own commodities? what will become of our Ships, Mariners, Munitions, our poor Artificiers and many others? doe we hope that other Countreys will afford us money for All our wares, without buying or bartering some of theirs? this would prove a vain expectation; it is more safe and sure to run a middle course by spending moderately, which will purchase treasure plentifully.[32]

Mun vouchsafes no definition of plentiful in this connection but in later chapters he developed further his ideas about the relation between the balance of trade, the supply of money and the level of economic activity.

He was considering the common argument that it was necessary to import treasure because it was necessary to have reserves and, in particular, that it was necessary for the Crown to have a reserve, i.e., basically the war-chest argument. Rather grudgingly he conceded this was necessary and that the Crown should be thrifty and lay up stores of treasure. He hastened to add, no doubt with an eye on the strained financial relationships between the king and Parliament at the time he was actually writing, that if the Crown needed any money in excess of that provided by existing taxes it should be obtained through Parliament.[33]

Admitting this, Mun observed that the important question arose of how much treasure the King could lay up each year without damaging his subjects. This led Mun into an analysis of the damaging deflationary consequences of a budget surplus.

[31] Ibid., pp. 135–9. In this connection his eulogy of the policy of the Duke of Tuscany in allowing free export of the precious metals and reference to the plentiful supply of such metals in his realms is illuminating.

[32] Ibid., p. 180. For an interesting discussion of Mun's contribution to the theory of the international mechanism for the distribution of the precious metals see Gould.

[33] Ibid., Ch. XVII.

Mun's explanation was simple but was not new: if the King put by a sum greater than the net inflow of treasure from the balance of trade he would reduce the amount of money in circulation, and hence lead to depression of economic activities. Mun's explanation seems to be the fullest given by early English mercantilist writers and may be regarded as a classic and is well worth quoting in full.

> This business doth seem at the first to be very plain and easy, for if a Prince have two millions yearly revenue, and spend but one, why should he not lay up the other? Indeed I must confess that this course is ordinary in the means and gettings of private men, but in the affairs of Princes it is far different, there are other circumstances to be considered; for although the revenue of a King should be very great, yet if the gain of the Kingdom be but small, this latter must ever give rule and proportion to that Treasure, which may conveniently be laid up yearly, for if he should mass up more mony than is gained by the overballance of his forraign trade, he shall not *Fleace*, but *Flea* his Subjects, and so with their ruin overthrow himself for want of future sheerings. To make this plain, suppose a Kingdom to be so rich by nature and art, that it may supply it self of forraign wares by trade and yet advance yearly 200000L. in ready mony: Next suppose all the King's revenue to be 900000L. and his expenses but 400000L. whereby he may lay up 300000L. more in his Coffers yearly than the whole Kingdom gains from strangers by forraign trade; who sees not then that all the mony in such a State, would suddenly be drawn into the Princes treasure, whereby the life of lands and arts must fail and fall to the ruin both of the publick and private wealth?

If, Mun declared, the King wants more treasure than the net inflow from the balance of trade, he must accept the fact that goods can be as useful as treasure and spend any additional balance of income or receipts on armaments and the accumulation of stores.

> Neither are all the advances of Princes strictly tied to be massed up in treasure, for they have other no less necessary and profitable wayes to make them rich and powerfull, by issuing out

continually a great part of the mony of their yearly Incomes to their subjects from who it was first taken; as namely, by employing them to make Ships of War, with all the provisions thereunto belonging, to build and repair Forts, to buy and store up Corn . . . for a Prince (in this case) is like the stomach in the body, which if it ceases to digest and distribute to the other members, it doth no sooner corrupt them, than it destroys itself.[34]

It will be noticed that it follows from Mun's argument (though he does not make the point) about the safe limits of accumulation by the Crown that an inflow of precious metals could be retained if it were hoarded and thus did not affect prices.

It is evident that Mun was as opposed to deflation as he was to inflation and regarded, as many others did, changes in the supply of money as of crucial importance to the level of economic activity. It will be noticed that Mun's argument in the passage just quoted is based only on the relationship between government changes in hoarding or spending and the level of activity. He does not appear to have considered that similar activities by individuals had any implications for economic activity in general terms, though he evidently regarded private hoarding as apt to be a foolish waste of opportunities. For instance he refers in one place to the piling up of treasure by merchants not as a cause of stagnation but as a result of stagnation and consequent lack of opportunities to invest. This latter passage is connected with a discussion of the rate of interest and is discussed more fully in Part 2 of this study, but it may perhaps reflect a genuine distinction in his mind between the significance of individual action and government action. If so he differed from his contemporary Misselden on this matter and a number of the later writers.

This conviction that changes in the supply of money affected the level of economic activity, continued to influence many writers in the later as in the earlier part of the seventeenth century. Typically it continued to be argued that a certain quantity of money was necessary as a circulating medium for a given level of economic activity. It was dangerous therefore to decrease the supply of money for it would depress economic activity and cause

[34] Ibid., Ch. XVIII, pp. 188 and 189–90. See Viner, Ch. I, sect. IV on the earlier writers on this topic.

unemployment. This view was of course implicit, and also sometimes explicit, in the proceedings of the various commissions and committees on trade and writers referred to earlier in this study.

Petty explained the dangers of having too little money in his *Treatise on Taxes* thus:

> the mischief thereof would be the doing of less work, which is the same as lessening the people, or their Art or Industry; for a hundred pound passing a hundred hands for Wages, causes 10,000 pounds worth of Commodities to be produced, which hands would have been idle and useless, had there not been this continual motive to their employment. (Vol. I, p. 36.)

But Petty also pointed out that there could be too much money as well as too little. He expressed it particularly succinctly in his *Verbum Sapienti*:

> Nor were it hard to substitute in the place of Money (were a competency of it wanting) what should be equivalent unto it. For Money is but the Fat of the Body-politick, whereof too much doth as often hinder its Agility, as too little makes it sick. (Vol. I, p. 113.)

Recognition that too much money was harmful, did not prevent Petty favouring an inflow. Excess money could be turned into plate and ornaments and formed a reserve.

There was considerable interest in the question of what determined the quantity of money needed to support a given level of activity at given prices. Petty's attempt to estimate how much money was required 'for such revolutions and circulations thereof as Trade requires', was much quoted. It was based on various assumptions about the frequency of payments of wages, rents, and taxes.[35] Sir Dudley North pointed out that the quantity of coin required varied with circumstances and that 'Wartime calls for more money than time of Peace, because everyone desires to keep some by him, to use upon Emergencies'. But North tried to show by the analogy of the buckets that any money in excess

[35] Petty, *Treatise on Taxes and Contributions*, 1662, Ch. 3 and *Verbum Sapienti* (written about 1665, publ. 1691), Vol. I, pp. 112–13. Petty also made calculations on similar lines in his *Quantulumcunque concerning Money* (written about 1682, publ. 1695) Vol. II, p. 446.

of the requirements of the circulation would be melted down, and vice versa, so that the supply of money would adjust correctly. He explicitly, however, decided not to discuss in this connection the problem of whether there might be an insufficient supply of bullion in the country to maintain the circulation, 'for that [he said] is a state of Poverty, and will not be until we are exhausted, which is besides my subject'.[36]

Neither Davenant nor Locke seemed to regard the problem as so simple as North seemed to, and their views are particularly relevant to the discussions of the rate of interest.

Davenant extended the discussions beyond the confines of the circulation of metallic money. In his *Discourses on the Publick Revenues*, published in 1698, he was much disturbed by the stagnation of the economy following the end of the war with France.[37] He pointed out that 'both before and since the War, the general Trade of this Country, has been more carry'd on by Credit, than manag'd with the Species of Mony' (Part II, p. 161). He then went on to examine the question of how much cash would 'be sufficient to give Life and Activity to this huge Body of Credit, which at present seems in a languishing Posture' (Part II, pp. 169–70), for he explains that 'there must be a quick Stock running' 'to put a Value' on the real economic resources of the country and 'to put Life and Motion to the Whole'. Thus although Davenant recognised that various types of credit instruments could to some extent take the place of money he argued that 'Mony and Credit must mutually help one another, Mony is the foundation of Credit; Where there is none, there can be no Credit; and where Credit obtains, Mony will circulate the better'. (Part II, p. 170.)

Two things were necessary to maintain 'that general Credit which is so necessary to support the Government, and carry on our Matters here at Home' confidence in the ability of the Government to pay its debts and that

there is, and shall be, kept within the Kingdom, a sufficient

[36] *Discourses upon Trade*, 1691. Postscript. The question of the influence of hoarding (instead of investing) savings on the quantity of money in circulation was discussed by many writers in connection with the rate of interest see pp. 46–9 below.

[37] Op. cit. All page references are to the original 1698 edition published in two parts.

quantity of the Species to turn in Trade, in the Payment of Rents and Taxes, and in the Manufacturers, and whereby to keep the Wheels of the Machine in Motion. (Part II, pp. 171–2.)

Davenant was confident of recovery and prosperity. It is not inconsistent with this view that he should claim that when as during the war with France

the Mony is carry'd out of the Kingdom, . . . 'tis the Riches of the Whole People, consider'd in a Body together, that goes away. However, in a long and expensive War, this is not to be avoided. (Part II, pp. 163–4.)

He recognised that a country could as well have 'too much as too little of this Kind of Treasure' if it were not used properly, by which he meant used as a trading commodity or used to employ people (Part II, pp. 62–4).

Locke took a more complicated line as part of his examination of the question of whether the rate of interest should be reduced. He set out his views in a paper probably written between 1670 and 1672 which he did not publish until 1692 when the rate of interest was again of current concern.[38] He was alarmed lest the lowering of the official maximum rate of interest, as suggested by Child and others, should lead to increased hoarding and repatriation of Dutch capital and the export of native capital. Such export of capital would lead to unfavourable exchanges and export of bullion, and like increased hoarding to deflation and trade depression, he argued.[39]

Locke started from the quantity theory of money. He explained that in a closed economy anything would do for money and the actual quantity of money was unimportant. Nevertheless, since at any time there was a necessary 'stock of money', a decrease in the quantity of money by depleting that stock would disrupt the flow of economic activity. Following along the same

[38] Locke, *Some Considerations of the Consequences of the Lowering of Interest and Raising the Value of Money.* All page references are to the second edition 1696. At the time of publication the question of restoration of the worn-out currency was also of importance, and Locke used his analysis of money in relation to this problem also in his controversy with Lowndes.

[39] Ibid., pp. 14–20.

lines as Petty he explained what determined the 'necessary stock' at any time thus:

> The Necessity of a certain Proportion of Money to Trade, (I conceive) lyes in this, that Money in its Circulation driving the several Wheels of Trade, whilst it keeps in that Channel (for some of it will unavoidably be dreined into standing Pools) is all shared between the Landholder whose land affords the Materials; The Labourer who works them; the Broker (i.e.) merchant and shopkeeper, who distributes them to those that want them; and the Consumer who spends them. Now Money is necessary to all these sorts of Men as serving both for Counters and Pledges. . . .[40]

In an open economy the situation was more complicated for the possibility of maintaining any particular 'necessary stock' of money depended on the relation between the internal price level and the price levels of other countries. Hence the quantity of money in the country is not a matter of indifference. As he explained:

> any quantity of that Money will not serve to drive any quantity of Trade; but there must be a certain proportion between their *Money* and *Trade* . . . because to keep your *Trade* going without loss, your Commodities amongst you, must keep an equal, or, at least, near the Price of the same Species of Commodities in the Neighbour Countries: Which they cannot do, if your *Money* be far less than in other Countries; for then, either your Commodities must be sold very cheap, or a great part of your *Trade* must stand still; there not being Money enough in the Country to pay for them (in their shifting of hands) at that high price, which the plenty and consequently low Value of Money makes them at in another Country. For the Value of Money in general is the quantity of all the Money in the World in proportion to all the Trade; but the value of Money in any one Country is the present quantity of the Current Money in that Country in proportion to the present trade.[41]

Locke illustrates his general argument by an example of a

40 Ibid., pp. 30–1.   41 Ibid., p. 77.

sudden halving of the supply of money. This he says must either halve all prices, wages and rents, *or* it will halve employment and production. In an open system the former alternative would have the serious disadvantage that the terms of trade will become unfavourable; the latter might lead ultimately to emigration of unemployed labourers.[42]

Locke went beyond the conclusion that an unfavourable balance of payment was injurious; he also concluded that a favourable balance was an advantage. It seems to me, though it is not altogether clear, that his desire for a favourable balance was based on the terms of trade argument, not on the desirability of inflation as such. He appears to have thought like Malynes that an increasing supply of circulating medium by raising prices would continue to improve the terms of trade. His general argument implies that there was some magnitude of the 'necessary stock of money' consistent with full employment and consistent with 'appropriate' terms of trade. The precise definition of 'appropriate' terms of trade is lacking however, and the following passage though it only makes sense as a term of trade argument throws no light on an equilibrium concept.

> Nor indeed, things rightly considered do Gold and Silver drawn out of the Mine equally Enrich, with what is got by Trade . . . Riches do not consist in having more Gold and Silver, but in having more in proportion, than the rest of the World, or than our Neighbours, whereby we are enabled to procure to ourselves a greater Plenty of the Conveniences of Life than comes within the reach of Neighbouring Kingdoms and States, who, sharing the Gold and Silver of the world, in a less proportion, want the means of Plenty and Power, and so are Poorer.[43]

He hastens to explain that no one would be richer if the quantity of mined gold and silver in the world doubled.

The late seventeenth century had, of course, thorough-going inflationists like the first part of the century. Petyt the author of *Britannia Languens* provides a striking example.

Petyt has the merit of attempting to show the way in which increases in the supply of money would raise prices *and* increase

43 Ibid., p. 15.   42 Ibid., pp. 78–9.

economic activity. In 1680 when Petyt wrote his pamphlet he was convinced that the country was in a deep depression and suffering from a prolonged decline in wealth. In evidence of his contention he gave long illustrations from particular trades and also made complicated calculations about supplies of coins and bullion.[44] Petyt set out elaborately his view of the stimulating effects of continued increases in the supply of money. Trade, both domestic and foreign, he regarded as a basic cause of progress in wealth and power, power being dependent upon wealth. The only way in which people were stimulated into productive activity, he argued, was by the provision of markets for their output so that they would produce beyond their immediate necessities. This made possible increases in population which in turn were both a means and a stimulus to further production of wealth and with it the acquisition of power and further treasure. Trade stimulated production because it drove up prices and it could only do this if the supply of money was increased. Hence the importance of trade.

> For where there is an increase of *Treasure* in a Nation which hath *property*, this will ordinarily diffuse amongst the people by the necessity and succession of *Contracts*; and then the people having universally more money than before, the *Seller* will not be so *necessitous* for money as before, and will have a greater *choice of Chapmen*, who will be more able and ready to buy.
>
> These numbers of Chapmen will inevitably raise the Market one upon the other, as is demonstrable by common and undeniable Experience and Fact; And therefore I shall lay it as a ground in Commerce, That the *plenty of Chapmen* who have *plenty of money*, will cause a higher and quicker Market for any desirable Commodity . . .

and

> a Forreign Trade (if managed to the best advantage) will yet further advance the values of Lands, by necessitating a vast *increase of people*, since it must maintain great multitudes of

[44] Petyt, *Britannia Languens* published 1680 under the *nom de plume* Philanglus. In Sections XI to XIII the state of individual trades and changes in the supply of money are described in detail.

> people in the very business of Trade, which could not other-
> wise be supported . . .: All which having the Rewards of their
> Labours in their hands, will still enlarge the choice of Chap-
> men to the Sellers, and there being so many more persons to
> be fed and cloathed, there must be a far greater home Con-
> sumption of all the products of Land.

and

> From what hath been said, it is evident that *National Power* is
> not Chimerical, but is founded on *People and Treasures*; and
> that, according to the different conditions of these its true
> Pillars, it immediately grows more vigorous or languid; that
> sufficient stores of Treasure cannot otherwise be gotten,
> than by the industry of the people; and, That till they have it,
> they cannot pay.[45]

Although Petyt appeared to value treasure for its own sake, nevertheless he was as much concerned with the concept of the necessary stock of money as the other inflationists quoted in this study.
The inflationists differed from non-inflationist anti-deflationists
however in their use of the concept. They assumed, or argued,
that if the stock of money were increased to a size appropriate
to a higher level of activity with higher prices, that higher level
of activity would be brought about by the stimulus of higher
prices.

Thus seventeenth-century writers concerned with the necessary
stock of money, whether inflationists or not, considered that ensuring the stock of money appropriate for their purposes was an
important object of policy, and the balance of trade was important
for this reason in addition to any other reasons to which they
might attach significance.[46] Thus they had elaborated the traditional ideas and any theory of interest would have to be consistent
with them and any policy conclusions based on a theory of interest

[45] Ibid., pp. 290, 291 and 457–8. All page references are to McCulloch's
Early Tracts (see p. 13 n. 20 above).

[46] It seems to have commonly been assumed in this context that inflows
and outflows of the precious metals always caused adjustments in economic
activity, and were not themselves adjustments in the necessary stock of
money required by prior changes in economic activity. Discussions of actual
crises, however, frequently identified changes in the demand for exports as
the fundamental cause of unfavourable balances of payments!

would have to take into account the effect on the balance of trade. It so happened that scepticism about the favourable balance of trade theorem developed during the later part of the seventeenth century. This was important in controversies over the rate of interest between the traditional 'necessary stock of money' theorists and advocates of a theory of interest based on a different view of the role of the supply of money. It will be convenient therefore to summarise the main criticisms of the favourable balance of trade theorem that seem particularly relevant.

(iv) The Balance of Trade Policy Questioned

Neither Malynes, nor Mun's attempts to apply the simple form of the quantity theory of money to problems of the exchanges and the balance of payments seem to have attracted attention even after the publication of *England's Treasure* in 1664. The criticisms of the favourable balance of payments policy followed other lines. This may well have been due to changes in the economic background, for the post-Restoration period, despite various difficulties mentioned below, was broadly speaking characterised by optimism in England. The rather hopeless admiration of the Dutch typical of the early part of the century, and the appreciation of the acute difficulties of competing with them about the middle of the century had disappeared by the later decades. Instead there was a conviction that it was possible to emulate even the Dutch successfully. As the French in turn developed as trade rivals, successful competition with them was also considered to be possible. The natural resources of England became the subject moreover of frequent self-congratulation. The focus of interest had shifted from the economic anxieties of a backward offshore island to the prospects of, and projects for, increases in wealth in general. Home production and domestic trade as well as foreign trade were seen as sources of increase of wealth. All these changes mitigated the almost pathological concern with the balance of payments of the earlier period.

Despite this general attitude of optimism and progress, the post-Restoration period was not free from economic, accidental and political troubles any more than the earlier part of the century. The war with the Dutch, 1664 to 1667, led to great anxiety. The Plague in 1665 and the Great Fire of London of 1666 were followed by a serious economic crisis. This led to the appointment of committees of inquiry by the House of Commons in 1667 and the House of Lords in 1669, while the King appointed a Council of Trade in 1668. The major financial crisis which developed with the collapse of the government credit with the stop of the exchequer in 1671 seems to have been largely an internal crisis. It seems to have helped to increase appreciation of the importance to economic activity of the credit structure as distinct from the supply of metallic money. There were renewed agitations for and discussions about reductions of the rate of interest. Finally perhaps the war with France, 1688–97, should be mentioned; it caused much anxiety over finance and economic prospects generally, but it led also to much self-congratulatory calculations about the ability of the country both to provide the sinews of war and to increase its standards of consumption and comfort. All these matters led to much controversy and the famous debate between Locke and Lowndes over the re-coinage also belongs to this period.[47]

Traders had discovered that though a policy intended to obtain a favourable balance of payments was no doubt far superior to one of control over the foreign exchange market, it too could be inconvenient. It not only encouraged much interference with trading activities, but it also provided occasions for particular trades to be attacked by jealous rivals. The East India Company for instance was again the object of an attack at the end of the century.[48] Writers such as Davenant and North expressed doubts indeed as to the ability of the government to interfere usefully with the course of trade. They suggested that reliance on experience and the profit motive of the traders was more likely to be beneficial.[49]

*   *   *

Impatience with the traditional preoccupation with the balance of payments was early displayed by Sir Josiah Child. The

[47] It is not necessary to deal with this controversy; for the purposes of this study it is sufficient to note the fact of this recurrence of the revaluation problem.

[48] See for instance *England and East-India inconsistent in their Manufactures* by John Pollexfen, 1697.

[49] Charles Davenant, *An Essay on the East-India-Trade*, pp. 25–6, first published 1696. References are to the reprint added to Part II of Davenant's *Discourses*, op. cit. On North, see pp. 33 below.

balance of payments was cited too often as a reason for not reducing the rate of interest, a proposal strongly favoured by Child
from the 1660s onwards. At this time he was much concerned
about the economic difficulties and depression which occurred
after the war with Holland, the Plague and the Great Fire of
London. Child did not attempt to develop Mun's criticisms of the
favourable balance of payments policy. He did realise however
that a discovery by Sir William Petty could be used to cast doubt
on the infallibility of a favourable balance of trade as a test of
benefit from trade.

Petty's discovery was the by-product of his statistical investigations in Ireland. He discovered that Ireland had a permanent
export surplus and therefore should have been acquiring treasure
and, according to the popular version of the balance trade
theorem, should have been increasing in wealth and prosperity.
But, as Petty commented, 'Ireland exporting more than it imports doth yet grow poorer to a paradox', for the export surplus, as
Petty realised, reflected the transfer of incomes to absentee landlords and capitalists 'and such as draw over the profits raised out
of Ireland refunding nothing'. As is well known this discovery
did not lead Petty to doubt the general desirability of a favourable balance of trade or to explore the nature of the mechanism
which transformed transfers of income into an export surplus
of goods.[50] Child however pointed out that similar phenomena
developed wherever landlords or capitalists were absentees as,
for example, in Virginia and Barbados. He noted that this also
provided an explanation of the continued poverty of Cornwall
despite its substantial sales of tin and pilchards. He observed that
it followed that countries that attracted capital from abroad by
relatively high interest rates would thereafter have to export
annually without benefit of countervailing imports in order to
transfer the interest due to the absentee capitalists.[51] So he concluded that an export surplus was not necessarily a sign of wealth
but might be one of poverty, and it did not necessarily lead to an

[50] Petty, *Treatise on Taxes*, Vol. I, p. 46.

[51] Child, *Trade and Interest of Money Considered*, Ch. IX, 'Concerning the balance of Trade', the discussion of Petty's paradox, etc., is on pp.
145–7 of the 1775 edition to which all page references are made. Although
written at the time of Child's activities on the Council of Trade this essay
was first published as part of *A Discourse on Trade* in 1690. It seems to
have been intended as an expansion of his views on the rate of interest

inflow of bullion. Thus it was folly to treat the state of the balance of payments as a criterion of prosperous and beneficial trade.

Satisfied that he had shown that a favourable balance of trade was theoretically invalid as a proof that there would be inflows of bullion, Child went on to argue that in any case in practice it was impossible to calculate the balance; the statistical data simply were not there. Child also repeated the criticisms made earlier by Mun as to the fallacy of calculating balances for individual trades or areas. To his own satisfaction he had demonstrated the use of the balance of trade as a basis of policy, or as a test of the gains from trade, was both fallacious and impracticable. He was able then to argue that the test should be the growth of trades both in particular and general and, hence, policy should be devoted to encouraging trade without reference to the balance of trade.[52] These conclusions were of course useful to Child as a member of the East India Company as well as in relation to his campaign for a reduction of the rate of interest. It has never been questioned that Child was a skilful propagandist; it must I think also be granted that he had some analytical insight.

In 1690, just over a quarter of a century after the publication of Mun's *England's Treasure*, and more than half a century after it was written, Nicholas Barbon took up (in a more sophisticated way than Mun) the argument that the precious metals could be regarded as normal trading commodities. Barbon however used his demonstration as a proof that the balance of payments was irrelevant, not that the use of the precious metals as commodities could be advantageous to and consistent with a favourable balance of trade policy as Mun had.

On the basis of an important analysis of the relative nature of value Barbon showed *inter alia* that 'nothing has a price or Value in itself'. Hence, since values are determined by supply and

---

and the trade depression that he had published in 1668 in his *Brief Observations concerning Trade and Interest of Money Considered*. The 1690 edition contained a reprint of the Observations and other papers written between 1665 and 1670. It was reprinted as *A New Discourse of Trade* in 1693 and frequently reprinted thereafter. (The 1690 edition was published anonymously). These bibliographical details are taken from Letwin *Sir Josiah Child, Merchant Economist*. In his interesting study of Child, W. Letwin ignores the contribution to inter-regional trade theory which seems to me to indicate more analytical acumen than he credits Child with.

[52] *Trade and Interest*. Particularly pp. 152 et seq.

demand 'in Trade and Commerce there is no difference in Commodities when their Values are equal; that is, Twenty shillings worth of Lead or Iron to some Merchants is the same as Twenty shillings in Silver or Gold'.[53] Consistently with his version of the state theory of money he follows this out to argue that there is no special value in gold and silver. Hence, the idea of a special advantage being derived from a favourable balance of trade has no foundation, even if the statistical difficulties of estimating the balance of trade could be reliably overcome.

But if there could be an account taken of the *Balance of Trade*, I can't see where the advantage of it could be. For the reason that's given for it, *That the Overplus is paid in Bullion, and the Nation grows so much the richer, because the Balance is made up in Bullion*, is altogether a mistake; for Gold and Silver are but Commodities; and one sort of Commodity is as good as another, so be it of the same value.[54]

Although Barbon had found it necessary to develop the pure theory of value in order to deal with problems of money and the balance of payments, he was really concerned with employment problems and the effects of declines in exports on the levels of employment.[55] It is worth noticing perhaps that he was personally involved in home industry, particularly the rebuilding of London and fire insurance, not with foreign trade. The following passage illustrates his general interest.

The Prohibition of *Trade*, is the Cause of its Decay; for all Forreign Wares are brought in by the Exchange of the Native: So that the prohibiting of any Foreign Commodity, doth hinder the Making and Exportation of so much of the Native as used to be Made and Exchanged for it. The Artificers and Merchants, that Dealt in such Goods, lose their Trades: and the Profit that was gained by such Trades and laid out among other Traders, is Lost. The Native Stock for want of such

---

[53] Barbon, *A Discourse Concerning Coining the New Money lighter*, 1696, p. 11; this contains a summary of the arguments of his *Discourse of Trade* of 1690. See pp. 72 et seq. below on Barbon's contribution to value theory.

[54] Ibid., p. 40.

[55] *Discourse of Trade*, p. 35. Hollander's Reprint (to which all page references relate).

Exportation, Falls in Value, and the Rent of the Land must fall with the Value of Stock.

Barbon regarded the maintenance of employment as his main criterion and one possibly inconsistent with that of the favourable balance of trade. His indifference to the latter and his implication that the supply of the precious metals was irrelevant to employment is of particular significance, for he was by no means indifferent to the availability of credit in relation to employment and economic activity in general.[56] He was indeed a co-founder of a land bank in 1695 and also favoured lowering the maximum rate of interest, and seems to have regarded the supply of the precious metals as *not* being the fundamental determinant of the amount of credit available. Barbon's critique of the balance of payments criterion was symptomatic of the growing conviction that a banking system might free the economy from dependence on the supply of the precious metals, and, therefore, on the balance of payments. The problems of paper money and bank credit were already beginning to rival those of the supply of metallic money as a major focal point for economic discussion.[57]

North, whose *Discourses upon Trade* was published a year after Barbon's first *Discourse*, was also drawn into consideration of the balance of trade during the controversies over the renewed proposals to reduce the rate of interest and the problems of the re-coinage. He believed that an understanding of the nature of trade was essential to correct conclusions about interest, money and coins.[58] Like Barbon he argued that gold and silver were in no way different from other commodities and that therefore a favourable balance of trade was of no particular importance. As every student knows he concluded that the mutual gain from

[56] Since this is concerned only with particular aspects of a few writers' views on the relation between employment and balance of trade policies, the vast literature on this subject must be ignored here. See on this: Viner, op. cit. Ch. I, v; E. S. Furniss, *The Position of the Labourer in System of Nationalism*, Ch. III; T. E. Gregory, 'The Economics of Employment, 1660–1713', *Economica* (1921).

[57] See p. 41 below on Barbon's views on interest. On land banks see Horsefield, *British Monetary Experiments, 1650–1710*, Ch. 16, pp. 196 et seq.

[58] Ibid., p. 516 of McCulloch's *Early Tracts*, op. cit. All page references are to this edition.

trade was independent of a favourable balance of trade, insisting that 'A Nation in the World, as to Trade, is in all respects like a City in a Kingdom, or Family in a City'.[59] In contrast to Barbon's attack on the balance of trade policy, North's was an integral part of a general critique of regulation of economic activity; it was an attempt to show in a simple way that an economic system with free markets needed no guidance. North's critique of government intervention implied of course that better use of resources would occur through unrestricted trade. This idea was more explicitly developed in two anonymous pamphlets of the period which require brief mention. In 1677, that is fourteen years before North's *Discourses* appeared, the author of *England's Great Happiness* not only recognised a similarity between domestic and foreign trade as the schoolman Ricardus had done long before, but he also attacked intervention on the ground that the advantage of obtaining things from abroad was that our resources were freed for more profitable use.[60] This resource allocation thesis was developed still more clearly in relation to the export of bullion in 1701, ten years after North's *Discourses*, in another anonymous pamphlet, *Considerations on the East-India Trade*, published in answer to Pollexfen's attack on the East India Company.[61]

There can be no doubt about the gradual decline in unanimity about the importance of the balance of payments towards the end of the seventeenth century in England, analytically incomplete though the criticisms were. The mere fact that criticisms were made seems to me to indicate increasing confidence in the country's potential for economic growth and, also, a growing unwillingness to accept the traditional view that growth must be limited by the requirements of a favourable balance of trade and the supplies of the precious metals. The implications of all this for the development of theories of the role and determination of

[59] Ibid., pp. 527, 531 and p. 528, respectively.

[60] Op. cit., pp. 261 and 260, respectively, of McCulloch's *Early Tracts*, op. cit. The pamphlet is attributed to John Houghton. On Ricardus see pp. 3–4 above.

[61] Ch. II, particularly pp. 558–9 of McCulloch's *Early Tracts*, op. cit., and Ch. X, pp. 579–80, 581, and 582. Davenant had also pointed out that it was advantageous to supply our wants cheaply from abroad in defending the East India Company in *An Essay on the East-India-Trade*, op. cit., pp. 31–2.

the rate of interest are of great importance. They will become evident in the next part of this study and will I hope be regarded as of sufficient interest to justify this preliminary survey of certain aspects of the development of theories of money and trade which has necessarily meant going over ground familiar in some contexts to many people.

PART 2   ANALYSIS OF INTEREST AS AN ECONOMIC PHENOMENON IN THE SEVENTEENTH CENTURY

Usury is a *Concessum propter Duritiem Cordis.*
BACON

I averr that high Interest will bring Money out of Hoards.
NORTH[1]

(i) Introduction

Theories of interest emerged in seventeenth-century England mainly in connection with discussions at various times of whether the legal maximum rate of interest should be lowered. It is possible to distinguish certain broad approaches to the problem. On the one hand some people regarded the rate of interest as a primarily dependent variable reflecting the demand and supply for loans which were themselves dependent on the general level of activity and the supply of money. On the other hand, some people regarded the rate of interest as a price which could be treated as an independent variable which, through its effect on the quantity of loans demanded, played the major role instead of the supply of money, influencing the general level of activity. It is because these differences figured so largely in the discussions of the rate of interest in the seventeenth century in England, that at the cost of repeating the familiar, Part 1 of this study was devoted to illustrating the background of views about the necessary stock of money and the supply of money and the balance of payments. The discussions of the various issues are mixed up with each in the literature and in order to disentangle them they have as far as practicable been dealt with here in separate sections.

Attention may conveniently be drawn to one general matter here. The main controversies over the role and determination of

---

[1] See pp. 36–7 and p. 48 below on Bacon and North, respectively.

the rate of interest in so far as they were concerned with the supply of money ran in general in terms of metallic money, the precious metals. The discussions of credit, banking and paper money which increased in volume and importance as the century went on seem to have been affected by, rather than affecting, the main discussions of the rate of interest with a few significant exceptions. A brief section at the end of the study draws attention to these developments.

(ii) What Interest is Paid For

Although as late as 1625 religious objections to usury were mentioned in Parliament,[2] seventeenth-century writers in England were relatively little concerned with the traditional moral arguments against it, and they displayed remarkable unanimity about the answers to the questions of what interest is paid for and why it is paid. Interest was regarded as the price paid for money loans, *not* as the income earned by a factor of production capital as wages were the income earned by the factor of production labour. In this the tradition of earlier discussions of usury was followed without question. Numerous seventeenth-century writers went to great pains to explain that, apart from consumption loans, money was borrowed in order to purchase labour and goods for the purpose of production and trade, and money was often described as artificial stock in comparison to land described as natural stock.

Malynes, for instance, pointed out in 1622 that the speculative investment of funds in foreign exchange bills prevented investment in the ships and tackle required in the fishing industry. Sir Thomas Culpepper the Elder complained in his *Tract against the High Rate of Usurie* that a high rate of interest made investment in agricultural improvements and afforestation unprofitable. In the later part of the century Petyt *inter alia* drew attention to these aspects. Barbon was among the most explicit; this was perhaps because he considered that there was nothing particularly important about the precious metals and was concerned to show this. Thus he wrote:

> Interest is commonly reckoned for Mony, because the Mony Borrowed at Interest is to be repaid in Mony; but this is a mistake; for the Interest is paid for Stock: for the Mony borrowed,

[2] See e.g. Lipson, op. cit., p. 225.

is laid out to buy Goods, or pay for them before bought.[3]
bought.[3]

Locke argued that traders would pay anything for a money loan rather than miss a good trading opportunity. He declared also that anything that hindered lending hindered trade.[4]

These efforts to show that money was not borrowed because it was wanted *per se* may be regarded either as propaganda against possible revival of the moral condemnation of money loans on the scholastic ground that money was barren, or as attempts to dispel any confusion about the nature of loans still remaining.[5] The similarity is obvious between these seventeenth-century statements and those of Cantillon at the beginning of the eighteenth century and Adam Smith at the end. Cantillon emphasised the same point explaining that money itself produced nothing, but since it was 'a pledge in exchange' it enabled people to buy stock for trading.[6] Adam Smith explained:

> Almost all loans at interest are made in money, either of paper, or of gold and silver. But what the borrower really wants, and what the lender really supplies him with, is not the money, but the money's worth, or goods which it can purchase. . . . By means of the loan, the lender, as it were, assigns to the borrower his right to a certain portion of the annual produce of the land and labour of the country, to be employed as the borrower pleases.[7]

The reason why interest had to be paid was equally generally agreed. Bacon perhaps put it most succinctly.

I say this onely, that *Usury* is a *Concessum propter Duritiem*

[3] Malynes, *Maintenance of Free Trade*, e.g. p. 42. Sir Thomas Culpepper (the Elder), *Tract against the High Rate of Usurie*, 1621, pp. 4–5. See note 10 below for further detail about Culpepper. Petyt, pp. 318–19. Barbon, *Discourse of Trade*, p. 20.

[4] Locke, op. cit., pp. 11–14.

[5] By avoiding discussion of the scholastic concept of interest as the price of time, the seventeenth-century writers, however, missed an opportunity of extending the scholastic discussion for money loans to consideration of the role of the capital as a factor of production.

[6] Cantillon, *Essai sur la Nature dir Commerce en Général*, Part II, Ch. IX. Royal Economic Society edn, to which all references are made.

[7] *Wealth of Nations*, Vol. I, Bk II, Ch. IV, p. 333.

Cordis: For since there must be Borrowing and Lending, and Men are so hard of Heart, as they will not lend freely, *Usury* must be permitted. . . . But few have spoken of *Usury* usefully. It is good to set before us, the *Incommodities*, and *Commodities of Usury*; That the Good may be, either Weighed out, or Culled out.

These Incommodities and Commodities to Bacon are practical matters not moral and after his discussion of them he concludes:

That it is a Vanite to conceive, that there would be Ordinary Borrowing without Profit; And it is impossible to conceive the Number of Inconveniences, that will ensue, if Borrowing be Cramped. Therefore to speak of the Abolishing of *Usury* is Idle. All States have ever had it, in one Kinde or Rate, or other.[8]

This type of explanation was frequently given in the seventeenth century, for instance by Malynes, Mun, Petty and North, while Cantillon and Adam Smith illustrate the same view in the eighteenth century.[9]

To sum up there was no difference between these seventeenth-century writers themselves and between them and Adam Smith as to why money was borrowed or why interest had to be paid. It may be noticed also that the resource allocation function of interest was understood. On the other hand the question whether the level of the rate of interest was a cause or a consequence of wealth provided a highly controversial issue of policy during the seventeenth century. It is appropriate to start the account of the controversy by considering the arguments put forward by Sir Thomas Culpepper the Elder in his early seventeenth-century campaign

[8] Bacon, *Essay of Usurie*, Golden Treasury Series reprint of *Bacon's Essays*, pp. 168–9 and 170.

[9] Mun, *England's Treasure*, Ch. XV, pp. 178–9. Malynes, *Consuetudo vel Lex Mercatoria*, frequently reprinted, 1622 edit. pp. 300. This passage is worth quoting in full, for Malynes expressed the commonsense view of an ordinary person lending money, viz: 'If I deale with a merchant that maketh gain of my money with his trade and commerce, and is well able to pay mee againe, being chiefly enriched by my meanes; why should I not in reason have part of his benefit and advantage when by my goods hee is growne rich?' Petty, *Treatise of Taxes*, Vol. I, pp. 47–8. North, particularly pp. 521–2. Cantillon, p. 201. Adam Smith, Bk. I, Chs. VI and IX, Vol. I, pp. 54, 90, 97, respectively.

for the reduction of the maximum legal rate of interest from its current level of 10 per cent. It should be pointed out that in these discussions it was apparently commonly assumed that the maximum legal rate was an effective rate in the sense that the rates on different types of loans were geared to it and not to some lower rate.

(iii) The Level of the Rate of Interest: Cause or Consequence of Wealth?

The predominantly agricultural character of the seventeenth-century economy and the political importance of the landed interest naturally affected the approach to many discussions on economic problems, including the rate of interest. It is particularly interesting that Sir Thomas Culpepper the Elder was a member of a family with estates in the Weald of Kent who were not only landed proprietors but also ironmasters. His *Tract against the High Rate of Usurie* was the first attempt at an orderly reasoned argument to show that the level of the rate of interest affected the growth of wealth. The *Tract* was published at the time of the great depression of 1619–23 when Parliament was discussing the lowering of the maximum rate of interest.[10] It was notable *inter alia* for its attempt to show that the landed and trading interests were identical with regard to the rate of interest, and that a lowering of the rate would be beneficial and was practicable. He assumed that the maximum legal rate was also the effective rate. His main arguments in favour of reduction can be summarised:

(a) The high rate of interest increased the difficulties of debtors and made it difficult for them to clear their debts. This led to stagnation. In particular the high rate of interest by lowering the

---

[10] Sir Thomas Culpepper (the Elder), 1578–1662, originally published his *Tract against the High Rate of Usurie* in 1621. He reprinted it in 1624 with some additions. Another reprint during his lifetime in 1641 contained an additional section setting out the benefits that he considered had accrued from the reduction of the rate of interest from 10 per cent to 8 per cent in 1625. He maintained that the good work of trying to secure further reductions must continue until the English rate was as low as that of our chief competitor: i.e. the Dutch. His son, also Sir Thomas, reprinted his Tract in 1668 together with a Preface, written by himself. Sir Josiah Child also included a reprint the same year in his *Brief Observations concerning Trade and Interest of Money*, see p. 29, n. 51 above.

capital value of land made it difficult for the landed interests to pay off their debts by the sale of some of their land. A low rate of interest would greatly assist debtors and by facilitating repayment of debts would help to reduce the need for further borrowing.[11]

(b) Investment in agriculture and forestry was discouraged by a high rate of interest. Improvements in agriculture and afforestation were investments with a slow return and were necessarily discriminated against by a high rate. The landed interests were thus doubly hit; the high rate of interest discouraged them from improving the productivity of their land and therefore from increasing the income from it, and it also diminished the number of years' purchase at which that land was valued. In directly relating the number of years' purchase of land to the rate of interest Culpepper was in agreement with numerous other writers of the period.[12]

(c) The rate of interest affected foreign trade. Traders who had to borrow at interest could only engage in those foreign trades in which the return gave them a margin over the rate paid on borrowed funds. Interest was a cost and since the rate of interest was lower in Holland than in England the Dutch had a cost advantage over the English. This was an important reason for the difficulties the English experienced in competing in foreign trade and therefore partly accounted for the lack of prosperity and the depression in foreign trade. In particular the decline of the fishing industry, so important as a nursery for the navy, was attributable to this trouble. The English rate of interest therefore ought to be lowered to the level of that of our chief competitor.[13]

(d) The rate of interest also affected business enterprise. An argument which figured prominently in Culpepper's *Tract*, and which was apparently taken seriously at this time, was the effect of the rate of interest on the supply of business enterprise or, as we would say today, on the supply of the entrepreneural factor. A high rate of interest, Culpepper pointed out, made it difficult for people without stock, or without much stock, to set up in business or to expand their business. This was not merely a hardship for such people but damaging to the general economy. Further, a high rate of interest made it possible for people with stock to retire early from business, or to refrain from entering it, as they could

[11] *Tract* (1621), p. 14. [12] Ibid., pp. 4–8. [13] Ibid., pp. 2–3.

live on the proceeds of their stock merely by lending it. A low rate
of interest had thus a positive advantage by increasing as it were
at both ends the supply of business enterprise.[14]

It is worth noticing various points in Culpepper's arguments.
First, the entrepreneural function was distinguished from that of
the ownership of stock or capital in any form. This distinction
which figured so largely at this time was not of much interest
to the classical economists except Adam Smith and J. B. Say.
Second, because interest was regarded as the price of money loans
it was not treated as a return to a factor of production. It was
only a cost to those entrepreneurs who had to borrow. This
approach was of course maintained by Adam Smith. Third, the
total supply of entrepreneurship was regarded as sensitive to the
rate of interest.

Culpepper's effective and orderly method of presentation of his
arguments made his *Tract* the reference work for other seventeenth-century writers. To Culpepper the Elder reduction in the
rate of interest continued to be a crusade throughout his life. He
bequeathed this mission to his son, also Sir Thomas; in 1668
when the latter felt the time was ripe he launched his attack.[15]
Culpepper the Younger again advocated a reduction in the rate
of interest as a cure for depression in trade and economic activity
generally. Culpepper the Younger added emphasis and some
generalisations to his father's arguments. Generalising the beneficial effects of the reduction of the rate of interest he claimed
that it would 'revive our dying Manufactures by making the
Stock of it cheap, and the Market quick' and that it would
increase employment generally and facilitate the rebuilding of
London after the destruction of the Great Fire. This rebuilding
he claimed was hampered by the then current maximum legal
rate of 6 per cent.[16]

By putting the level of the rate of interest into the forefront as
determining the stimulus to investment and economic activity, the

[14] Ibid., pp. 1–2 and 4.

[15] Sir Thomas Culpepper (the Younger), 1626–97, '*A Discourse showing
the many Advantages that will accrue to the Kingdom by the abatement
of Usurie*', 1668, Section III, pp. 10 et seq. He also published in 1670 a
reply to Manley's *Usury at 6 per cent Examined*, called *The Necessity of
Abating Usury Reasserted*.

[16] *Discourse*, Section III, p. 25. The maximum legal rate of interest
had been reduced from 8 per cent to 6 per cent in 1651.

Culpeppers implicitly denied the traditional view that changes in the supply of money *se ipse* were the factor of major significance in this connection. Such concern as they expressed with the supply of money was, as we shall see presently, vaguely and ambiguously expressed.

The Culpeppers were by no means alone in considering that a low rate of interest was beneficial to economic activity. Henry Robinson for instance urged the reduction of the rate of interest during the Commonwealth using similar arguments.[17] Child using Culpepper's and Robinson's argument agitated for a reduction of the rate of interest at about the same time as Culpepper the Younger and also later in the century. Child argued that the Dutch were prosperous because they had a low rate of interest and that it was this low rate that was the cause of their prosperity. He concluded that a similarly low rate would create wealth and prosperity in England as easily as in Holland. He did not mince his words: thus he said:

> This, in my poor opinion, is the *causa causans* of all the other causes of the riches of that people; and that, if the interest of money were with us reduced to the same rate it is with them, it would in a short time render us as rich and considerable in trade as they now are.[18]

In the last decade of the century, when agitation for the reduction of the legal rate was again renewed by Child and others in a period of uncertain trade and difficulties of war finance, much the same arguments were used. Barbon for instance followed the Culpeppers' argument closely. He argued further that the profit on the export industries (which would be helped by a reduction in the interest rate) was spent on domestic goods and services. This stimulated economic activity and employment. This is one of the few attempts to show how low interest might stimulate economic activity as distinct from individual investment projects.[19]

[17] Henry Robinson, *England's Safety in Trades Encrease*, 1641, pp. 6–8, and *Certain Proposals in Order to the People's Freedome and Accomodation . . . etc.*, 1652, p. 10.

[18] Child, *Discourse concerning Trade*, pp. 7 and 13–17. See also W. Letwin, *The Origins of Scientific Economics*, pp. 5–15 on Child.

[19] Barbon, *Discourse of Trade*, pp. 38–42 and p. 35, and see pp. 31–2 above. Barbon was one of those writers who declared from time to time

Although Culpepper, and those who may be called perhaps his disciples, regarded the rate of interest as the variable of primary importance rather than the supply of money, not everyone who considered a low rate of interest an advantage followed the Culpepper line. Misselden, contemporary with Culpepper the Elder, had argued that a low rate of interest was beneficial but denied that lowering the legal rate was either necessary or practicable. A low rate of interest was he argued simply *one* of the advantages of a plentiful supply of money. He certainly seems to have considered the mild inflation arising from plentiful supplies of money as a more important stimulus to economic activity than a low rate of interest. Malynes for once agreed with Misselden. Both of them followed the tradition of preoccupation with the direct effect of changes in the supply of money on the level of activity.[20]

The argument that high interest was injurious so forcibly urged was by no means universally accepted. Mun for instance had argued in *England's Treasure by Forraign Trade* that low interest was not sufficient to stimulate trade when it was depressed; opportunities for profitable investment were more important than the level of the rate of interest.

So that for these, and some other reasons which might be alledged, we might conclude, contrary to these who affirm, that

---

that the consumption of the rich was necessary for the employment of the poor. He summarised this opinion in his *Discourse of Trade* in the often quoted sentence: 'A Conspiracy of the Rich Men to be Covetous, and not spend, would be as dangerous to a Trading State, as a Foreign War' (p. 32). He did not suggest however that any such conspiracy existed or was likely, or that there was any inherent tendency to underconsumption in the system. He was simply arguing against the view that thrift as such was desirable by pointing out in effect that if people ceased to demand goods, luxuries as well as necessities, demand would collapse and with it employment. Like Locke (and Adam Smith later) Barbon pointed out, in his discussion of the nature of demand in connection with his analysis of value, that the provision of necessities accounted for only a very small proportion of economic activities (see pp. 73–4 below).

[20] Malynes, *Maintenance of Free Trade*, pp. 98–9. Misselden, *Free Trade*, pp. 29–30 and 116. See also pp. 10–11 and 13–14 above. Neither Malynes nor Misselden, however, seems to have been concerned with the problem of hoarding in connection with a lowering of the rate of interest. This may be due either to their simply not thinking about it at all, or because they assumed that increases in the supply of money, such as they wished for, would offset any increases in hoarding.

Trade decreaseth as Usury increaseth, for they *rise and fall together.*

Mum, it should be noticed however, was not concerned with the question of long-period investment in agricultural improvements like his contemporary Culpepper the Elder.[21]

Like Mun, Davenant seems to have been little interested in the rate of interest in general; his concern seems to have been limited to its effect on the cost of government borrowing. For instance, in his lengthy discussion of the necessary stock of money in his *Discourses* already referred to, he was concerned with the economic stagnation following the end of the war with France, but he did not mention the rate of interest.

Manley arguing against the Culpepper's and Child late in the 1660s elaborated further on the theme of the importance of profit prospects rather than the rate of interest. He drew attention to the problem of the size of changes in the rate of interest in relation to the rate of profit expected. He argued specifically for instance that changes in the rate by 2 per cent, such as those under discussion, were too small in relation to the expected profits from improvements in agriculture of the type suggested by the Culpeppers and Child to make any difference to investment decisions. Even more definitely, as one actually engaged in rebuilding London, he claimed that the current rate of interest was not high enough to hamper rebuilding either then or in the future. It was, he claimed, dwarfed by the expectation of profits from site values and could in any case be offset by reducing the quality of the buldings. He considered that the cost of labour, and the recent increases in wages, were far more important than the rate of interest in hampering investment in general and successful competition in foreign trade.[22]

21 Mun, *England's Treasure*, Ch. XV, p. 179.
22 Thomas Manley, *Usury at 6 per cent Examined*, 1669, p. 7, pp. 47–9, pp. 18–19 and 24–5 on wages. It will be remembered that Adam Smith in a notable passage (Bk. I, Ch. IX, pp. 99–100) apparently held the opposite view about wages. 'In reality high profits tend much more to raise the price of work than high wages.... In raising the price of commodities the rise of wages operates in the same manner as simple interest does in the accumulation of debt. The rise of profits operates like compound interest. Our merchants and master manufacturers complain much about the bad effects of high wages in raising the price, and thereby lessening the scale of their goods both at home and abroad. They say nothing about the bad

Although it is clear that Manley was obsessed by the increasing cost of labour his arguments as to the relative importance of interest as a cost, and changes in it as insignificant, are of considerable interest. Locke seems to have been broadly of the same opinion as Mun and Manley; he noted that high interest and thriving trade went together and that people would pay whatever interest was necessary rather than miss a good trading opportunity. North also held the view that low interest was not the cause of economic activity and declared that low interest was simply the effect of increased wealth increasing the supply of loans. Thus after arguing that the rate of interest was simply determined by the supply and demand for 'stock' he concluded 'Wherefore it is not low Interest makes Trade, but Trade increasing, the Stock of the Nation makes Interest low'.[23]

Mun paid very little attention to the rate of interest, and it seems evident that problems connected with the supply of money in relation to the circulation and prices were of far more concern to him. But some later writers just quoted were much concerned with the danger that the legal rate might be set so low that the supply of loans and/or the supply of money might be diminished and the balance of payments be made unfavourable. It was indeed fears of such consequences that appeared constantly in the course of inquiries and Parliamentary Debates on lowering the rate of interest.[24] The attempts made to deal with these problems by Culpepper and his disciples are outlined in the next section.

(iv) *The Supply of Loans and Money*

(a) *Money, Dutch capital and the balance of payments*
Culpepper the Elder found it easy to be eloquent about the advantages that might be expected from a reduction of the rate of interest, but it was also essential to show that these advantages would not be frustrated by a reduction of the supply of loans. In

---

effects of high profits. They are silent with regard to the pernicious effects of their own gains. They complain only of those of ther people.'

[23] Locke, op. cit., pp. 106–7 and North, op. cit., pp. 517–18.

[24] See on this for instance Lipson, op. cit., Vol. III, pp. 222 et seq. and for the part played by Child in the Parliamentary debates see Letwin, op. cit., pp. 4 et seq.

this connection, moreover, traditional analysis of the direct relation between the changes in the supply of money and the level of activity, the necessary stock of money approach, and the importance attached to the balance of payments on this and other acounts, needed to be considered. Naturally people like Misselden and Malynes who regarded a low rate of interest as just one of the benefits flowing from increases in the supply of money were not involved in such difficulties on this account.

The Culpeppers and Child made no attempt to deal analytically with the general question of money by showing it was unimportant. Indeed Culpepper the Elder admitted that money must be plentiful in order 'to make money easy to be borrowed', but considered that the condition was satisfied in contemporary circumstances. Child too implied acceptance of Culpepper's view that the supply of money was in some way relevant, for he claimed that there was sufficient money in the country to support a lower rate of interest. He said that there was obviously more money about at the time he was writing than at the time of the previous reduction of the rate of interest. He dismissed complaints of the existence of a shortage of money by asserting simply that everyone always complained of this.[25] Barbon's analysis, however, of the nature of the precious metals as a mere trading commodity, outlined already in the first part of this study, enabled him to argue that the supply of metallic money was irrelevant to the rate of interest. The supply of credit could he considered be adjusted to the requirements of the rate of interest through the establishment of appropriate banks. Barbon it will be remembered was a co-founder of a landbank.[26]

Child's attempt to show that the balance of payments was irrelevant we have seen already was based on different arguments from Barbon's.[27] Although Child stressed the irrelevance of the balance of payments, nevertheless he felt it to be desirable to show

[25] Culpepper, 1st edn, pp. 14–17, and 1624 edn, pp. 13–17. Child, *Discourse concerning Trade*, op. cit., Preface, p. xxx.

[26] See p. 32 above. During the 1690s the credit of the government was particularly low. This led to fears that the government would not be able to borrow if the maximum rate of interest were reduced. Barbon therefore suggested that the Government should be allowed to borrow at some selected rate above the proposed reduced maximum. (*Discourse of Trade*, pp. 41 etc., et seq.)

[27] See pp. 28 et seq. above for details and for other critics.

that in particular the supply of Dutch loans to England would not be affected by the proposed reduction of the rate of interest and lead to a loss of money. He claimed therefore that since the proposed reduction would still leave the English rate 1 per cent above the Dutch rate this would be sufficient to maintain supplies. At the same time however he accepted the Culpepper thesis (strengthened by his own extension of Petty's Irish paradox) that withdrawal of Dutch loans would not be disadvantageous, since payment of the interest was a deduction from England's wealth.[28] Thus he attempted to meet all possible objections of this type. These arguments were not of course universally accepted and some of the counter arguments will be outlined in the section on the total supply of loans. In the meantime the question of hoarding must be examined.

(b) *Hoarding and the elasticity of supply of loans*
Awareness of the phenomenon of hoarding was a natural consequence of the slow development and ill-organised state of the capital market in England. The development of an internal bill market and goldsmith banking demonstrated the practical desire of the seventeenth-century business world for a means of both enabling and tempting people with surplus funds to lend them. The preoccupation of some of the banking projectors with inventing suitable securities against which loans could be made was recognition of another aspect of the problem. These were fundamental difficulties in an economy in which decisions by savers to hoard or to invest could not be offset through a banking system. Savings and surplus funds generally were most easily held in the form of precious metals; this was the accepted, and for many people, indeed the only way of holding savings. For instance, North explained that people and nations

> supply themselves with what they have occasion for from abroad; which done, the rest is laid up, and is Silver, Gold, etc., for as I said, these being commutable for everything, and of small bulk, are still preferr'd to be laid up, till occasion shall call them out to supply other Necessaries wanted.[29]

Observant writers were naturally concerned with the circum-

28 See references for Culpepper in note 25 above, Child, pp. 13–17.
29 *Discourses*, p. 517.

stances under which hoarding would or would not be increased or decreased.

Concern with the effect of hoarding on the supply of loans led to discussions about the influence of the rate of interest on people's decisions to lend or to hoard their savings and temporarily surplus funds. It will be recognised from the account already given of ideas on the 'necessary stock of money', that hoarding in these discussions was not confused with the demand for money for transactions and emergencies.

The contrast between the views of seventeenth-century writers and those of the late eighteenth and early nineteenth as to the importance of hoarding can be simply illustrated. In 1776 Adam Smith was able to state 'What is annually saved is as regularly consumed as what is annually spent, and nearly in the same time too'. In 1820 Malthus could declare that 'No political economist of the present day can by saving mean mere hoarding'. It will be remembered that the *Wealth of Nations* contains a quite lengthy description of the contemporary banking system of England and Scotland.[30]

It seems to me no accident therefore that the problem of hoarding in relation to the rate of interest was a subject of general speculation in the seventeenth century, but disappeared from view at first with the development of banking and the capital market, only to be rediscovered much later within the banking system.

Culpepper disposed of the question of hoarding very simply. He argued that native loans will continue to be lent at reduced rates of interest because there will be no alternative. Child and Barbon also assumed something like total inelasticity of the supply of native loans in relation to the rate of interest. Thus Barbon argued in his *Discourse of Trade* that if it is impossible to lend above 5 per cent will lend at that rate rather than forgo any interest at all.[31] Manley however, who was also concerned with

[30] *Wealth of Nations*, Vol. I, p. 320 and Bk. II, Ch. II. Malthus, *Principles of Political Economy*, 1st edn (1820), p. 32.

[31] See pp. 39–40 above on Culpepper's belief shared by Child that people would have to stay in business longer if interest rates were lower and would thus be less likely to hoard their savings. Culpepper also apparently believed that owing to the general relief of indebtedness there would not be an increased demand for loans. The possibility that wealth and prosperity would not be increased if there were not a net increased

loans for expansion, argued that if treasure was already locked in misers' chests when the rate was 6 per cent still more would be locked up if the rate was reduced.[32]

North agreed with Manley, stating his opinion with emphasis.

> But I averr, that high Interest will bring Money out from Hoards, Plate, etc. into Trade, when low Interest will keep it back.

> Many Men of great Estates, keep by them for State and Honour, great Quantities of Plate, Jewels, etc., which certainly they will be more inclin'd to do, when Interest is very low, than when it is high.

North's general thesis on the rate of interest was that it should be left to the free market to settle. Thus it followed that there would be untoward consequences if the legal rate of interest diverged from this. He pointed out specifically that if the legal rate were lowered below the free market level, and it was not evaded, traders would not be able to obtain so many loans and 'so much of trade is lopt off; and there cannot be well a greater obstruction to diminish Trade than that would be'. North did not discuss the question of changes in the hoarding and investment of savings in relation to the circulation as such.[33]

Locke, like North, considered that reduction of the rate of interest would 'discourage men from lending' and opposed the contemporary proposals for reduction. Nevertheless he seems to have been more concerned that this would 'be a Loss to the Kingdom, in stopping so much of the Current of Money, which turns the Wheels of Trade'.[34] It is understandable that Locke should be more anxious about maintaining the 'necessary' circula-

---

demand for loans seems to have been overlooked. For references on Culpepper and Child see note 25 above and also pp. 38–9 above on Culpepper. Barbon, p. 41.

[32] Manley, pp. 6–7.

[33] North, pp. 519–20 and pp. 521–2 and p. 44 above.

[34] Locke, p. 18, see also pp. 22–4 above. Locke also introduced the following curious argument in connection with a reduction of the legal rate of interest. If it were reduced bankers would be 'content to have more money lye dead by them than now', because they would make so much profit on loans charged at more than the legal rate for which they would expect to receive a substantial risk premium (p. 7). Bankers were apparently not regarded as profit maximisers by Locke!

tion than North with his faith in automatic adjustments. It is natural therefore that he should have been the one to perceive that all changes in hoarding, whether connected with investment or ordinary spending, had an influence on circulation and there fore *se ipse* according to his analysis on the level of activity. Locke thus found himself faced with the problem of the relation of the rate of interest via the supply of loans to changes in the supply of money and the level of the circulation and, hence, to the level of prices and activity. Locke's attempt to solve this problem can be conveniently considered in the next section in connection with the ideas of other writers as to the dependence of the rate of interest on supplies of money.

(c) *The total supply of loans*
The consideration of the immediate effects of the rate of interest on the supply of loanable funds in relation to hoarding and inter national movements of capital naturally focused attention on the importance of supplies of money. For hoarding and dis-hoarding were in practice a physical process of putting the precious metals into treasure chests and cellars, or taking them out, or of turning them into plate or other ornaments or melting them down. It was also recognised that international capital movements were likely to result in movements of the precious metals. It was thus not unusual for the supply of money to be regarded as a determinant or limiting factor on the supply of loans. Thus Misselden stated: 'The *Remedy* for *Usurie* may bee plenty of *Money*. . . . For as it is the scarcitie of *Money* that maketh the high rates of Interest; so the plentie of *Money* will make the rate low, better than any Statute for that Purpose.' While Petty argued that 'the natural fall of Interest, is the effect of the increase of Mony'.[35] Even Child found it necessary to try to show that there was enough money to support a low rate of interest. The author of the anonymous pamphlet *Interest of Money Mistaken*, published in 1668, declared 'for without plenty of money interest cannot be low'. Manley fully shared this view.[36]

These writers did not explain however why or how changes

---

[35] Misselden, *Free Trade*, p. 116–17. Petty, *Political Arithmetic* (written 1671–6, publ. 1690), Vol. I, p. 304. Child, see p. 45 above.
[36] *Interest of Money Mistaken*, Anonymous, 1668, p. 18. Manley, pp. 68–69.

in the supply of money as such affected the total supply of *potential* loanable funds. This problem was a major preoccupation of Locke. It has been shown that the fear that the flow of activity would be broken was an important reason for Locke's opposition to reduction in the rate of interest. We have seen that he thought that reductions in the rate would reduce the amount of money in circulation by encouraging hoarding at the expense of lending. It would, also, probably lead to repatriation of Dutch capital and export of English capital which would necessarily result in an export of the precious metals and a reduction in the supply of money.

Locke tried to disentangle the function of money as a circulating medium from its function as a loanable fund. He pointed out money had a value as a medium of exchange, its purchasing power, and also a value or price called interest, and that this duality led to confusion. The former Locke saw as determined by the quantity theory of money. In order to elucidate it he regarded it as necessary to examine the general problem of the determination of value in terms of supply and demand.

> 'I shall begin first', he says, 'with the Necessaries or Conveniences of Life, and the Consumable Commodities subservient thereunto; and shew, That the *Value of Money* in respect of those depends only on the Plenty and Scarcity of Money in proportion to the Plenty and Scarcity of those things and not what Interest shall by Necessity, Law, or Contract be.'[37]

Locke goes on through a careful analysis of the factors affecting the value of individual goods and demonstrates the correctness of the quantity theory of money. From this he is able to conclude that changes in the rate of interest *se ipse* alter neither the quantity of money, nor of land, nor of any good and therefore cannot alter the purchasing power of money, 'the measure of that is only the *Quantity* and *Vent*, which are not immediately chang'd by the Change of Interest'. This is not the end of the matter, however, for in so far as a change in interest is conducive to trade and to importing or exporting more money or goods and so in time 'varying their Proportions . . . so far the change of

[37] Locke, p. 46.

Interest as all other things that promote or hinder Trade may alter the Value of Money in reference to Commodities'.[38]

Locke had had no difficulty in showing that changes in the total quantity of money spent affected prices; his difficulty was to distinguish between the stream of money spent directly and that which was spent by borrowers which had interest as its price and how the *latter* expenditure was affected by the supply of money. He explained how the lending and borrowing of money arose by analogy with rent of land. The latter was due to the fact that some people had more land than they wished to use, and some less, hence the latter hired it from the former for a rent if they thought it profitable to do so. This was hiring natural stock. In the same way some people had more money than they wished to use, and some less, and so the latter hired it for interest if they thought it profitable to do so. This was hiring artificial stock. The contrast in the natures of the two types of stock is made clear:

> Land produces naturally some thing new and profitable, and of Value to Mankind; but Money is a barren thing, and produces nothing, but by Compact, transfers that Profit which was the Reward of one Man's Labour into another Man's pocket.

Locke ultimately concludes:

> The natural Value of Money, as it is apt to yield such a yearly Income by *Interest*, depends on the whole of the then passing Money of the Kingdom, in proportion to the whole trade of the Kingdom (i.e.) the general vent of all the Commodities. But the natural Value of Money, in exchanging for any one Commodity, is the quantity of the Trading Money of the Kingdom designed for that Commodity, in proportion to that single Commodity and its Vent.[39]

It seems to me that Locke himself was not really satisfied by this conclusion.[40] Cantillon in the next century certainly was not. He attempted to clear the matter up by distinguishing between cases in which an increase of the supply of money would lower interest and cases in which it would raise it. He argued that an increase of money in the state 'will doubtless bring down' the

---

[38] Ibid., pp. 48–9.   [39] Ibid., pp. 55–6 and pp. 72 et seq. respectively.
[40] Keynes, despite his admiration for Locke, considered that Locke had not resolved the problem. Keynes, op. cit., pp. 343.

rate of interest if the increase is initially in the hands of money-lenders. If however it is in the hands of spenders he contends it will raise the rate of interest by stimulating entrepreneurs to borrow more. They will do this in order to take advantage of the increased opportunities of business provided by the increase of spending. In the one case the supply of loans is increased in the other the demand for loans. In all cases, however, an increase in the supply of money would increase prices and vice versa 'without any necessary connection with the rate of interest'.[41]

Another aspect of the problem of the supply of loans must be mentioned, that is the supply of saving. As Tucker's important study *Progress and Profits in British Economic Thought, 1650–1850* makes clear, saving was commonly regarded as depending on the general growth of wealth and the prevailing sociological attitude towards thrift.[42] It was not regarded as dependent on either the rate of profit or the rate of interest. Indeed it was argued, by analogy with the Dutch experience, that both the rates of profit and interest would tend to fall with the growth of wealth *but* that the volume of saving would increase. It is possible to read into the co-existence of this view of the determinants of saving and the seventeenth-century treatment of hoarding, a theory of the influence of the supply of real saving on the supply loans via the rate of interest. North's explanation of hoarding and of the relation of the growth of 'stock' to the growth of wealth in relation to the rate of interest can be, I think, possibly interpreted in this way.[43] I do not really think however that such a theory can be regarded as even unconsciously assumed in the general discussions on hoarding.

Another facet of discussions on saving must also be mentioned, for its relation to a belief that the supply of money affected the supply of loans and the rate of interest is puzzling. It is well known that the idea was not uncommon that a favourable balance of payments, and the consequent inflows of the precious metals, indicated net saving by a nation. The conclusion drawn from this was that the saving increased the supply of money in the country.[44] It appears of course to follow that it is saving which affects *both* the supply of loans and the supply of money, *not* the supply of money which affects the supply of loans. This thesis

---

[41] Op. cit., p. 215.   [42] Tucker, pp. 20 et seq.   [43] See pp. 44 and 49 above.
[44] See Viner, pp. 32–3, or Mun, Misselden, Davenant, etc.

could have been fitted into the treatment of hoarding in relation to the rate of interest. As far as I know however this line of thought was not suggested except possibly by North.

The problem I am interested in here is why this emphasis on the possible saving/supply of money relation did not destroy the belief that the supply of money determined the supply of loans and therefore the rate of interest. Locke does not discuss the issue. I suggest that the explanation may be that Locke and others were looking at the whole problem of the rate of interest from such an entirely different angle that they did not notice the possible relevance of the other line of thought. Starting as they did from the basic inherited assumption that changes in the supply of money influenced the level of activity, the problem of the supply of loans might be seen by them as an integral part of that level of activity and therefore dependent on the supply of money. The problem then would be to show the way in which the supply of loans and the rate of interest were adapted to the level of activity. The apparently obvious conclusion might well seem to be that the change in the supply of money that affected the level of activity also naturally affected the supply of loans in the same way. The problem was to explain just how and this of course is what Locke tried to do. This plane of discourse was entirely different from that concerned with the effect of real savings on the balance of payments and hence on the supply of money.

(v) *Supply and Demand: the Natural Rate of Interest and Government Control*

One way and another those seventeenth-century writers who regarded the supply of loans as varying with the rate of interest treated the rate of interest as being determined by supply and demand for loans. Locke and North pointed out that their analysis was an extension of supply and demand theory from the determination of commodity prices to the determination of the price of loans at which supply and demand would be in equilibrium.[45] In the terminology of the period the price that would be reached in this way in the absence of Government intervention was regarded as a 'natural' price. Thus Locke wrote "by *natural Use* I mean that Rate of Money which the present Scarcity of it makes

[45] Locke, p. 6 and North, p. 518.

it naturally at'.[46] The concept clearly implied economic laws in the modern sense. Thus Petty in his discussion of the way in which the rate of interest varied according to circumstances in the *Treatise of Taxes and Contribution*, wrote:

> Now the Questions arising hence are; what are the Natural Standards of Usury and Exchange? ... I see no reason for endeavouring to limit Usury upon time, any more than that upon place, which the practice of the world doth not, unless it is that those who make such Laws were rather Borrowers than Lenders: But of the Vanity and fruitlessness of making Civil Positive Laws against the Laws of Nature, I have spoken elsewhere, and instanced in several particulars.[47]

As Tucker points out in his *Progress and Profits in British Economic Thought 1650–1850* even Child was obliged to indicate that his arguments in favour of government policy of lowering the rate of interest did not go against nature. Child argued:

> Laws against Nature, I grant, would be ineffectual; but I never heard before, that Laws to help Nature, were against Reason.

and

> *The same thing may be both a Cause and an Effect ... The Abatement of Interest causeth an encrease of Wealth, and the encrease of Wealth may cause a further Abatement of Interest.* But that is best done by the Midwifery of Good Laws.[48]

Further it was generally recognised that the actual rates prevailing in practice on loans varied with the reputation of the borrower and the type of project he was financing. It was indeed argued by some, as by Adam Smith later, that an unduly high rate would encourage lending to rash enterprises at the expense of sounder schemes, because the former would be willing to offer to pay high rates.[49] Thus no one rate of interest could be satisfac-

[46] Locke, p. 8. Locke explained that the natural rate in a market implied also that the market was not distorted by what he like some of his contemporaries, e.g. Child, regarded as the monopolising activities of bankers.

[47] Petty, *Treatise on Taxes*, Vol. I, p. 48.

[48] Child, *Trade and Interest of Money*, Ch. I, p. 70 and pp. 58–9, respectively. See also Tucker, pp. 21–2. (My italics.)

[49] For instance Petty, *Treatise on Taxes*, Vol. I, pp. 47–8, and *Quantulumcunque concerning money*, Vol. II, pp. 447–8. Manley, p. 41. See also

tory. It was also noted as a difficulty, for instance by Locke, that the conditions of supply and demand varied with great rapidity in the market for loans so the natural rate would fluctuate and inevitably any legal rate would frequently diverge from it.[50] In so far as the legal rate was not evaded it was realised, as we have seen, that either borrowing would be unnecessarily restricted if the rate was too high, or loanable funds would be unnecessarily reduced if the legal rate was too low. These complications led Petty and North to the conclusion that the regulation of the rate of interest by setting an actual rate was futile; North stated his views briefly and unambiguously.[51]

> Thus when all things are considered, it will be found best for the Nation to leave the Borrowers and the Lender to make their own Bargains, according to the circumstances they lie under.

In fact, however, the actual policy issue was concerned with whether the maximum rate should be changed and relatively few writers argued about complete freedom from restriction. Approval of the imposition of a maximum rate, provided that it was at a level that was reasonable in relation to the so-called natural rate, was common. The long-standing arguments about the hardships caused by 'biting' usury still had force and a legal maximum was regarded as a means of preventing exploitation. It was also argued that it discouraged loans for wild-cat schemes at the expense of more worthy borrowers. Finally, a known rate was considered desirable for use in contracts in which no individual rate had been mentioned.[52]

(vi) Bank Credit, Paper Money and the Rate of Interest
Most of the discussions of the relation between the rate of interest and the supply of money so far considered were concerned with metallic money and the precious metals. But the

---

H. J. Habakkuk, 'The Long-Term Rate of Interest and the Price of Land in the Seventeenth Century', *Economic History Review*, 2nd series, V (1951–2).

[50] Locke, pp. 51–2.
[51] For Petty see p. 54 above. North, p. 521.
[52] E.g. Locke, pp. 103 et seq. Barbon, *Discourse of Trade*, p. 20.

seventeenth century was a time of active experiment in and speculation about banks and paper money.[53] The example of continental countries in establishing banks long before had not been copied
in this country. Banks had however been advocated by a number
of English writers of the first part of the century, by Malynes,
Misselden and Mun, for instance, as a means of increasing the
efficiency with which the supply of money was used. In Mun's
view, of course, this would increase the supply of precious metals
available for use as trading commodities. During the Commonwealth there was an outcrop of important pamphlets on banks,
emphasising their usefulness as a means of facilitating expansion
of trade by increasing the basis of credit. Proliferation of promis-
sory notes based on paper obligations created in the course of,
trade, for example, was proposed by William Potter in 1650.
Samuel Hartlib, in 1653, proposed that a Bank of England should
be established similar to the Bank of Amsterdam; he also proposed the use of land mortgages as a basis for the extension of
credit.[54] The post-Restoration period was even more enthusiastic
and there was a plethora of projects too numerous to be listed
here.

There were also writers who believed that the great obstacle to
expansion and growth was the lack of market realisability of real
resources owned by the potential customers of a bank.[55] The
latter's object therefore was to set up mortgage banks and Lom-
bards issuing loans to individuals depositing their real titles
to wealth, particularly trading stock. There were also innumerable projects for land banks such as Barbon's in which loans were
to be made on security of titles to lands.[56] The last two methods

[53] See Horsefield, op. cit., Part IV for a detailed and most illuminating
account. Also Lipson, Vol. III, pp. 208–48 for a short account of the
growth of capital and the development of banking.

[54] Henry Robinson, *England's Safety in Trades Encrease*; William
Potter, *The Key of Wealth*; Samuel Hartlib, *A discoverie for Division or
Setting out of Land* ... etc.; also *An Essay upon Mr Potter's Design con-
cerning a bank of Lands*.

[55] E.g. by Henry Robinson, 1652; Edward Chamberlayne, 1667, etc. See
Horsefield, Ch. 10.

[56] E.g. by Hugh Chamberlen, John Briscoe, John Asgill and Barbon,
to mention only some the best-known projectors. See Horsefield, Chaps.
14, 15, 16, 17. A Lombard may be described as a glorified pawnshop;
all kinds of goods, including trading stocks, would be accepted and the
receipts issued passed as money.

would directly increase the effective supply of loans by credit creation and tend to reduce the rate of interest. For Barbon this was a major objective, but for some projectors merely a by-product. Increases in the supply of money, *paper or metallic*, would be a necessary consequence.[57] Other projectors took the view that some form of credit money could be issued related to what they believed to be the unlimited or evergrowing wealth of the country. Its creation would release the economy from the straitjacket imposed by the limited supplies of metallic money. That the issue of such credit money required in some way to be limited in relation to the real resources backing it, was implicit in the plans for basing banks on the security of some type of real resources. This problem was explicitly pointed out in the criticism made in the Scottish Parliament in 1693 in relation to a proposal of Hugh Chamberlen for setting up a land bank in Scotland. It was pointed out that, if money were multiplied at the rate Chamberlen's scheme involved, the prices of all commodities and wages would rise. Inflation not the increase of real wealth would thus develop.[58]

Scotland was equally cautious about what was perhaps the most grandiose scheme of all: John Law's project for the creation of in effect unlimited wealth by the issue of paper money on the basis of the real wealth of the nation.[59] The disaster following its acceptance in France not merely discredited get-rich-quick schemes for several decades but also demonstrated, in an extreme way, that the relation of credit creation of any sort to the growth of wealth was more complex than hitherto realised by some enthusiasts.

The projects for banks and paper money thus also illustrate the divergence of views as to the nature of the relations between the rate of interest, the supply of money and the level of economic activity or growth, which appeared in the controversy over the question of whether the rate of interest should be lowered. However, even the numerous projectors who accepted the traditional view that the supply of money was the independent variable and the rate of interest the dependent variable held one important

---

[57] See on this Horsefield, particularly p. 102.

[58] Horsefield, Ch. 14, Section III.

[59] His plan was set out in his *Proposals for Supplying the Nation with Money* (1705).

idea in common with the non-traditional school. They believed that the level of activity and the rate of growth could, and should, be independent of the supply of metallic money and hence of the requirements of any policy connected with the balance of payments.

(vii) Conclusions

This study set out to reconsider the theories of interest that emerged in the seventeenth-century discussions in England in the light of their peculiar institutional and analytical background: the final acceptance of interest as an economic phenomenon late in the preceding century, the absence of a banking system and paper money and the heritage of ideas about problems of money and foreign trade. These last had developed partly as a result of analysis, partly by the drawing of conclusions without analysis from observation of apparently associated phenomena during the long period during which interest was discussed in moral, not economic, terms and was not in any way included as an integral part of the economic system. Hence the seventeenth-century heritage of ideas on monetary problems was without a theory of the role and determination of the rate of interest or any indication that this could affect conclusions about monetary problems.

During the seventeenth century the analysis of the relation between the supply of money and the level of activity was developed and refined by one group of writers, whom I have for obvious reasons called traditional, round the concept of the necessary stock of money. This concept was developed in such a way that the acceptance of the quantity theory of money in general terms did not lead to the conclusion that changes in the supply of money would only affect the general level of prices. The traditional view that changes in the supply of money affected the level of activity as well as, or instead of, the price level was retained without elucidation of the determinants of any particular combination of effects.

It has been pointed out that the traditional writers on the theory of interest naturally treated interest as a phenomenon that must fit into the established framework of monetary analysis or ideas. The rate of interest was treated by them therefore as a basically dependent variable – a price determined by the supply of loans, which depended in some way on the supply of money, and by the demand for loans which depended on the level of activity but might or might not be interest-elastic. Looked at in this way the rate of interest appeared to be fundamentally a subsidiary phenomenon having primarily a micro-allocative function. But it was not quite so simply seen, for the supply of loans was regarded as interest-elastic influencing the well-recognised phenomena of hoarding and dis-hoarding and international capital flows. Some writers realised that in this way rate of interest would have a feed-back effect on the quantity of money in circulation and the balance of trade.

In elucidating these matters in connection with the controversy of whether the legal rate of interest should be lowered, a concept of a 'natural' rate emerged as the rate equating supply and demand in a *free* market. In some sense it was seen as an optimum rate, for divergences due to government policy were considered to have untoward effects on the supply and demand for loans, and hence on the supply of money and the level of activity and also on the supply of money.

(A parallel concept of a 'natural' price for a good also developed as part of the general theory of value as will be seen in the next study.)

It was noticed that writers differed as to whether the actual level of the 'natural' rate of interest had any secondary effect on the economy according as to whether the demand for loans was regarded as interest-elastic or inelastic. The analysis was adapted for use by writers who favoured inflation as well as by noninflationist anti-deflationists.

The problem of how changes in the supply of money directly affected the supply of loans, as the traditional writers believed, was not resolved, nor was a theory of the relation of real saving to the supply of loans, or to the supply of money, integrated into the analysis except to some extent by North. There was nevertheless a widespread belief that saving was dependent not on the rates of profit or interest but on the growth of wealth and sociological attitudes.

Without over-interpreting the views of these traditional writers it can be said, I think, that they had some concept of aggregate demand as a result of their acceptance of the theory of a relation between changes in the 'necessary stock of money' and economic activity. Naturally perhaps this appears more definite in the seventeenth than in earlier centuries. It cannot be concluded from this that these writers had any theory of or even belief in an inherent tendency to a deficiency of aggregate demand. Even the inflationists within the traditional school referred to in this study did not attempt to show that there was an inherent tendency to deficiency of aggregate demand. It has been noted that they were each writing at times of actual or believed crises in export markets and did not distinguish between such causes of unemployment and general causes of permanent unemployed resources. The non-inflationist anti-deflationists seem to have considered that if mistaken policies leading to deflation were avoided there was no inherent problem of inadequate demand. I do not think therefore that it is possible to build into the stated views of the writers included by this study in this group a genuine theory of inadequate aggregate demand as an inherent attribute of the economic system, whether or not any of the inflationists believed it to exist.

The emergence of the non-traditional school of Culpepper and his followers has been shown to be of particular interest. Not only did this group break away from the traditional preoccupation with monetary problems, but their break arose from the conviction that it was the rate of interest not the supply of money that was all-important with regard to activity and growth. The rate of interest was seen as an important cost affecting both investment and enterprise and also competition in international trade. Investment was singled out, for I believe the first time in the English literature, as the mainspring of activity and growth. An inexhaustible range of opportunities for investment was clearly believed to exist, the development of which was hampered by the level of the rate of interest. Hence they claimed that the government could increase the wealth of the country merely by reducing the rate of interest. In consequence they had to attempt to show that the supply of loans was interest-inelastic and foreign borrowing undesirable. No attempt to explain what determined the total supply of loans seems to have been thought necessary. The question of how the supply of loans would increase in response to an increased demand was therefore not explicitly discussed but Child seemed to imply that the initial increase in wealth expected would solve their problem. The concepts of the natural rate of interest and aggregate demand were not of analytical concern to them and their ambiguity about the supply of money may have been partly due to their lack of interest in the concept of aggregate demand. Their views on money may perhaps be fairly summarised by saying that they believed, though they could not prove it, that the supply of money was either unimportant or would in some way be adjusted. The logical conclusion for members of this group who were also concerned with banking was of course that it could be adjusted by the use of bank money and supplies of bank credit. For the group the favourable balance of trade policy was a nuisance in so far as it was used as an argument against reduction of the rate of interest. They naturally contributed to the criticisms of the policy. They can be regarded as early supporters of the view that the level of domestic activity could and should be independent of the requirements of the balance of trade. In contrast of course the traditional writers either hoped to adjust the balance of trade to the requirements of domestic policy or regarded the latter as less important than the former.

The significance of the approach of banking projectors to problems of money and interest has been emphasised. Some of them were concerned with increasing the volume of credit and/or providing bank money as an alternative or supplement to metallic money. Broadly speaking they were concerned *inter alia* with releasing the activity and growth of the economy from what they conceived to be the straitjacket of the supply of the metallic money and the balance of payments. Those that bothered with the rate of interest, rather than simply the supply of money and credit, considered that the increase in the supply of loans would lower the rate of interest. To some this seems to have been a major objective and they, like Barbon, really belong to the Culpepper group; others seem to have considered a fall in the rate of interest merely as a consequential advantage. Whatever their detailed prognostications they were characterised by an optimistic belief that there was plenty of opportunities for growth; it was not lack of aggregate demand that was their concern, but the technical monetary and banking problems of providing the means for realising it. It seems to me that most were more concerned with the supply of money than with the rate of interest and to this extent they had affinities with the traditional school.

These comparisons of the approaches to the problem of the rate of interest show that far more was involved than the question of whether the legal maximum rate of interest was too high – the issue which provided the occasions for much of the discussion. What was really involved was the question of the role of the rate of interest considered as a purely economic phenomenon.

The analytical incompleteness or inadequacy of the theories put forward seem to me to be less remarkable than the recognition of so many of the important questions relating to the rate of interest. This outburst of economic speculation in England, which affected other fields of economic theory as well, must I think be at least partly attributable to the critical situation of an economy in the early stages of potentially rapid economic development without appropriate financial experience or institutions.

It is perhaps proper to close this study by drawing attention to the striking difference between Adam Smith and the seventeenth-century writers with respect to the importance attached to questions connected with the rate of interest compared to the rate of profit. Adam Smith was far more concerned with the latter and in particular with the causes and consequences of the tendency of the rate of profit to fall. His evident belief that hoarding was not a significant economic phenomenon combined with his *a priori* denial of any influence of the changes in the total supply of money on the level of activity and the supply of loans is important in this connection. It enabled him to treat the supply of loans as entirely dependent on real factors – social attitudes and the growth of wealth. The demand for loans was treated as dependent solely on the rate of profit. He concluded that the rate of interest was therefore simply a dependent variable, reflecting the relation between the growth of real wealth and the fall in the rate of profit with the growth of real wealth. Thus he argued in the chapter 'Of Stock lent at Interest' that the supply of loans, the savings of 'the monied interest', will necessarily increase with the increasing total stock of society. Therefore as supply increases, interest, the price of loans, will necessarily tend to fall 'not only from those general causes which make the market price of things commonly diminish as their quantity increases, but from other causes which are peculiar to this particular case', i.e. the tendency of the rate of profit to fall.[60] The rate of interest thus had only an allocative role and did not influence the level of activity, and throughout the *Wealth of Nations* the rate of interest is treated as a secondary phenomenon, for instance it is 'always a derivative

[60] *Wealth of Nations*, Vol. I, p. 335.

revenue'.[61] So much for the free market rate; the legal rate below this rate would, if it could be enforced (Adam Smith argued) have the same effects as the total prohibition of interest. A legal rate substantially above the free market rate however would distort the allocation of loans in favour of 'prodigals and projectors' leading to waste of stock. Thus only incorrect intervention in the market for loans could give the rate of interest any importance. Rightly or wrongly the economic universe with which the *Wealth of Nations* is concerned is entirely different from that with which the seventeenth-century English writers were concerned and this is reflected in the change in the importance attached to the price of loans as well as to the supply of money.

[61] Ibid., p. 54. See also Tucker, pp. 49–50.

II *The development of Value Theory in the Seventeenth Century: a by-product of the Theories of Money, Trade and Interest*

> Only what is rare is valuable, and water, which is the best of all things . . . is also the cheapest.
>
> PLATO

(i) The Seventeenth-Century Heritage[1]

The reasons for the emergence of speculation about economic matters by the great Schoolmen of the thirteenth century and the continued concern with them in subsequent centuries is not difficult to comprehend. Feudal society was, it might be said, no sooner established and a tolerable approximation to the rule of law realised, than its economic basis began to dissolve. Relatively settled conditions facilitated the development of trade and this broke down the local self-sufficiency of economic units. With trade, credit transactions developed and ownership of wealth as

---

[1] This study is an expansion and revision of my article in *Economica* (May 1963), 'Some Seventeenth Century Contributions to the Theory of Value'. It is intended on the one hand to clarify the relations between seventeenth-century developments and the work of the schoolmen, on the other hand to provide a more secure foundation for considering the eighteenth-century contributions. The main additions and alterations are: additional material at the beginning and end of Section i; a short discussion in Section ii, footnote 23, of Locke's treatment of value in his *Civil Government*; the discussion on the measure of value (originally section IV now section iii) has been developed and is entirely new except for the first two paragraphs; a new and longer concluding section v replaces the old section V. The old section III is now section iv without its concluding paragraphs as the problems raised in them are considered in the last study in this book 'Aspects of Wages and Profit Theory'. I am grateful to the editors of *Economica* for permission to reprint the appropriate parts of the original article.

distinct from original status began to become influential. In short economic development broke down, or rather threatened to break down, customary and legal economic relationships. The church was obliged to consider the applicability of its teaching to these circumstances and to formulate an approach to current economic and social problems. The centuries during which feudal society had been becoming established were not notable for analytical discussions of the ethical implications of the economic organisation of society. The centuries during which it began to decay forced such discussion upon the church. Hence the concern of the Schoolmen from the twelfth century onwards with economic questions. It is important to appreciate that among the Schoolmen were men whose intellectual ability would have been outstanding in any age. They were not foolish men fumbling emotionally for rules of thumb. They were capable of, and indeed carried through, elaborate abstract analysis in economics as well as in theology.

The sources of information and of authority available were the classical philosophers, Roman Law and ancient custom, precedent, the Bible and the Christian Fathers and other writings and edicts of Christian authorities. The Schoolmen thus did not start their investigations of price from a *tabula rasa*. Certain aspects of the phenomena of exchange value or price have been well understood from the beginning of economic speculation in the works of the Greek philosophers. It had been a commonplace since antiquity that any good having exchange value must be capable of satisfying a want and be limited in supply in relation to that want – usefulness or utility on the one hand, scarcity on the other. It is of course obvious that anyone engaged in buying and selling, or governments or officials concerned with the problems of maintaining supplies, were well aware that the market price of goods, if left unregulated, was determined by demand and supply. Philosophers observing the commonplace facts of the market had noted that usefulness, or utility, in the ordinary sense of some inherent capacity to satisfy some practical or essential need, did not necessarily result in a high exchange value. On the contrary, conveniences and luxuries were normally more valuable in the market than necessities. The diamond/water paradox was recognised. This apparently flagrant divergence of market values from commonsense values led to the obvious conclusion that exchange values must depend upon the relation between wants (and the incomes and enthusiasms of those having the wants) on the one hand, and scarcity on the other. No new words were introduced to distinguish between the inherent capacity of a good for satisfying some requirement, its use value (which might be graded in relation to the type of want that could be satisfied) and its exchange value.

Plato for instance observed, somewhat caustically perhaps, that 'only what is rare is valuable, and water, which is the best of all things... is also the cheapest'[2] Aristotle merely noted the difference between value in use and value in exchange pointing out that the value of anything is determined according to men's need to use it.[3] A Greek explorer of the second century B.C., Agatharchidas, explained the way use and scarcity were taken into account in determining exchange value by peoples abounding in gold, as follows:

> They exchange gold for three times as much as bronze, and for iron they give twice as much gold, whilst silver is worth ten times what gold is. Their method of fixing value is based on abundance and scarcity. In these things the whole life of men considers not so much the nature of the thing as the necessity of its use.[4]

In the second century A.D. Sextus Empiricus, the sceptic philosopher, found the subject of value an appropriate illustration of relativity, stating

> Rare things too we count as precious, but not what is familiar to us and easily got. Thus if we should suppose water to be rare, how much more precious it would appear to us than all the things which are accounted precious! Or, if we should imagine gold to be simply scattered in quantities over the earth like stones, to whom do we suppose it would then be precious or worth hoarding?[5]

Realisation of the obvious fact that demand and supply, usually stated in terms of use and scarcity, provide an explanation of actual exchange value, or price, is equally evident throughout the

[2] *Euthydemus*, p. 304 B. quoted by Pufendorf in *De Jure Naturae et Gentium Libri*, Classics of International Law edition, Vol. II, p. 680.
[3] *Ethics*, IX.
[4] *De Mari Rusio*, Ch. XLIX, quoted by Pufendorf, p. 683.
[5] *Outline of Pyrrhonism*, I, Ch. XIV, p. 85, Loeb Classical Library edn.

scholastic period. Thirteenth-century Schoolmen, such as Albertus Magnus and Ricardus of Media Villa, seem to have appreciated fully the philosophers' conclusions on the relative nature of exchange value.[6] Neither philosophic comments on the nature of exchange value in free markets, nor the Biblical exhortations to Christians to display charity in all their dealings, nor the structure of society implied, however, that the interaction of demand and supply would naturally result in a desirable price structure. On the contrary, prices determined in this way were frequently regarded as inconsistent with popular or other more objective criteria of welfare, particularly of course if they diverged violently from customary prices in the case of necessities of life. The great discussions on the *just price* by the Schoolmen, from the thirteenth to the sixteenth centuries, were fundamentally examinations of the circumstances under which the prices established by demand and supply, use and scarcity, were or were not consistent with a Christian concept of justice in exchange. The problem was to discover what ensured that the criterion of commutative justice, that is equivalence of values in exchange, was satisfied. Inevitably these discussions considered whether the costs of production had any connection with the just price and if so what were the cost items to be included: should they include for instance the just rewards for labour or other services?[7]

The discussions as to whether the just price should cover legitimate rewards for the services required to maintain supplies implied an underlying recognition of one of the functions of prices. It pushed the problem of the just price back to the stage of determination of legitimate rewards and identification of services to be rewarded. The determination of legitimate rewards, however, was not seen as a market problem but rather in terms of maintaining the providers of services according to their customary standard of living. On this line of reasoning the just prices of goods were determined by the parameters of the customary distribution of wealth deriving from the hierarchy of the social system. This determined the costs recognised as just.[8]

[6] See Demant, *The Just Price*, pp. 62 et seq. on Albertus Magnus.

[7] See Demant, pp. 64–5 on, for instance, Duns Scotus on the relation of costs to the just price.

[8] See G. O'Brien, *Medieval Economic Teaching* and Schumpeter, *History of Economic Analysis*, pp. 93 et seq.

The other main line of inquiry pursued by the Schoolmen was that of trying to identify market situations in which price would be unfair, or as we might say, involved exploitation. It was argued for instance, by Aquinas that the special need of a buyer for a good might not be taken into account; the utility of a good for the purpose of the fair price was the utility to the ordinary buyers. Advantage was not to be taken of the position of the particular individual. Similarly, the seller was not allowed to take advantage of a particularly advantageous position in which he might be vis-à-vis the market as a whole. Forestalling and regrating and engrossing were thus condemned.[9] From such considerations the idea had emerged by the fifteenth century that the just price should be fixed by *communis aestimatio*, that is by the common opinion of the well-informed body of buyers and sellers; they would take into account the utility of the good to buyers in general, its supply and the cost of the supply. St. Antoninus of Florence (1389–1459) identified the just price with the market price. This was finally defined as the price which could be obtained in a market supposing common knowledge of conditions and the absence of fraud and compulsion (St. Thomas, Cardinal Cajetan (1468–1534)). This idea was explained by De Soto (1494–1560) as the price as 'reckoned by prudent men and the market'.[10] Such a price was clearly regarded as equivalent to that which would have been established in a free and competitive market. The question of the relation of such a price to long-run or normal supply price was not closely considered, despite the emphasis laid by some of the writers, such as for example Duns Scotus, on the relation between the just price and costs. It was not until the late sixteenth century that more careful attention was given to this problem. Molina (1535–1600) and Lessius (1554–1623) for example, while accepting the price of a competitive market as the just price, had some conception of the dependence of the maintenance of supplies on the price-cost relationship.[11]

The Schoolmen's new conclusions were of major importance. The price reached in a competitive and informed market satisfied the welfare criterion of the just price. This criterion was identified with the absence of exploitation arising from imperfec-

[9] See G. O'Brien.   [10] See on this Demant, pp. 68–73.
[11] See B. W. Dempsey, *Interest and Usury*, Chs. VI–VIII and Schumpeter, pp. 97–9.

tions of the market. Finally it was considered that this market price should in some way normally conform with expenses of supply. The analytical relationship between price and cost of supply tended to be concealed because the discussions were commonly in terms of whether a trader had a moral right to recompense; this in turn required justification in terms of identifying the services rendered. It was this approach which left *lacunae* in the analysis as to the causal connection between divergences in just price determined by demand and scarcity in a competitive market, that is actual market price, and the just price taking into account the costs of supply. The existence of this gap seemed to have been rather incompletely recognised by the later Schoolmen.

(ii) The Theory of Value – a By-product of the Theory of Money
The seventeenth-century writers thus started out from a reasonably clear body of analysis with regard to the nature of exchange value and its determination in the market, and some indications of the function of the long-term supply price in maintaining supplies. Since, however, the value elements in long-run supply price were written in from data given by the framework of law and custom, there was effectively nothing to help them in the application of value analysis to factor prices. Nor was there any indication of the possibility, or desirability, of an economic analysis of income distribution based on factor valuations.

The views on value and price of seventeenth-century authors appear most often because they were (or were thought to be) essential to the analysis of the particular practical problem of policy they were discussing. Monetary problems, the foreign exchanges, the regulation of interest and the measurement of value seem to have been the chief among these problems.

The great discussions of the foreign exchanges and the balance of payments of the early part of the century provide familiar source material for the history of the theory of the exchanges and the distribution of the precious metals. They have been discussed already from that point of view in the first of these studies. It is not commonly realised that they also provide information about the explanations of value accepted at that time, and the use to which the analysis of value was put. The main practical problem of policy was how to stop the outflow of the precious metals. The question to be resolved was whether attention should be concentrated on control of the exchange rate for sterling or on the balance of payments. The most famous writers in the debate – Malynes, Misselden and Mun – found themselves involved in consideration of the determination of prices. Put briefly, the main point at issue between Misselden and Mun on the one hand, and Malynes on the other, was whether or not the foreign exchange rate was a price for sterling determined like other prices by supply and demand.

In *A Treatise of the Canker of England's Common Wealth* Malynes had stated that the price of individual commodities depended on 'the plentie or scarcitie of the things themselves, or the use of them.'[12] Misselden held much the same view. Thus in *The Circle of Commerce: or, the Balance of Trade*, in reply to Malynes, he declared: '... but it is the plenty or scarcitie of Commodities, their use or *Non-use* that maketh them rise or fall in price.'[13] And he makes clear the application of this principle to the foreign exchange market:

> *The plentie or scarcitie of moneys*, which perpetually doth cause the Exchanges to rise or fall: and which doth as certainly, in forraine parts where moneys goe uncertaine, rule their Values or denomination, as the plenty or scarcitie of Commodities does their Prices.[14]

The relevance of the use/scarcity analysis of price to the foreign exchange market is perhaps made even more obvious in the following passage. Here Misselden is referring to Malynes's argument that the foreign exchange rates ought to be precisely equal to the ratios of the metallic contents of currencies, the *pars pro pari* of Malynes:

> For there would be no advantage left, neither to him that delivereth nor him that taketh, when mony must be answered with mony in the same *intrinsique* value. For as it is the goodness of a Commodity that directeth the price: yet that price is greater or lesse, according to the use of that thing, or the judgement of the buyer and seller: even so it is the fineness of money, that directeth the price or value of the Exchange,

---

[12] See p. 11 n. 17 above   [13] 1623 edition, p. 21.   [14] Ibid., p. 69.

yet this price is greater or less according to the occasions of both parties contracting for the same.[15]

The particular merits of Malynes's and Misselden's arguments about the foreign exchanges have been discussed in the first study in this book. What is of interest here is that they started out with similar explanations of the determination of the exchange values of goods, which both regarded as so much a commonplace as to need no proof, but argued whether this also applied to the price of sterling in the foreign exchange market.

Mun displays a similar basic assumption about the determination of value in his *England's Treasure by Forraign Trade,* and explicitly uses the same sort of argument as Misselden about its applicability to the foreign exchanges. Thus he argues:

> it is not the *power of Exchange* that doth enforce treasure where the rich Prince will have it, but it is the money proceeding of wares in Forraigne trade that doth enforce the exchange, and rules of the price thereof high or low, according to the plenty or scarcity of the said money.[16]

It was on the basis of this argument, as to the application of demand and supply analysis that both Mun and Misselden tried to prove that the foreign exchange market should be free from control. This was of course the main point of the controversy; but all three writers had something to say about the effect of the price of exports on the demand for them. Mun's statement, very near the beginning of his book, is of particular interest:

> In our exportations we must not only regard our own superfluities, but also we must consider our neighbours necessities, so that upon the wares which they cannot want, nor yet be furnished thereof elsewhere, we may (besides the vent of the Materials) gain so much of the manufacture as we can, and also endeavour to sell them dear, so far forth as the high price cause not a less vent of the quantity. But the superfluities of our commodities which strangers use, and may also have the same from other Nations, or may abate their vent by the use of some such like wares from other places, and with little inconvenience; we must in this case strive to sell as cheap as possible we can, rather than lose the utterance of such wares.[17]

[15] Ibid., pp. 97–8.   [16] Op. cit., p. 175.   [17] Ibid., p. 128.

This was shrewd advice to give to his son to whom the *Treasure* was originally dedicated, and was backed up by examples from his experience which would serve today as simple illustrations of the factors affecting the elasticity of demand.

These merchants' statements on the nature and determination of exchange value – actually market price in an uncontrolled market – were clearly not the result of new theoretical analysis. They were applications of the accepted explanation of the determination of prices. There are however some other interesting points about the controversy. The first is that in it a bold attempt was made to use the explanation of exchange value, i.e. price, as a tool of analysis in solving a particular problem of commercial policy. The second point of special interest is that the debate had in fact turned on an issue fundamental to the theory of value. The case for freedom of the foreign exchange market had focused on the argument that there was no absolute or objective basis for value in exchange, either with or without ethical implications, for it was simply the consequence of a relation between scarcity and wants. This principle was discussed with great elaboration in the last decade of the seventeenth century by Nicholas Barbon and John Locke. Further, both Misselden and Mun implied that the price determined by supply and demand in the exchange markets was the correct price in the interests of the smooth working of the whole system of foreign trade and finance. In some sense it was regarded as an equilibrium price. This price in practice seems to be the same as the just price of the later Schoolmen whether defined in terms of *communis aestimatio*, or of the competitive market price, but its welfare interpretations are different, the Schoolmen's being ethical concerned with the welfare of men's souls.[18]

In the latter part of the seventeenth century problems of the legal rate of interest and the re-coinage replaced the foreign ex-

[18] This interpretation can be supported by the frequent allusions to the importance of the absence of monopoly. For instance, Misselden defined the evil of monopoly as restricting 'the liberty of commerce to some or a few persons', which results in 'the setting of the price of the monopolist for his private benefit' (*Free Trade; or, the Means to make Trade Flourish*, op. cit., p. 57). Although this passage occurs in one of Misselden's attacks on the privileges of the trading companies, he is openly making use of the argument that price reached by demand and supply in a free and unmonopolised market is consistent with the public welfare. Mun also goes to great

changes as a centre of debate. The principle of the relativity of value was applied in an outstanding manner quite deliberately to the solution of these problems by Barbon and Locke in the last decade of the century. They both found it necessary to examine in an orderly way the nature of demand and the significance of the relative nature of value in exchange in relation to monetary problems.

In 1690 Barbon's *Discourse of Trade* provided a systematic analysis of value, money, credit and interest, employment and trade theory and policy. In particular, Barbon was concerned with the nature of money in connection with the contemporary controversy over the re-coinage and the discussion of the lowering of the rate of interest, and ultimately with foreign trade policy and the level of economic activity and employment. He observed that there was an analytical connection between the nature of value and certain problems of money, riches and trade.[19] The arrangement of the *Discourse of Trade* displays his general line of thought. The first section is headed 'Of Trade, and the Stock or Wares of Trade', the second 'Of the Quality and Quantity of Wares'. This leads to the section of particular interest for this chapter, 'Of the Value and Price of Wares', followed by 'Of Money, Credit and Interest'. From here he goes straight on to his three sections on trade and employment using his analysis of value and money to criticise the favourable balance of trade policy.

Barbon's treatment of the determination of value in exchange, in contrast to the earlier seventeenth-century writers cited, is a deliberate analysis. Mere acceptance, or assumption, of the scarcity/utility and supply and demand theorems would have been inadequate to establish with sufficient emphasis the relativity of all values in exchange, including those of the precious metals. His discussion is based on an interesting and detailed discussion of the nature of wants which leads him to conclude that they depend mainly on psychological rather than physical requirements. It is the sort of discussion so much admired by Jevons,

---

pains to demonstrate that individuals could not manipulate the foreign exchange rates in a free competitive market for their own benefit (op. cit., Chs. XIII and XIV).

[19] This connection is made particularly clear in his 1696 pamphlet, *A Discourse Concerning Coining the New Money Lighter*, in the statement of 'The Contrary Propositions in Answer to Mr Locke'.

though Jevons does not appear to have known of it. The section on value starts off with familiar commonplace: 'The value of all wares arises from their Use; Things of no Use, have no Value.'[20] This leads him into the discussion of the difference between 'wants of the body' and 'wants of the mind' and his discourse on the nature of wants:

> The Use of Things, are to supply the Wants and Necessities of Man: There are Two General Wants that Mankind is born with; the Wants of the Body and the Wants of the Mind; To supply these two necessities, all things under the Sun become useful, and therefore have a Value . . . Wares useful to supply the Wants of the Body, are all things necessary to support Life; such are in Common Estimation; . . . But if strictly Examined, nothing is absolutely necessary to support Life, but Food; . . .
>
> Wares, that have their Value for supplying the Wants of the Mind, are all such things that can satisfie Desire; Desire implies Want. It is the Appetite of the Soul, and is as natural to the Soul, as Hunger to the Body.
>
> The Wants of the Mind are infinite, Man naturally Aspires, and as the Mind is elevated, his senses grow more refined, and more capable of Delight; his Desires are inlarged, and the Wants increase with his Wishes, which is for every thing that is rare, can gratifie his Senses, adorn his Body, and provide the Ease, Pleasure, and Pomp of Life . . .

and so on (pp. 13–15).

After this elaborate discussion, Barbon introduces scarcity in the traditional way to determine price or value in exchange:

> The Price of Wares is the present Value; And ariseth by Computing the occasions or use for them, with the Quantity that serves that Occasion; for the Value of things depending on the use of them, the *Over-plus* of Those Wares, which are more than can be used, become worth nothing; So that Plenty with respect to the occasion, makes things cheap; and scarcity, dear (p. 18).

Although we are thus back at the usual scarcity/utility formulation, Barbon goes on to state explicitly the significance of the

[20] *Discourse of Trade*, p. 15. All references in this study are to the 1690 edition.

conclusion with regard to the nature of value, a conclusion which we have seen Mun and Misselden had used with less formal explanation in connection with the value of sterling. Barbon declares: 'There is no fixt Price or Value of anything for the Wares of Trade . . .' (p. 18). The implication with regard to the freedom of prices from control is clearly brought out in the following passage at the end of the section:

> But the Market is the best Judge of Value; for by the con-course of Buyers and Sellers, the Quantity of Wares, and the Occasion for them are Best known; Things are just worth so much, as they can be sold for, according to the old Rule, *Valet Quantum Vendi Potest* (p. 20).

This analysis of the relative nature of value is applied explicitly to money in the section following 'Of Money, Credit and Interest'. Here Barbon argues that gold and silver have no certain intrinsic value, for their values are determined by the same causes as the values of other goods. 'Nothing in it self, [he says] hath a certain Value; One thing is as much worth as another: And it is time, and place, that give a difference to the value of all things' (p. 27). Having disposed in this way of the idea that gold and silver have any particular inherent value, he is able to develop his views on trade and employment without bothering about the effects on the balance of trade. Barbon thus elaborated the theory of the relative nature of value to the point at which he could use it to justify certain policy suggestions.

It will have been noticed that though Malynes, Misselden and Mun all held essentially the same view of the determination of value as Barbon, they did not pursue its application so far as to conclude that it showed there was no particular importance to be attached to gold and silver in trade, or Malynes's and Misselden's reasons for wanting inflows. It is worth pointing out however that they were discussing determination of value in relation to a different problem in a different context – the choice of a policy for checking the adverse exchanges and outflow of bullion.

In his *Discourse Concerning Coining the New Money Lighter*, Barbon went to even greater pains to make clear the relativity of exchange value and the relevance of this to problems of money. This *Discourse* was published six years later and was a reply to Locke's proposals on the re-coinage. In it he declares:

There is nothing that troubles this Controversy more, than for want of distinguishing between Value and Vertue.

Value is only the Price of Things: That can never be certain, because it must be then at all times, and in all places, of the same Value; therefore nothing can have an Intrinsic Value.

But Things have an Intrinsic Vertue in themselves, which in all places have the same Vertue (p. 6).

He then goes on to illustrate the nature of 'vertue' as the inherent physical properties of goods, and finally summarises his theory of value in five rules:

1. That nothing has a Price or Value in itself.
2. That the Price or Value of every thing arises from the occasion or use for it.
3. That Plenty or Scarcity in respect to their occasion, makes things of greater or lesser Value.
4. That the Plenty or Scarcity of one Commodity do's not alter the Prices of other Commodities which are not for the same uses.
5. That in Trade and Commerce there is no difference in Commodities when their Values are equal; that is Twenty shillings worth of Lead or Iron to some Merchants is the same as Twenty Shillings in Silver or Gold (pp. 10–11).

Locke, he argues, is wrong because he has failed to appreciate the full significance of the relativity of exchange value and has, thus, been led to attribute an intrinsic value to silver (p. 9). In this second *Discourse* Barbon goes on, as in his first, to use his analysis of value to show that there is no advantage in a favourable balance of trade.

Locke's main discussion of value is better known than Barbon's. It occurs in *Some Considerations of the Consequences of the Lowering of Interest and Raising the Value of Money* (published in 1692). Locke finds that it is necessary to elucidate the difference between the value of money and the price of money, i.e. interest. This requires a statement of the nature and determination of exchange value. He starts with a statement of demand and supply as determinants of price; thus 'the price of any Commodity rises or falls, by the proportion of the number of *Buyers* and *Sellers*'. This, he says, is a universal rule and the same thing as saying that price is determined by 'vent' and quantity.[21] From this point he goes on like Barbon to an analysis of the nature of demand:[22]

> The Vent of any Thing depends upon its Necessity or Usefulness, as Convenience, or Opinion guided by Phancy or fashion shall determine . . .
> . . . Men give any Portion of Money for whatsoever is absolutely necessary, rather than go without it. And in such things the Scarcity of them alone makes their Prices.

He illustrates this in terms of the demand for grains:

> By the like proportions of Increase and Decrease, does the value of Things, more or less convenient, rise and fall in respect of Money, only with this difference, that things absolutely *necessary* for Life must be had at any rate; but Things *convenient* will be had only as they stand in preference with other Conveniences: And therefore in any one of these Commodities, the value rises only as its quantity is less, and vent greater, which depends on its being preferr'd to other Things in its Consumption. For supposing that at the same time there is a great scarcity of Wheat, and other Grain, there were a considerable quantity of *Oats*, Men, no questions, would give far more for Wheat than Oats, as being the healthier, pleasanter, and more convenient Food: But since Oats would serve to supply that absolute necessity of sustaining Life, Men would not rob themselves of all other Conveniences of Life by paying all their money for Wheat, when Oats, that are cheaper, though with some inconvenience, would supply that Defect.

This is on numerous counts an illuminating passage. It indicates the reasoning behind the idea of elasticity of demand in more general terms than Mun had done, though there is, of course, no formal statement of the concept. It also outlines in general terms the process of distribution of expenditure between different uses to maximise satisfactions, and shows that this distribution will be affected by changes in prices of commodities.

The relative nature of exchange value is developed somewhat

---

[21] *Some Considerations* . . ., p. 45. John Law pointed out that Locke should have used the word 'demand' not 'vent' since 'vent' could not differ from the amount sold, but demand could. He does not doubt, however, that Locke had meant demand. Law, *Money and Trade Considered*, 1705, Ch. I.   [22] Ibid., pp. 46–8.

later. Locke distinguished clearly between what Barbon called 'vertues' and value by means of an example displaying the circumstances under which water or air will have prices. This is essentially the same type of treatment as that, for instance, of Sextus Empiricus which had been quoted with approval by Pufendorf in 1672. Locke's exposition is so lucid that it deserves full quotation:

> The Being of any *good*, and useful *quality* in anything neither increases its *Price*, nor indeed makes it have any Price at all, but only as it lessens its quantity or increases its vent, each of these in proportion to one another. What more useful or necessary things are there to the Being, or Well-being, of Men, than Air and Water, and yet these have generally no Price at all, nor yield any Money. Because their quantity is immensely greater than their vent in most places of the World. But, as soon as ever Water (for Air still offers itself everywhere, without restraint or inclosure, and therefore is no where of any price) comes any where to be reduced into any proportion to its consumption, it begins presently to have a Price, and is sometimes sold dearer than Wine. Hence it is, that the best, and most useful things are commonly the cheapest; because though their Consumption be great, yet the Bounty of Providence has made their production large, and suitable to it (p. 63).

After explaining that improvements in the quality of a good will not affect its price unless it affects the demand in proportion to its quantity, Locke sums up his analysis of value in the following propositions:

> 1. That the Intrinsick Natural worth of any Thing consists in its fitness to supply the Necessities or serve the Conveniences of human Life; and the more necessary it is to our Being, or the more it contributes to our Well-being the greater is its worth: But yet ...
> 2. That there is no such thing as Intrinsick Natural settled value in any Thing, as to make any assign'd quantity of it, constantly worth any assigned quantity of any other.
> 3. The Marketable value of any assign'd quantities of two or more commodities are *pro hic and nunc*, equal, when they will exchange one for another.

4. The change of the Marketable value of one Commodity in respect of another Commodity . . . is not the altering of any intrinsick value or quality in the Commodity; . . . but the altering of some proportion which that Commodity bears to something else.

5. This proportion in all Commodities . . . is the proportion of their quantity to the vent. The Vent is nothing else, but the passing of Commodities from one owner to another in Exchange: (pp. 66–7).

Locke goes on immediately to apply this analysis to a comparison of the factors affecting the demand for goods with those affecting the demand for money. The similarity between Locke's analysis of value and Barbon's is obvious. Whatever the latter might think about Locke's application of it to money, he clearly was not justified in claiming in general terms that Locke failed to recognise the relative nature of exchange value. Locke, it will be noticed, graded the usefulness of goods like Plato, distinguishing between necessities and conveniences or luxuries.[23]

John Law's *Money and Trade Considered* showed that he shared Barbon's and Locke's conviction that the theory of value in general was the key to the theory of money, and he accepted

[23] Locke is sometimes credited, or debited, with a labour theory of value on the strength of the following passage from his *Civil Government*, par. 42: 'Let us but trace some of the ordinary provisions of life . . . and see how much they receive of their value from human industry. Bread, wine and cloth are things of daily use and great plenty, yet notwithstanding, acorns, water, leaves, or skins must be our bread, drink, and clothing, did not labour furnish us with these more useful commodities. For whatever bread is worth more than acorns, wine than water, and cloth or silk than leaves, skins or moss, that is wholly owing to labour and industry.' This passage occurs in Locke's discussion of the origin of property and the passage is evidently a simple illustration of the fact that the application of labour to natural resources makes them more useful by improving their physical attributes to enable them to satisfy wants more effectively. 'Useful' and 'worth' are obviously used here in the ordinary sense of inherent physical properties. This is perfectly consistent with his theory of value set out in his pamphlet *Some Considerations of the Consequences of lowering Interest*, and just described in the last few pages, for Locke emphasised that 'value in use' in the usual sense did not determine value in exchange. (See for instance his fourth proposition already quoted.) If this interpretation of the passage in *Civil Government* is accepted Locke did not put forward a labour theory of value and there is no inconsistency between this passage and his pamphlet.

the former as laid down by them. He explained this in his introduction, and appropriately heads his first chapter *How goods are valued, of barter, of silver; its value as a metal; its qualities fitting it for money;* . . . He stated the essential thesis that value is determined by utility and scarcity, reformulating Locke's wine/water illustration in terms of diamonds and water, thus:

> Goods have a value from the uses they are applied to; and their value is greater or lesser, not so much from their more or less valuable or necessary uses, as from the greater or lesser quantity of them in proportion to the demand for them. Example: water is of great use but of little value; because the quantity of water is much greater than demand for it. Diamonds are of little use, yet of great value, because the demand for diamonds is much greater than the quantity of them.[24]

Law clearly is not contributing anything new either in ideas or method of formulation. Barbon and Locke must however be regarded as having illumined the problem of value. The basic concept of the dependence of value on utility and scarcity was not, it has been shown, in any way original to them. Many of their illustrations, and even of their elaborations, of the concept of the relative nature of exchange value, and its significance, can be found in earlier work. Even the use of this characteristic as a tool for analysis of problems of policy had been clearly demonstrated in the controversies of the earlier part of the seventeenth century. Nevertheless, the deliberate setting out and demonstration of the nature of exchange value, and of the nature of the factors affecting demand, as a necessary preliminary to the investigation of problems of economic policy must, I think, be regarded as a major contribution to the development of scientific economic analysis independent of any incidental originality in the expositions.[25] Although, in the discussions on interest, the effect of lowering the legal rate of interest on the supply of loans was debated, the emphasis of their contributions to the theory of value was on the demand blade of Marshall's scissors.

[24] Law, op. cit., p. 4.

[25] Molina at least had made an orderly exposition in the late sixteenth century as part of his inquiry into the just price (see Dempsey, and Schumpeter). There is, however, no evidence to show that Barbon and Locke were familiar with Molina's work.

The problems with which these seventeenth-century writers on value were concerned did not require analysis of the influences affecting supply of goods and services, or of the function of the price system in the allocation of productive resources. It is obvious from the general literature that it was taken for granted that if losses were made constantly in an occupation, producers or merchants would leave it; if profits were particularly high, producers or merchants would try to enter. This seems to have been regarded as sufficient information. Barbon actually has a pregnant passage in his *Discourse of Trade* which implies, perhaps, the effects of differences between the actual prices realised in the market and those which would result in a profit sufficient to maintain supplies, but he does not develop this aspect. He explains that the merchant reckons the price he hopes to receive in terms of 'prime cost, charges and interest', and the artificer in terms of the cost of materials and the time spent working them up. The price of 'time' varied with 'the value of the art and the skill of the artist'. Both would reckon they lose by their trade, he says, 'if the prices of their wares so alter either by plenty or change of use, that they do not pay the merchant his interest, nor the artificer for his "time"'.[26] Barbon goes on merely to reiterate that it is the market that is 'the best judge of value'.

From the point of view of subsequent developments of the resource allocation aspects of the theory of value, the examination of value by Pufendorf in 1672 is of some relevance. Pufendorf's discussion of value and price in *De Jure Naturae et Gentium Libri* is part of his study of the law of contract. He is concerned with the nature of exchange value and the distinction between legal determination of price and 'natural, common or ordinary price'. Accidentally, almost, this has significance in the development of economic analysis, and is worth some discussion here. It brings out the contrast between market price and what is effectively regarded as a supply price based on costs.

Pufendorf's explanation of the nature of value and the determination of price was essentially the same as those of Barbon and Locke: 'The foundation of price in itself is the aptitude of a thing or action, by which it can either mediately or immediately contribute to the necessity of human life, or to making it more advantageous or pleasant. This is why in ordinary speech things

[26] *Discourse of Trade*, pp. 19–20.

of no use are said to be of no value.'[27] He goes on to explain
however that this is not a sufficient cause of price which depends
also on scarcity, so that price is determined by scarcity in relation
to the desire for particular goods.[28] This conclusion is reached
after an elaborate examination of the views of numerous philosophers and other authorities. Pufendorf goes on to a discussion of
the distinction between legal and 'natural, common or ordinary'
prices in contrast to the price which may actually exist at any
time in the market, owing to the immediate degree of scarcity in
relation to demand. Although the discussion is part of an investigation of the *just price* in relation to contracts, it is of particular
relevance. The 'natural, common or ordinary' price is that which
will normally rule in a market where there is no legal price. It is
apparently settled by the general informed opinion of the market
as a fair price so as to take into account the expenses 'commonly'
incurred by merchants; merchants can include in their estimates

> . . . the time they have spent, the plans they have formed, and
> the troubles they have met in acquiring, preserving, or distribu-
> ting their merchandise, as well as all necessary expenses for the
> labour of their servants. And it would surely be inhuman, and
> likely to destroy the industry of men, to try to allow a man for
> his business, or any sort of occupation, no more profit than
> barely permits him to meet his necessities by frugality and
> hardships.[29]

This 'natural, common or ordinary' price forms the focal point of
the just price; Pufendorf is clearly describing essentially the same
concept as that used by the more advanced schoolmen when using
costs as a basis of just price. Pufendorf does not provide a formal
exposition of the relation between this price and the price that
happens to exist at any moment, but his examples make clear
that the latter are to be regarded as temporary aberrations. The
mechanism by which these prices are adjusted is not discussed.
Not only, however, is the contrast between the two types of prices
clear, but the identification of the 'natural, common, or ordinary
price' with a supply price based on costs makes the gap peculiarly

[27] Pufendorf, p. 676, Vol. II of Classics of International Law edition, to
which all page references are made.

[28] Ibid., pp. 680–1, 683 et seq. and 688.   [29] Ibid., pp. 678–9.

obvious. The relation between Pufendorf's and Adam Smith's treatment of prices is considered in a later study in this book.

(iii) The Measure of Value

It was consistent with the interest in the theory of value in relation to problems of money, interest and trade, that some seventeenth-century writers should be concerned with trying to find a measure of value. Two attempts, those of Rice Vaughan and Petty, are of special interest against the background of the discussions on value, and also because of the thread of ideas which links them to the eighteenth-century discussions of Cantillon and Adam Smith in particular.

Rice Vaughan set out in his treatise *On Coins and Coinage* of 1623 (published in 1655) to measure changes in the value of money that were not attributable to changes in its metallic content. In particular he wanted to know how much of the change in the value of money was due to increases in the supply of precious metals. He opens Chapter IV, *Of the Proportions held between Gold and Silver, Ancient and Modern*, with the following statement:

> *Use* and *Delight*, or the opinion of them, are the causes why all things have a Value and Price set upon them, but the Proportion of that value and price is wholy governed by Rarity and Abundance: And therefore the Proportion of Value between *Gold* and *Silver* must needs differ in several Times and Places, according to the scarcity or abundance of those Metals.[30]

This is obviously a lucid if brief statement of the familiar utility/scarcity concept; and Vaughan, like other writers of the period stated it as though it were a well-known commonplace. It led him to the conclusion that prices of goods would vary with changes in conditions of supply, such as inventions, good and bad harvests, etc., and changes in conditions of demand due to fashion and fancy. Hence the prices of goods as such could not be used to measure change in the value of money due to changes in the supply of money. He decided:

> ... there is only one thing, from whence we many certainly

[30] Ch. IV, p. 18 of the 1933 reprint of McCulloch's *Old and Scarce Tracts on Money.*

track out the prices, and which carries with it a constant result-
ant of the Prices of all other things which are necessary for a
Man's life; and that is the price of Labourers and Servants
Wages, especially those of the meaner sort . . .

. . . Besides; that Reason doth convince that there must be a
convenient Proportion between their Wages and their Food
and Raiment, the Wisdom of the State doth confirm it, which
doth always direct the Rate of Labourers and Servants to be
made with a regard of Prices of Victuals, Apparel and other
things necessary to their use.[31]

Thus Rice Vaughan tried in reverse the modern idea of using
changes in a number of prices to measure changes in real wages.
He took money wages of the meaner sort of labour as the measure
of changes in the value of money.

Petty's reason for trying to find a measure of value was rather
different. He came upon the problem in connection with the
valuation of land in Ireland for taxation. He dealt with it initially
in *A Treatise of Taxes and Contributions* published in 1662 and
again in *The Political Anatomy of Ireland* written some ten years
later. He required to capitalise rents but, like Rice Vaughan, he
recognised that the value of money was apt to vary over time with
changes in the metallic content of the coinage and changes in the
quantity of money without changes in the metallic content of the
coinage. He concluded that land valuations based on money rents
could be misleading and that instead rents should be valued in
real terms i.e. in terms of its products. This required a means of
valuing the individual products without using money in order that
the quantities of the different products could be added together.
Petty chose the inputs of physical resources, land and labour, used
for each product as being the 'two natural Denominations' for
he considered 'that Labour is the Father and active principle of
Wealth, as Lands are the Mother'. In order to add inputs of land
and labour together he required a conversion factor between
them, as he explained

we should be glad to finde out a natural Par between Land and
Labour, so as we might express the value by either of them
alone as well or better then by both, and reduce one into

[31] Ibid., p. 59.

the other as easily and certainly as we reduce pence into pounds.[32]

In this way Petty's attempt to find a method of land valuation, which would be independent of changes in the general value of money, led him to introduce a method of measuring the values of all commodities in terms of the inputs of the resources of land and labour converted into each other by the Par. In *The Political Anatomy of Ireland* the Par is described in detail (pp. 181–2). as the quantity of land required to produce the 'easiest gotten food' required to support a labourer on an average in any place. 'Wherefore [he explains] the days food of an adult man, at a Medium, and not the days labour, is the common measure of Value.' He goes on to attempt to show how this measure can be modified to allow for the use of tools and inventions. Petty like Rice Vaughan regarded the subsistence of the labourer as something constant and unchanging in real terms and therefore suitable to measure changes in the value of money. The great search for an invariable measure of *real* value distinct from nominal or money value had thus been launched in the seventeenth century with suggestions about the *subsistence of labour* and *inputs of land and labour combined* as in some way clues. The question was destined to provide a major preoccupation for the most distinguished classical economists and to lead to lengthy and often acrid arguments.

It is not in Petty's measure of value that the labour theory of value sometimes attributed to him is to be found, for his measure is based on inputs of *both* land and labour and the conversion factor of a day's subsistence is simply his method of reckoning one factor in terms of the other according to a constant physical scale. There are however some passages which, particularly if taken out of their context, can be read as suggesting that Petty had a labour input theory of value. For instance in the paragraphs leading up to his explanation of labour *and* land inputs as the basis of the measure of value in his *Treatise on Taxes and Contributions* (pp. 43–4), he explains that the corn rent of land is the surplus over the subsistence of the farmer and his other expenses of production. He states that its value in silver (money) will be equal to the

[32] *Treatise of Taxes.* See Vol. I, pp. 43–5, for the whole discussion; the quotation about land being the father of wealth etc. is however from p. 68.

surplus in silver obtained by a silver miner by working for the same time, after deduction of subsistence and other expenses. He applies the same reasoning to show the rate at which gold and silver should exchange for other. Later on, after again explaining that changes in the quantity of money change the prices of goods, he states that the 'natural' price of corn in terms of silver is the amount of silver that can be produced in the same time as a bushel of corn (p. 50). No proof or attempt at proof is provided for any of these statements; they seem to be intended more as preliminaries to the introduction of his solution of the problem of the valuation of land in terms of his measure of value than as general statements of a theory of value. It is of course difficult to reconcile a labour theory of value with Petty's general statment that 'all things ought to be valued by two natural Denominations, which is Land and Labour' (p. 44).

Fortunately it does not matter for the purposes of this book whether Petty intended to put forward a labour theory of value. His statements may have been interpreted in this way and thus may have had an influence on later writers; for instance they may have influenced the discussion of the labour theory of value in the *Wealth of Nations* though this does not seem to me very likely. Cantillon, however, it is obvious ignored Petty's silver miners and concentrated wholly and explicitly on the concept of land *and* labour measure of value and built his theory of value upon it.[33]

(iv) Factor Prices

The pricing of the factors of production did not attract attention as a problem of value in the seventeenth century any more than in the sixteenth. With the doubtful exception of Petty's discussion of the relative earnings of the silver miner and the farmer, there seems to have been no attempt to consider the price of labour as connected with the theory of value. There is, however, a voluminous literature about the price that was, or ought, to be paid for labour. Some of it will be discussed in the sixth of these studies in connection with Cantillon's and Adam Smith's treatments of wages.

Discussions of the rate of profit were equally divorced from

[33] See study III, pp. 95 et seq. and pp. 117 et seq., respectively, in connection with the influence of Petty on Cantillon and Adam Smith in this matter.

value theory. Profit, it was assumed, was necessary to get people to advance their stock and undertake the troubles and risks of business. There was a tendency to assume some customary rate necessary to maintain the merchant, such as had been accepted in preceding centuries. Beyond this it was recognised that profit in practice would fluctuate in particular occupations and markets with the state of trade in them. The analytical connection with the allocation of resources was not pursued. There was, however, a tendency to argue that the rate of profit must fall as the quantity of capital (stock) in the system increased. The Netherlands were regarded as providing an illustration of this tendency. No systematic explanation of this secular trend was attempted; it was regarded merely as a natural consequence of increased supply.[34]

It can be said perhaps that the problem of rent attracted more interest, possibly because the effect of any suggested policy on the landed interest was politically important. Rent was recognised sometimes as being price-determined; Petty and Locke perceived this characteristic as resulting from its fixed supply. References generally, however, were in terms of the effect of changes in the rate of interest on the price of land.[35]

However much this account is expanded in detail, it is impossible to reach any conclusion except that factor prices were not regarded as a problem of value analysis. This is not surprising in a century in which the economic system was slowly emerging from centuries of regulation of wages, and also of profits, by law or custom, and when the leading writers on the theory of value were engaged on problems far removed from factor pricing or the distribution of income. Nevertheless, it is of importance that such consideration as seems to have been given to the general levels of wages and profits tended to be in terms of a search for institutional or physical explanations of prices of factors. It is the natural consequence of the fact that writers on these subjects were working in an economic environment in which it had been customary to regard factor prices as data in the system. Variations were recognised as occurring owing to temporary or local conditions of demand or supply; but these minor manifestations of demand and supply were not of much interest. In these circumstances the

[34] See Tucker, op. cit., for a discussion of seventeenth-century opinion on secular trends in the rate of profits.
[35] Locke, pp. 94–6; Petty, *Treatise on Taxes*, Vol. I, pp. 48–9.

imputation problem, of such interest after the middle of the nineteenth century, was naturally simply unrecognised. The questions which seemed chiefly to interest the seventeenth-century writers, mainly in conection with labour, were: What ought factor prices to be in relation to some policy? What secular, institutional, or physical influences might affect factor prices in the long run?

(v) Conclusions

The Schoolmen's work on the theory of value had established a number of important principles before the seventeenth century. The relative character of exchange had been demonstrated and the Schoolmen had considered under what conditions a market price determined by supply and demand or, as generally formulated, by scarcity and utility, might be regarded as a just price. They had concluded either *aestimatio communis* or conditions of what more modern economists call perfect competition led to a price which might be regarded as just. They had also become involved with the relation of the just price to the costs of supplying goods and had tried to define the costs which might be legitimately included. Rather vague indications had been given by a few of the later Schoolmen as to the relation between the just cost or supply price and the just market price. The just price however in so far as it was determined by costs depended on the prices paid for factors being themselves just. They assumed that in the society in which they lived such just prices were in fact established by law or custom and were data provided to the price system.

It might have been supposed that during the seventeenth century three lines of inquiry might in consequence have been pursued. Attention might have been directed to trying to solve more clearly the relationship between market and supply or cost prices and this might have led to consideration of the resource-allocation function of the price mechanism. Some thought might have been given to the problems of the determination of factor prices, particularly of labour, in a world in which regulation by law or custom was breaking down. Conclusions about prices determined under various conditions might have been examined in the light of new philosophical ideas which might affect traditional criteria of economic welfare.

The first problem listed in the last paragraph was pursued to some extent in relation to just prices by a few Schoolmen in Roman Catholic countries, but did not lead to a solution (Pufendorf provided an account of the conclusions effectively accepted). In England on the other hand the direct contributions of value theory dealt with none of these problems. Instead the discussions developed in connection with the perennial problems of trade and monetary policy. Although their reasons for considering problems of value theory were therefore different from those which stimulated the schoolmen, they worked with the same concepts of the relative nature of exchange value and its determination in the market by scarcity and utility or supply and demand. This does not mean that the contribution of the English seventeenth-century writers on value was unimportant – quite the contrary. They showed the applicability of these ideas to problems of policy connected with the foreign exchanges and trade and money. In the course of these applications they developed further the theory of demand and demonstrated in an orderly way the relative nature of exchange value, but they did not go so far as to formulate a law of diminishing marginal utility. Neither the analysis of supply and of long- and short-period prices, nor the resource-allocation function of the price mechanism was germane to their problems, and their contributions to these subjects were naturally insignificant. The traditional views of factor prices remained unchanged.

Entirely new ground was broken however in connection with the measurement of changes in the value of money. This too arose out of monetary problems for it had long been recognised that changes in the quantity or in the metallic content of money affected prices. Attempts to find scientific methods for measuring changes in the value of money and to eliminate the vitiating effects of such changes on comparisons of value over time were, as far as I am aware, new and characteristic of the seventeenth century. Both Rice Vaughan and Petty seem to have been influenced by the interest in quantitative methods associated with the scientific approach of the seventeenth century. The introduction of these 'scientific' methods of measurement of changes in value had far reaching effects on Cantillon's and also on classical economics.

Perhaps the most significant aspect of Petty's approach for economic analysis was that he explicitly raised the issue of the relation between the quantities of real resources used in the production of a commodity and its price. It was this, or rather its implications for resource allocation, that appears to have influenced Cantillon. Neither Petty, nor any other seventeenth-century economist took up this question that I can discover; indeed they do not appear to have been aware of it. Naturally therefore the possibility that there might be some difference between this resource-input approach and the supply-price approach of some of the Schoolmen was not noticed. Like the formulation of the law of diminishing utility, the problems of factor pricing and the resource-allocation function of the price mechanism were left over to be dealt with later.

In contrast to the discussions of interest in the seventeenth century those on value raised (and examined) no new fundamental questions except accidentally in connection with the measurement of value. The most obvious explanation is that discussion on value and price as economic problems had been going on for centuries, while the traditional discussions about interest had centred round its sinfulness. Another simple partial explanation is that new major problems did not obtrude themselves on people's notice as of urgent practical importance. Similarly the possible complications of contemporary developments in philosophy for establishing new criteria of economic policy were still to be formulated, though fragmentary references were appearing before the end of the century.

III *Alternative Approaches to the Price Mechanism in the Eighteenth Century: Cantillon to Adam Smith*

with an Addendum on the Just Price and Adam Smith's Natural Price.

> Mr Locke ... like all the English writers on the subject has looked only to market prices.
>
> CANTILLON[1]

> The natural price, therefore, is, as it were, the central price, to which the prices of all commodities are continually gravitating. Different accidents may sometimes keep them suspended a good deal above it, and sometimes force them down even somewhat below it. But whatever may be the obstacles which hinder them from settling in this center of repose and continuance, they are constantly tending towards it.
>
> ADAM SMITH[2]

(i) Introduction

It has been pointed out that the seventeenth-century discussions of the theory of value concentrated on market price.[3] In contrast the most important novelties in the discussions of price in the eighteenth century related to long-run price, or supply price, with interest centred on the significance of the differences between it and market price as the stimulus to the allocation of resources between uses – in short the nature and functions of the price mechanism. It is symptomatic of this change of emphasis that the term 'natural' was used by Adam Smith and his classical successors to describe this long-run price, while English seventeenth-century writers used it to describe the price in any market that was freely competitive. It will be remembered that it has been pointed out that Petty was an exception to these generaliza-

[1] Op. cit., p. 117.   [2] *Wealth of Nations*, Vol. I, Bk. I, Ch. 7, p. 60.
[3] See pp. 88–9 above.

tions about the seventeenth-century English writers' interest, while Pufendorf on the continent provided a striking example of the continued scholastic type of interest in legal or long-run customary price to which he applied, like Adam Smith after him, the term 'natural'.

The contributions of Pufendorf and Petty respectively are of great relevance to this essay. It is concerned with contrasts between Adam Smith's and Cantillon's attempts to explain the price mechanism and its functions in relation to resource allocation. The essay is also concerned with the extent to which the explanations depended on parameters determined outside the price system and the gradual trend towards the construction of a self-contained micro-model in which all prices and resource allocations could be demonstrated in terms of reactions to economic stimuli, given tastes, technology and natural resources.

The highly abstract analysis of the relative nature of exchange value, which was typical of English seventeenth-century discussions, was geared, it will be remembered, originally to problems of money. It was in the work of Barbon and Locke that it reached its most refined form. The analysis highlighted the significance of demand and the nature of demand in terms of individual valuation of the utility of goods and services. It distinguished between the physical capacity of goods to satisfy particular wants, the conventional grading of the importance of different wants and the valuation of those goods in the market. It did not analyse the supply functions or the nature of supply; thus it did not lead to a theory of long-run supply price or an examination of the function of the price mechanism in relation to resource allocation. It will be remembered that, though Barbon did point out there that must be some connection between the price actually received in the market and future supplies, he did not pursue the topic.

Pufendorf's discussion however led to a distinction between market price (explained in seventeenth-century terms similar to those of Barbon and Locke) and long-run price; he called the latter, when not established by regulation, the 'natural' price. He explained the principles upon which prices should be regulated in scholastic terms of the costs of production, and claimed that the natural price in a free market would be determined in the same way. He implied, but did not elaborate, the relationship between market price and long-run supply prices. In essence Pufendorf's discussion was a seventeenth-century gloss on the work of the later Schoolmen which occasionally implied, though it did not explore, the resource-allocation properties of the price mechanism.

I shall argue presently that Adam Smith's Glasgow *Lectures* and the *Wealth of Nations* can be regarded as a direct attempt to develop Pufendorf's implications and that Adam Smith can properly be regarded as in the direct line from the schoolmen.

Petty's emphasis on the physical sources of wealth, land and labour, and his statement that the value of goods ought to be measured by the land and labour used in their production emphasised the importance of physical inputs in relation to value. It will be remembered of course that he found himself involved in finding a par between land and labour. He left unresolved the problem of the relationship between market values and values calculated on the basis of land and labour inputs. This problem seems to be that which Cantillon set out to resolve in his analysis of the price mechanism. This brings me to one of the contrasts I want to pursue: Cantillon approached the problem of long-run price and the price mechanism from Petty's angle of physical resources, while Adam Smith approached the problem from Pufendorf's angle of supply prices (i.e. the price at which people will maintain the supply of a particular good).

There is another contrast which is of interest, I think, to keep in mind. Cantillon assumed the structure of a society dominated by private land ownership. He was concerned to explain its economic working, including *inter alia* how the wealth of that society was provided by the allocation of land and labour between uses, for 'The Land is the Source or Matter from whence all Wealth is produced. The Labour of man is the Form which produces it.'[4] This of course is Cantillon's version of Petty's statement 'Labour is the Father and active principle of Wealth, as Lands are the Mother'.[5]

Adam Smith on the other hand framed his problem in different terms both in the *Lectures* and in the *Wealth of Nations*. The section of the *Lectures* dealing with economics is headed in Cannan's edition 'Cheapness or Plenty' and the first sentence of this section is:

In the following part of this discourse we are to confine our-

---

[4] Op. cit., p. 1.   [5] *Treatise of Taxes*, Vol. I, p. 68.

selves to the consideration of cheapness or plenty, or, which is the same thing, the most proper way of procuring wealth and abundance.[6]

Similarly in the *Wealth of Nations*, or to give it its full title *An Enquiry into the Nature and Causes of the Wealth of Nations*, he immediately raised the question of supply, pointing out that the greater the total wealth is in relation to the *numbers of consumers* so 'the nation will be better or worse supplied with all the necessaries or conveniences for which it has occasion' (p. 1). As every reader of the *Wealth of Nations* knows, Adam Smith goes on to explain that the wealth of a nation depends on the productivity with which its resources are used, in particular the skill and dexterity with which labour is employed and the proportion of productive to unproductive labour. Thus from the very beginning, while Cantillon is concerned with the defined problem of the economic mechanism of societies based on private land ownership, Adam Smith is concerned with the problems of the level of wealth per head of society as a whole. Thus Cantillon and Adam Smith approached the study of the price mechanism for different purposes. Cantillon needed to explain how physical inputs were organised in response to the wants of a particular type of society. Adam Smith wanted to investigate how far the wants of men could be, or were, satisfied, and by what means.

(ii) Cantillon's Analysis of the Price Mechanism

Cantillon starts the *Essai* with a picturesque description of the structure of settled societies based on private individual ownership of land. The first six chapters of Part I describe the relationships between the uses of land, the establishment of a network of villages, market towns, cities and capital cities and the physical flows of goods and services through the network, geared to satisfy, ultimately, demands of the landowners. This brings him to the question of the means by which the right quantities of resources are devoted to different purposes. The order in which he sets out this analysis helps, I think, to conceal the ideas that he is working out, for he starts his exposition with a discussion of the problem of the valuation of different types of labour in Chapters

[6] *Lectures of Adam Smith*, p. 157. Cannan's edn to which all page references relate.

VII, VIII and IX of Part I. Once the problem of the relative earnings of different grades of labour is solved he goes rapidly through the analysis of the price mechanism: Chapter X on price and intrinsic value, Chapter XI on the par between land and labour. Chapter XII demonstrates the role of landowners in determining aggregate demand and the circulation of wealth, and Chapter XIII sets out the role of the entrepreneur. These chapters contain the essence of his theory of the price mechanism. In the vitally important Chapter XIV, however, he shows that similar resource allocations, in relation to an unchanged demand by landowners, can be obtained either through a free market system and the price mechanism, or by over-all pre-planning by the landowners. The object of this last chapter is of course to show precisely how the whole system depends on the demands of the landowner; its significance however is very much greater than this, for it provides a demonstration of the alternative mechanisms of allocating resources in relation to a given demand. Finally, in Chapter I of Part II of the *Essai*, he explains the significance of what he has done and the problem of translating from real to money terms.

Cantillon's definition of intrinsic value is really his theoretical starting point, together with the concept of the par between labour and land. Chapter X of Part I is headed 'The Price and Intrinsic Value of a Thing, in general, is the measure of the Land and Labour which enter into its Production'. This concept is more fully defined in the text of the chapter, the most unambiguous definition coming on page 29, 'the Price or intrinsic value of a thing is the measure of the quantity of Land and Labour entering into its production, having regard to the fertility or produce of the land and the quality of the Labour'. In the actual world the current or market price may diverge from this intrinsic value and he continues, 'But it often happens that many things which have actually this intrinsic value are not sold in the Market according to that value; that will depend on the Humours and Fancies of men and on their consumption'. Finally on page 31 he states, 'There is never a variation in intrinsic values, but the impossibility of proportioning the production of merchandise and produce in a State to their consumption causes a daily variation, and a perpetual ebb and flow in Market Prices.'[7]

[7] This implies that wage differentials are unchanging. We shall see that

Cantillon explained that it is the function of the entrepreneur to make continual adjustments in supplies under the stimulus of profit or loss (determined by the excess or deficit of market compared to intrinsic values). Thus the entrepreneur brings about as accurately as possible an allocation of land and labour to correspond with the requirements of demands for goods and services. This is explained briefly in Chapter X and set out at length in Chapter XIII 'The circulation and exchange of goods and merchandise as well as their production are carried on in Europe by Undertakers, and at a risk'.

It is of course necessary to have some means of comparing the intrinsic values of different goods with each other and with their market prices – hence the need not only for explanation of the wage differentials of different types of labour, but also for a conversion factor or 'par' between land and labour. Cantillon's approach to the discussion of this 'par' demonstrates that he had recognised the problem of relating market values to physical resource inputs that Petty had indicated but had not resolved. Indeed Cantillon considered that Petty had failed because although he

> considers this Par, or Equation between Land and Labour, as the most important consideration in Political Arithmetic, but the research which he had made into it in passing is fanciful and remote from natural laws, because he has attached himself not to causes and principles but only to effects, as Mr Locke, Mr Davenant and all the other English authors who have written on this subject have done after him (p. 43).

It is the analysis of the determinants of the differentials between the wage rates of different types of labour that provides Cantillon's famous contribution to wage analysis which was taken over by Adam Smith and re-stated as the theory of net advantages. It occupies the three chapters of Part I (Chapters VII–IX) leading to the analysis of intrinsic value naturally enough, for they are intended to explain the way in which wage differentials provide the means of allowing for the influence of different *qualities* of labour on intrinsic value. For this purpose he investigated

---

they are not determined by any means wholly by physical inputs and that a more complicated approach and assumptions about the basis for the invariability of intrinsic value are needed (See pp. 97–9 and 102 et seq. below).

the causes determining the supply of labour for each occupation. He took into account the costs of training and the loss of income while training on the one hand, the expected income, utilities and disutilities, risks, dangers and responsibilities associated with particular occupations on the other hand. All these considerations are presumed to affect the willingness and ability to enter different occupations. Hence the supply of skilled labour of each type must, he argued, be 'proportioned' to the demand so as to receive these appropriate differentials. Estimation of the differentials in wage rates necessary to compensate for these factors he seems to have regarded as based on custom and tradition, though loss of income while training, and some costs of training, can be regarded as precisely calculable. Cantillon summed up his discussion by claiming that by examples from 'ordinary experience it is easily seen that the difference of price paid for daily work is based upon natural and obvious reasons' (pp. 21–3).

Cantillon allowed specifically for the case in which a shortage of the supply of a skilled type of labour was so great that wage rates might move significantly (p. 261, Ch. VIII). In all other cases he seemed to have considered that for skilled labour and unskilled labour adjustment to changes in demand would take place not through price movements, but through changes in supply. He envisaged men who could not get sufficient employment to maintain their customary standard of living at the customary wage rate postponing marriage or moving from one place to another. The inflow of new recruits to an occupation he seemed to have thought would be quickly affected by such considerations and he evidently assumed that this would have a fairly rapid effect on the total supply of labour in it (Ch. IX). This was probably not an unrealistic assumption in the eighteenth-century world in view of the very high death rate at all ages. The natural wastage from an individual occupation and from the total labour supply by death must have been, by modern standards, very high.

In Chapter XI, 'Of the Par or Relation between the Value of Land and Labour', he tackles the working out of the Par initially in a planned economy, considering the problems of 'a Proprietor of a Great Estate' who keeps its management in his own hands and works it with slave labour (p. 33). The problem is stated in terms of the numbers of slaves required with different degrees of training, in order to provide for the demands of the landowner himself and the needs of the slaves. The limiting factor is the quantity and quality of the land, for the landowner must allow 'labouring' (i.e. unskilled) slaves 'their subsistence and the where-withal to bring up their Children. The Overseers must be allowed Advantages proportionable to the confidence and Authority which he gives them.' Further the craftsmen and overseer craftsmen cost more in resources as they have to be maintained during their period of training and given a better maintenance during their working life, 'since the loss of an Artisan would be greater than that of a Labourer and more care must be taken of him having regard to the expense of training another to take his place' (p. 33).

Allowing for translation from a free to a planned system the differentials have some things in common. The cost of training and the risk of not recouping that cost in a working life are the same. The utilities and disutilities of particular types of work seem to apear however only in the slave state with reference to the responsibilities of overseers, though perhaps too much impor-tance should not be attached to lack of reference to special risks and dangers etc. in the slave state.

Cantillon argued that the labour of an adult unskilled slave must be 'worth at least as much as the quantity of Land which the Proprietor is obliged to allot for his food and necessaries' *plus* sufficient to enable him to bring up enough children to maintain the size of the unskilled working population (pp. 33–5). Hence the 'par' between labour and land must be, Cantillon concluded, equivalent to the produce of the land allocated to the support of unskilled labourers, doubled to allow for bringing up the number of children necessary to replace them. The labour of craftsmen slaves may similarly be appraised at twice the produce of the land they consume themselves to allow for bringing up their replace-ments.

It is of interest to see how Cantillon translated the concept of the 'par' from the planned slave estate to the real world. He had to show first how the 'par' between unskilled labour and land is established, from this the 'pars' for different types of labourers followed automatically from the differences in wage rates; hence the importance of the wage differentials.

Cantillon admitted that this 'par' varied greatly as the stan-dards of living of the meanest type of labourer differed greatly as between different countries in Europe, between different periods of history and between different types of civilisations. He claimed however that the ratio will always be twice the produce of land required to support an adult labourer or a skilled worker, respectively, in order to enable him to bring up his replacements just as in a slave economy (p. 39). It is evident that he cannot explain what determines the standard of subsistence required, only observing that it seemed to depend not only on technology but also on customs. Given this standard however, Cantillon believed that the numbers of labourers must depend on the total amount of land allocated to their support (in the planned estate allocated directly by the landowner, in a market economy indirectly). This conclusion was based on Cantillon's conviction that population was limited only by the total subsistence available and customary standards of living. As he put it in a later chapter 'men multiply like mice in a barn' if there is unlimited subsistence (Pt. I, Ch. XV, p. 83).

The reward of the entrepreneurs, master-craftsmen and farmers who correspond to the slave overseers presented peculiar difficulties for some get rich and others go bankrupt, but the 'majority support themselves and their Families from day to day'. There is another difficulty in valuing their labour, Cantillon thinks, for the number of workers each could supervise may be much greater than the number they do in fact, for this is determined by the size of their farms or the number of their customers. Nevertheless he argued that their labour will in fact have a value which can be related to land by means of the amount of the produce of the land they consume (p. 41).

In Chapter XIV Cantillon sets out to show that there will be the same resource allocation whether it is pre-planned by the landowners or left to market forces, provided that the real income and the tastes of landowners are unchanged. The relevance of his concept of intrinsic value to his problem immediately becomes clear. Given the same technology, the same quantities of land of different sorts and labour of different sorts will be required to produce each product under the planned as under the market system; intrinsic values will be the same, for it is merely the sum of these resource requirements. In the planned marketless system intrinsic value provides (or is identical with) the essential accounting unit for the plan. In the market economy the interplay of market prices and intrinsic values provide the mechanism by which the accounting is translated in resource allocation to satisfy the given demand. Thus all that Cantillon needs to show is: (1) the conditions under which resource allocation will be the same under the two systems; (2) that the allocation will be stable unless there are changes in landowners' demand and that such changes will bring about appropriate changes in resource allocation. The purpose is to demonstrate that the demand of the landowners is always the controlling force in resource allocation in the economy. The heading of the chapter indicates both the form of argument and its object, viz.: *The Fancies, the Fashions and the Modes of Living of the Prince, and especially of the Landowners, determine the use to which Land is put in a State and cause the variation in the Market Prices of all Things.*

Cantillon examines a large estate which in the best academic manner he intends 'to consider here as if there were no other in the world' (p. 59). The use of the estate is planned by its owner to satisfy his own wishes. These will determine the numbers of labourers of different sorts, overseers, etc. required and the allocation of land to provide for their needs 'according to the way he wishes to maintain them', and also to provide for the parks and gardens and products he wants himself. The amount of land is the fixed factor, the supply of labour can be adjusted by the landowner. In order to demonstrate his thesis, Cantillon considers a change in the way the landowner runs his estate.

> Let us [he says] now suppose that to avoid so much care and trouble he makes a bargain with the Overseers of the Labourers, gives them Farms or pieces of Land and leaves the responsibility for maintaining in the usual manner all the Labourers they supervise, so that the Overseers, now become Farmers or Undertakers, give the Labourers for working on the land or Farm another third of the produce for their Food, Clothing and other requirements, such as they had when the Owner employed them.[8]

He supposes a similar bargain made with the 'Overseers of the Mechaniks' who become 'Master Craftsmen'. The landowner selects silver as money. He ensures his own income at the same

[8] Ibid., p. 59. It will be remembered that Cantillon divides the product into three equal 'rents', one of which goes to the landowner, one to the farmers and one to agricultural labourers.

level as before by requiring the newly created farmers to pay in silver a third of the produce of their farms as rent (pp. 59 and 61). He also supposes that prices can be selected such that the 'Master Craftsmen' (entrepreneurs) receive the same income as they did when 'overseers', and so

> The merchandise which they have made, Hats, Stockings, Shoes, Cloaths, etc., will be sold to the landowner, the farmers, the Labourers and the other Mechanicks reciprocally at a price which leaves to all of them the same advantages as before; and the Farmers will sell, at a proportionate price, their produce and raw materials.
>
> ... We suppose then that after this change all the people on this large Estate live just as they did before, and so all the portions and Farms of this great Estate will be put to the same use as it formerly was (p. 61).

He goes on to argue that this must be so, for if some of the farmers change the quantities of their various crops, they will find, as there has been no change in demand, that there will be too little of something and too much of another which they will not be able to sell. Hence they will be unable to pay their rents in silver. They will therefore try to adjust matters the following year 'for Farmers always take care to use their land for the production of those things which they think will fetch the best price at Market' (p. 61). The profit motive, backed up by the contractual requirement of paying the appropriate rent, ensures that land will be allocated in the same way as before. Only if there is a significant change in demand, Cantillon argues, will farmers have an incentive to change the use of land. Since such significant changes, according to the basic sociological thesis, are normally only made by landowners, changes in land use will occur in the market as in the planned system only with changes in the landowners' demand. The following quotation will be sufficient to illustrate this well-known thesis of Cantillon:

> The Owner, who has at his disposal the third of the Produce of the Land, is the principal Agent in the changes which may occur in demand. Labourers and Mechaniks who live from day to day change their mode of living only from necessity. If a few Farmers, Master Craftsmen or other Undertakers in easy

circumstances vary their expenditure and consumption they always take as their model the Lords and Owners of the Land. . . . If the Land owners please to wear fine linen, silk or lace, the demand for these merchandises will be greater than that of the Proprietors themselves (p. 63).

Finally at the end of the chapter he generalises his conclusion:

If all the Landowners of a State cultivated their own estates they would use them to produce what they want; and as the variations of demand are chiefly caused by their mode of living the prices which they offer in the Market decide the Farmers to all the changes which they make in the employment and use of the land (p. 65).

It is evident that Cantillon's comparison of the planned and market systems depends on certain conditions being satisfied. These can be stated in relation to the overriding requirement that the landowner gets the same real income as before equivalent to a third of the produce of the land. In order that he should get the same bundle of products as before:

   (i) Intrinsic values must be the same under both systems so that resource requirements for producing the same goods will be identical.

  (ii) In order for intrinsic values to be the same the 'par' between unskilled labour and land and all the wage differentials must be the same, and the levels of overseers' wages and entrepreneurs' profits, under both systems. These determine the resources that must be allocated to provide the labour of any type required in the production of each product. They are the measures of the *quality and quantity* of labour required which along with the land required determines intrinsic value. Put another way, the distribution of income among different types of labour reflects the valuation differentials of different types of labour which affects the intrinsic value of the commodities in which it is used.

 (iii) The ratios of market prices expressed in silver must tend to equality with the ratios of intrinsic values.

 (iv) The rent for each farm must be set at a level based on the intrinsic values of the former planned output of each farm

converted into silver (money). This ensures that the farmer can only pay his rent if he continues to use the land
in the same way as when it was planned by the landowner.

How many of these conditions does Cantillon include? The first
follows from his definition of intrinsic value, provided the second
condition is satisfied. This latter is in fact explicitly stated in the
description of the bargain made by the landowner with the overseers, though it is not clear whether it is intended to form part
of the bargain or is assumed to follow from it from the workings
of the market system described in the earlier chapters on wages.
The third condition is an inherent part of Cantillon's theory of
price and value. The fourth condition seems to be implied only.
It is stated that the landlord requires that his third of the produce
of land (the share always allocated to the landlord by Cantillon)
be paid in silver and it is also stated that the farmer will not be
able to pay his rent if he alters the use of the land. This implies
that the rents be fixed as stated in the fourth condition, but this
is not explicitly stated. The argument thus appears to be complete
whether or not Cantillon deliberately intended to imply the
fourth condition. What is obscure is the precise way in which
Cantillon viewed the transition process from a planned to a market economy. He seems to have assumed that certain key incomes
and prices would be set to start with in addition to the landowner's. Whether he regarded this as necessary or merely a convenient method of demonstrating his argument is uncertain, for
he took pains to show in addition that the market system would
respond adequately to changes in the landowner's demand.

Cantillon's whole analysis, however, depends on the concept of
intrinsic value. It is to the question of the adequacy of this concept that we must now turn. Intrinsic value as defined by
Cantillon depends fundamentally on the use of the differences between wages of different types of labour to measure differences in
quality of labour used, and on the 'par' between labour and land.

The problem of the treatment of wage differentials is familiar
from later criticisms made of the practices of Adam Smith and
Ricardo. It arises because only some of the items influencing the
differentials can be regarded as inputs of physical resources tech-
nically necessary for the production for a particular type of
labour. Other items are utilities and disutilities associated with

particular occupations that have to be compensated by income prospects, and the evaluation of this compensation required may be based on custom, thus being given, otherwise it would involve a market valuation. This is unimportant with regard to Cantillon's concept of intrinsic value which is geared to resource allocation. All that Cantillon required was a means of calculating the extra amounts of the produce of land to be taken into account in measuring the resources of labour and land used in producing commodities, since different commodities require the use of different qualities (i.e. types) of labour. Cantillon was not concerned with any idea of intrinsic value of labour, and there is no difference in principle between his use of subsistence standards for unskilled labour determined by custom in determining the par between unskilled labour and land, and the use of wage differentials at least partly determined by custom for completing his calculations.

It seems to me that it is perfectly legitimate to use an existing constant set of wage differentials as a basis of coverting heterogeneous to homogeneous labour in labour theories of value, if regarded purely as explanations of the mechanism of resource allocation in an economy. When however labour input is treated as a source of value in some philosophical or ethical sense, then the introduction of custom-determined wage differentials may introduce an additional basis for valuation of labour and therefore of labour input inconsistent with an initial abstract concept of labour input as a source of value. It is this possibility that has to be considered in connection with Adam Smith's, and more particularly perhaps Ricardo's, use of the same type of explanation of wage differentials as Cantillon. A problem that must arise, however, in all cases of labour theories of value is that of the stability of the customs affecting differentials under changing circumstances.

Cantillon thus treated the wages of labour of unskilled labour as determined by customary standards of living and the differentials for different types of labour by costs of training and custom. This treatment, together with his view that the numbers employed tended to adjust to fixed wage rates, can I think be regarded as his interpretation of the experience of the consequences of contemporary customary wages and legal wage regulations. Its consequences for his analysis was of course that the equilibrium prices

of labour of all types were given as parameters determined externally to the price system to which all other equilibrium prices
adjusted. The variations by later economists on this theme are
one of the most interesting aspects of the history of wage theory;
Adam Smith's treatment of it is examined in the next section.

We must now look at the nature of the 'par' between land
and labour from the aspect of Cantillon's treatment of the differing fertilities (i.e. qualities) of land.

If land were completely homogeneous the 'par' would be an
unambiguous relationship and 'the quantity of the produce of
land' in Cantillon's phrase, could be written 'quantity of land'.
If land differed in fertility but the fertility ratios of all pieces of
land were uniform for all types of products, there would still be
no difficulty; any particular grade of land could be translated into
another and it would not matter which product was used for the
purposes of translation. Land however is not homogeneous either
in the obvious sense or in this pseudo- or more complicated sense,
and therefore it is impossible to convert one piece of land into
another piece of land in terms of some purely physical output
scale. It is necessary to introduce some scale of values or prices of
the different products of land. These cannot sensibly be based on
any customary scale determined externally to the price system like
some of the elements in wage differentials, for the determination
of the intrinsic values of the products of land is an integral part
of the whole pricing problem Cantillon set out to solve. Cantillon
however never discussed the problem of the relative prices or the
values of different pieces of land at all, he merely referred to taking
into account different quantities and fertilities of land in calculating intrinsic values. Thus he never considered the question
'What is to be done with heterogeneous land in relation to intrinsic
value, how is its quality to be assessed?' It seems that Cantillon
did not notice the existence of the difficulty. He therefore, presumably, did not notice that heterogeneous land could not be
handled in a physical input concept of intrinsic value and that
some means of pricing land, of valuation in the market sense, was
required. Hence he did not observe that the 'par' between land
and labour could only be found under special and unrealistic
assumptions about the fertilities of different pieces of land for
different purposes, and that the intrinsic values of two commodities
could only be compared under the same assumptions. It is evident

that this difficulty which destroys Cantillon's concept of intrinsic value as the general basis of a general theory of value has a marked family likeness to the difficulty arising from differing capital structures which upset Ricardo's Labour-input theory.

Cantillon's description of the price mechanism and its function seems to have been readily accepted by Postlethwayt and Joseph Harris among eighteenth-century writers. Postlethwayt is notorious for having incorporated large sections of Cantillon's *Essai* in his various publications from 1749 onwards. Joseph Harris, either cribbing from Postlethwayt or directly from Cantillon, incorporated a major part of his theory of the price mechanism and intrinsic value in a garbled way in his *Essay upon Money and Coins*, in 1757 (Part I, Chapter I). Neither of these writers appears to have had any difficulty about the nature of the 'par' between land and labour. They seem to have regarded it as obvious common sense that the intrinsic value of a commodity must be determined by the sum of the physical inputs, an idea which, after all, had been put forward by the famous and often quoted authority, Sir William Petty.[9]

(iii) Adam Smith – The Lectures
It is instructive to contrast Adam Smith's first approach to the price mechanism with Cantillon's. In the *Lectures*, it has already been pointed out, Adam Smith plunged immediately into his main theme, the causes which promote or retard opulence (pp. 157–61). We are introduced first to the general characteristics of the wants of mankind, the satisfaction of which is opulence. Then immediately he goes on to the division of labour as the main

[9] On Postlethwayt see Henry Higgs's essay on Cantillon in the R.E.S. edit. of the *Essai*, pp. 383 et seq. Andrew Skinner states that Steuart used 'real value' in the same sense as Cantillon in the latter's Part I, Ch. X (Skinner's footnote 2, p. 161 of Vol. I of his edition of Steuart's *Political Oeconomy*). Dr Skinner means that Steuart's 'real value' is the same as Cantillon's 'intrinsic value' for Part I, Ch. X of the *Essai* is about intrinsic value. This surely is not correct for Steuart defines 'real value' as made up of the quantity of labour time, the *value* of the workman's subsistence and expenses and the *value* of the materials. Thus he introduced value into the component of real value – this is quite different from 'intrinsic value' defined by Cantillon as the measure of the quantities and qualities (or fertilities) of the labour and land used in producing a commodity. Steuart also treated profits differently from, and more explicitly than, Cantillon. Steuart, Bk. II, Chs IV and X (Vol. I of Skinner's edition).

cause of the increase of opulence (pp. 161–8). This leads to the necessity of exchange to enable the division of labour to develop; exchange involves exchange values, i.e. price (pp. 168–73). This is not the same line of approach as that of Cantillon. Adam Smith's approaches exchange value directly as the price necessary to induce people to produce one commodity rather than another in response to demand. He starts immediately with the theme of the existence of market and natural prices as two distinct phenomena. Thus on page 173 it is stated:

> Of every commodity there are two different prices, which though apparently independent, will be found to have a necessary connexion, viz. the natural price and the market price.

Following Pufendorf it seems, Adam Smith analysed the natural price in terms of a long-run supply price. The nature of this price and its relationship with market price is the problem that Adam Smith recognises as needing to be resolved. His initial explanation is as follows:

> When men are induced to a certain species of industry, rather than any other, they must make as much by the employment as will maintain them while they are employed (pp. 173–4).

Moreover, he goes on to explain immediately, this amount will differ in different occupations and various reasons for differences in rates of earnings in different occupations are set out. Adam Smith's final conclusion on natural price is on page 176; it is worth quoting:

> A man then has the natural price of his labour, when it is sufficient to maintain him during the time of labour, to defray the expense of education, and to compensate the risk of not living long enough, and of not succeeding in the business. When a man has this, there is sufficient encouragement to the labourer, and the commodity will be cultivated in proportion to the demand.

As Cannan pointed out in a footnote to this passage, in his edition of the *Lectures*, there is evidently a hiatus in the notes and the sentence should have been completed as a phrase 'and sold at its natural price' (p. 176, Cannan's note 1).

There is no reference, it will be noticed, to stock or profits or land or rent in the discussion of natural price. This is the more remarkable in that the necessity for accumulation of stock for the division of labour is explained later in the lectures in the discussion of causes retarding the growth of wealth. Various types of land tenures and rents are discussed also in the same place and, also, in connection with taxes.[10]

Adam Smith contrasts the market price which he says is 'regulated by quite other circumstances'. When a buyer comes to the market, he never asks of a seller what expenses he has incurred in producing the goods (p. 176). Market price, he explained, is regulated by the relationship between the following influences: (1) 'the demand, or need for the commodity'; (2) 'the abundance or scarcity of the commodity in proportion to the need for it'; (3) 'the riches or poverty of those who demand'. This explanation of market price is closely similar to that of the traditional seventeenth-century analysis of value in exchange.[11] The action of the divergence between market and natural prices in causing re-allocation of resources in relation to demand is fully explained and illustrated. Adam Smith then reaches his major conclusion:

> Dearness and scarcity are in effect the same thing. When commodities are in abundance, they can be sold to the inferior ranks of people, who can afford to give less for them, but not if they are scarce. So far, therefore, as goods are a conveniency to the society, the society lives less happy when only the few can possess them. Whatever therefore keeps goods above their natural price for a permanency, diminishes [a] nation's opulence (p. 178).

Adam Smith now had the analytical tool, even if rather crude, that he required for his critique of restrictive policies. Restrictive policies prevented the price mechanism working to allocate resources between uses in response to demand and prevented goods being supplied at the lowest price which would ensure the maintenance of their supply, i.e., the natural price. It is clear that Adam Smith had filled the analytical gap in Pufendorf's work between market price and what Pufendorf described as the

[10] *Lectures*, pp. 222–3 on stock; pp. 224 et seq. on land tenures and rents; pp. 238 et seq. on taxes and rents.

[11] For a discussion of Adam Smith's treatment of utility see pp. 133–42 below.

natural, common, or legal price according to circumstances in the market, and that Adam Smith's natural price was the same as Pufendorf's. It will be remembered that the latter following in this one scholastic tradition considered that the legal, or natural, price should just suffice to cover the proper expenses of producing and maintaining a supply of the commodity and bringing it to market. Where the price was not fixed by law, he implied that the natural price should, or would, approximate to this level.[12]

The difference between Cantillon's and Adam Smith's approach is noteworthy and important. Cantillon had based his concept of value on quantities and qualities of physical resources used in production, and intrinsic value measured by the use of these resources. Exchange value could be related to intrinsic value but intrinsic value existed independently of exchange. In contrast Adam Smith emphasised that the 'natural price' was the price which induced people to maintain supplies of goods for exchange. It was not explained in terms of the physical inputs required but in terms of incentives. Nevertheless the exposition of the components of the natural price of a man's labour included not only his maintenance (undefined) but all the compensations needed for the expenses, risks, utilities and disutilities of particular occupations that had been set out by Cantillon in discussing differences of wage rates.[13] The purpose of this exercise was obviously different however, for Adam Smith was concerned with these items as affecting the incentive to carry on a particular form of production, not (as Cantillon) as a means of measuring different qualities of labour used and from this calculating the 'par' with land.

It seems evident Adam Smith must have adopted Cantillon's explanation of wages differentials by the time, probably 1763, that he gave these lectures of which we have the notes. But we seem to have no means of deciding how early he knew anything of Cantillon's work or how much he altered his own lectures between 1752, when he first gave them in Glasgow, and about 1763.[14]

[12] See pp. 81–3 above. The 'Early Draft of the Wealth of Nations' contains a summary of an intended chapter on price to follow a chapter on the division of labour. This summary is simply a summary of the treatment of market and natural price in the Glasgow lectures. See W. R. Scott, *Adam Smith as Student and Professor*, p. 319 and pp. 345–6.

[13] See pp. 181 et seq. below, for a more detailed discussion of wage theory.

[14] See Cannan's introduction to his edition of the *Lectures*, pp. xix–xx.

It is thus impossible to know whether Adam Smith got the idea of the resource-allocation function of the price mechanism from Cantillon or not. The problem of originality on this particular point does not seem to be of very great importance, for what we are concerned with is the difference in the two approaches to the price mechanism. Indeed one might perhaps say that if Adam Smith had originally derived the explanation of the function of the price mechanism from Cantillon, the difference in approach is still more noteworthy than if he had not.

(iv) Adam Smith – The Wealth of Nations

In the *Lectures* it is notable that Adam Smith has no trace of a labour theory of value, while labour as a measure of value is mentioned only in passing after a lengthy discussion of the way in which money evolved as a measure of value and medium of exchange – a discussion which included consideration of why the value of money itself varied.[15] It is followed by a section headed by Cannan 'That Natural Opulence does not consist in Money'. This opens with the following sentence:

> We have shown what rendered money the measure of value, but it is to be observed that labour, not money, is the true measure of value. National opulence consists therefore in the quantity of goods, and the facility of barter (p. 190).

Presumably the sentence should end 'not money'. This cryptic reference to labour as a true measure of value is the only reference in the *Lectures* to labour in connection with value. One of the unsettled problems in the history of economic thought is why Adam Smith paid so little attention to labour in the *Lectures* but traditionally is regarded as having introduced a labour theory of value into the *Wealth of Nations*. This is a subject with which we shall be concerned presently. Its discussion leads naturally to another question which seems to me important – the extent to which Adam Smith's treatment of prices of commodities and factors can be regarded conceptually as an integrated analytical investigation, or whether it is merely a series of disconnected theories as textbooks so frequently imply.

The relationship between the chapters in the *Wealth of Nations* on real and nominal price and on the component parts of price

15 *Lectures*, pp. 182–90.

(Bk I, Chs V and VI) and the chapter on natural and market price (Bk I, Ch. VII) has been in my opinion unduly neglected. It appears to me that these three chapters are intended to be an integrated examination of the problems of value listed at the end of Chapter IV and should be considered as such. At the end of Chapter IV Adam Smith points out, as many people had before him, that the exchange values of goods obviously do not conform to their utility or usefulness, i.e. 'value in use' in the common or ordinary sense of moralists and the man in the street who distinguish between wants which are for necessities, conveniences, and luxuries, and grade the usefulness or utility of goods according to which type of want they are capable of satisfying.[16] He then set out three questions, the answers to which will explain what determines exchange value:

> First, what is the real measure of this exchangeable value; or, wherein consists the real price of all commodities.
>
> Secondly, what are the different parts of which this real price is composed or made up.
>
> And, lastly, what are the different circumstances which sometimes raise some or all of these different parts of price above, and sometimes sink them below their natural or ordinary rate; or, what are the causes which sometimes hinder the market price, that is, the actual price of commodities, from coinciding exactly with what may be called their natural price (Vol. I, p. 30).

The next chapter, Chapter V, 'Of the Real and Nominal Price of Commodities, or of their Price in Labour, and their Price in Money', is precisely what it purports to be, a discussion of the differences between real and money prices and of the problem of measuring value. In it physical inputs are rejected as a measure of value. It also, incidentally, illuminates Adam Smith's preoccupation with the obstacles to supply. Chapter VI, 'Of the Component Parts of Price', is obviously intended to emphasise that he considers that a theory of value must take cognisance of capital as well as labour and land, in contrast with theories in the Petty tradition, and of course with his own Lectures. The chapter is also, I consider, intended to provide a demonstration that physical inputs cannot determine exchange values unless special assumptions are made. Once the chapter is read from this

[16] See pp. 133–42 below on Adam Smith's treatment of utility.

point of view, it appears to be deliberately arranged with this latter purpose in view, so as to justify the subsequent exposition of a theory of natural prices based on supply prices instead of physical inputs in the Petty–Cantillon tradition. The interpretation reverses the very common view that Adam Smith's theory of natural price was, as it were, a second string in his analysis introduced because he found himself unable to develop a labour-input theory of value for an advanced society. I emphasise that it seems to me much more reasonable to consider that Adam Smith was no more interested in the physical-input type of value-theory in the *Wealth of Nations* than he had been in the *Lectures*. But Cantillon's theory was already incorporated in the influential works of Postlethwayt and Joseph Harris. What could be more natural in those circumstances than that Adam Smith should try to show in the *Wealth of Nations* that a physical-input theory would only be valid with one scarce factor, a case which involved very special assumptions? Naturally Adam Smith would conceive the problem in terms of labour as labour was to him always a scarce factor for it involved disutility.

I propose to consider first Chapter V 'Of the Real and Nominal Price of Commodities, or of their Price in Labour and their Price in Money' in rather more detail than is customary in order to develop this opinion. The title suggests a development from the cryptic statement of the *Lectures* that the true measure of exchange value is labour. The opening paragraph of Chapter V provides Adam Smith's explanation of why labour not money is the real measure of exchangeable value of all commodities. The idea is clearly derived from the tradition of the importance attached to labour as the means of creating wealth from the natural resources of land emphasised by so many seventeenth- and eighteenth-century writers, for instance Petty, Locke, Cantillon, Joseph Harris and Sir James Steuart. Adam Smith's version of the idea may be summarised. It is quite simple. A man is rich according to the quantity he can enjoy of the necessaries, conveniences and amusements of life. After the division of labour 'has once thoroughly taken place' a man will only be able to provide himself to a very limited extent by his direct labour; his wealth will depend on how much of the labour of other people he can command or purchase. From this Adam Smith concludes that a commodity which an owner does not wish to use himself is worth to its owner the quantity of labour he can obtain in exchange for it, 'the quantity of labour which it enables him to purchase or command' (p. 32). Thus from the start he is not concerned with labour input but with labour commanded. He develops his argument as follows:

> Labour, therefore, is the real measure of the exchangeable value of all commodities.
>
> The real price of everything, what everything really costs to the man who wants to acquire it, is the toil and trouble of acquiring it. What everything is really worth to the man who has acquired it, and wants to dispose of it or exchange it for something else, is the toil and trouble which it can save to himself, and which it can impose upon other people.
>
> What is bought with money or with goods is purchased by labour, as much as what we acquire with the toil of our own body. That money or those goods indeed save us this toil. They contain the value of a certain quantity of labour which we exchange for what is supposed at the time to contain the value of an equal quantity. Labour was the first price, the original purchase-money that was paid for all things. It was not by gold or by silver, but by labour, that all the wealth of the world was originally purchased; and its value, to those who possess it, and who want to exchange it for some new productions, is precisely equal to the quantity of labour which it can enable them to purchase or command (Vol. I, pp. 32–3).

This is a deliberate statement of a labour-commanded theory of the measure of value, and only the sentence beginning 'They contain the value of a certain quantity of labour' suggests that labour input may influence labour commanded. There is no statement, it will be noticed, that a good has a value because it requires labour to produce it. It is important to notice also that it is labour as synonymous with 'toil and trouble' not as a natural resource, that Adam Smith regards it as providing a measure of value. He goes on to expound the idea of labour as involving pain, a disutility, so the pain of labour becomes the fundamental cost or price of acquiring wealth. Thus he obtains an absolute measure of value in terms of an invariable unit of disutility, the disutility of labour that is saved by the ability to exchange a commodity for command over labour. Adam Smith points out that different types of labour involve different pain costs and that it is not easy to find any accurate measure of the hardship and ingenuity of the labour involved. He goes on to claim without more than a superficial attempt at justification that in practice the market and custom will establish a conversion scale between quantities of labour of different sorts, taking into account the labour involved in acquiring skills etc.[17] Oddly enough in this exposition of a conversion scale he makes no reference to the much more thorough examination of the evaluation of different types of labour in Chapter X. His description or exposition of the disutility of labour which constitutes labour an *invariable* measure of value, runs as follows:

> Equal quantities of labour, at all times and places, may be said to be of equal value to the labourer. In his ordinary state of health, strength and spirits; in the ordinary degree of his skill and dexterity, he must always lay down the same portion of his ease, his liberty, and his happiness. The price which he pays must always be the same, whatever may be the quantity of goods which he receives in exchange for it (Vol. I, p. 35).

He winds up with the following conclusion:

> Labour alone, therefore, never varying in its own value, is alone the ultimate and real standard by which the value of all commodities can at all times and places be estimated and compared. It is their real price; money is their nominal price only. But though equal quantities of labour are always of equal value to the labourer, yet to the person who employs him they appear sometimes to be of greater and sometimes of smaller value (Vol. I, p. 35).

Adam Smith goes on to point out that labour will have a nominal price in terms of money and a real price in terms of what goods the money will buy, but that neither of these necessarily has any close connection with the cost to the labourer in terms of toil and trouble. This *constant* pain cost of labour to the labourer is thus a measure which is independent of money and of real wages in the ordinary sense. It is also something which is quite indepen-

---

[17] This seems to be a case in which reliance on custom or market forces for a conversion scale is of doubtful validity. It needs at least an excursion into disutility theory to justify it.

dent of the subsistence cost of labour. Adam Smith admits that few people will realise that because labour has a constant disutility to the labourer the true measure of value is labour. To most people the value of a good is represented either by its money price or by the quantity of other goods it exchanges for, and these will bear a different relation to the quantity of labour commanded by the good according to variations in rates of wages, both money and real. Adam Smith devoted the rest of the chapter largely to explaining the circumstances under which money on the one hand, or corn on the other, can be used as approximate measures of value in so far as at any particular time, or over a particular period, the price of labour in money, or in corn, may be constant. He noted, for instance, that equal quantities of corn are more likely to purchase equal qualities of labour as between different periods than equal quantities of gold or silver, and the reverse for short periods owing to the tendency of the price of corn to fluctuate markedly from year to year (pp. 37–9).

In all this there is no suggestion that labour input provides a measure of value as distinct from affecting possibly labour commanded. The latter suggestion is developed further in the explanation of the variations in the labour commanded by the precious metals from time to time. The explanation given is that the mines available at different times vary in their fertility and hence the labour input required to produce the precious metals also varies (Vol. I, p. 34). The actual circumstances under which labour input and labour commanded are equal are, of course, set out in the following chapter on the component parts of price.

Adam Smith's concept of the constant disutility of labour making labour an invariable measure of value, was not, as everyone knows, accepted into classical economics in general. Malthus, it will be remembered, did not consider Adam Smith was strictly correct in asserting the constant disutility of labour. Nevertheless he accepted his 'labour commanded' as the best measure of value since it measured 'the paramount cause of value which includes every other: namely, the state of supply as compared with demand'.[18] Ricardo rejected Adam Smith's concept without recognising that they wanted invariable measures of value for different

---

[18] *Definitions in Political Economy*, Ch. IX, partic. p. 226 and pp. 220–2. Kelley and Millman edn. He noted *inter alia* that Adam Smith's use of the word 'real' deliberately in two senses caused confusion. Ibid., Ch. III.

purposes. Hence he did not consider whether the disutility of labour was either constant or relevant to Adam Smith's own problem. It will be remembered that Ricardo rejected Adam Smith's 'labour-commanded' measure of value because he claimed that labour itself varies in value, *either* in terms of actual wages paid at any moment, *or* in terms of the cost of production of labour in terms of the cost of subsistence. Adam Smith however actually accepted, indeed he stated, that labour in terms of its wages varied in value. What he claimed, and what Ricardo could not accept of course, was that it was not the variability of the price paid for labour as such, nor the cost of producing labour as such that influenced the suitability of labour as a measure of value. It was the actual constant disutility of labour to human beings in Adam Smith's opinion which made it a standard of value independent of what happened to be paid for labour at any particular time.

The search for an invariable standard or measure of value which seemed so important to the classical economists for various reasons, was so obviously on a par with the search for the philosopher's stone or any other chimera, that historians of economic thought have shunned the controversies surrounding it. It is perhaps for this reason that the novelty of Adam Smith's suggestion of a psychological concept, the disutility of labour, as the measure of value has received little attention from historians.[19] It is not necessary to my purpose to pursue the tangled controversy over the measure of value. I am concerned with Adam Smith's proposal only in so far as it illuminates other aspects of his work and other aspects of the history of theory. I have already stressed that this discussion of it shows that he was not concerned primarily with physical inputs as the basis either of value or its measurement. He used the concept of the disutility of labour for a different purpose in his attack on the belief that the individual's supply curve of labour was backward-sloping, an attack that was most important for his own theory of wages. Jevons, it will be remembered, recognised the significance of Adam Smith's concept

[19] H. M. Robertson and W. L. Taylor's joint article 'Adam Smith's Approach to the 'Theory of Value', *E.J.* 1957, pp. 195–6 is one of the relatively few articles which draw attention to it. Another is V. W. Bladen's essay 'Adam Smith on Value' in *Essays in Political Economy in honour of E. J. Lerwick*, pp. 31–2.

of the pain cost of labour in relation to the individual's supply of labour. He opened Chapter V 'The Theory of Labour' in his *Theory of Political Economy* by quoting with approval Adam Smith's statement 'the real price of everything, what everything really costs to the man who wants to acquire it, is the toil and trouble of acquiring it . . . Labour was the first price' etc. With Jevons, of course, any idea of a constant disutility of labour disappears and the disutility of labour is incorporated within the general body of his analysis as his disutility of labour curve. Adam Smith's pain cost of labour influenced more than wage and labour supply theory however. It provided the basis of the 'real' cost tradition of English economics as illustrated by Senior's introduction of 'abstinence' as denoting a 'real' sacrifice or disutility involved in saving that would be parallel to the disutility of labour to the labourer.[20]

*   *   *

If Adam Smith had gone straight on from Chapter V on the measure of value to Chapter VII 'Of the natural and market prices of commodities', there would have been no question of a labour theory of value in the *Wealth of Nations*. It would have been clear that he was proceeding along the same lines as in the *Lectures* in considering natural price in terms of a supply price, not in terms of physical inputs, and that he was not particularly interested in the latter. If he had done this, however, he would not have shown that physical input theories of value were only applicable under special circumstances. The need to show this provides a reasonable explanation of the arrangement of Chapter VI. It starts with a statement of the labour-input theory of value in a primitive society. This requires only four quite short paragraphs, barely a full page in all (Vol. I, pp. 49–50). The argument is familiar.

Labour is always toil and trouble so that even in a primitive society people will not exchange the product of more labour for that of less labour. As demonstrated by the deer and beaver example in this primitive society with only labour as a scarce factor, land being a free good and no stock being used, goods will

[20] See pp. 180 and 197–8 below on the backward-sloping supply curve of labour, and Senior, *Political Economy*, 6th edn, pp. 58–9 on the 'real' sacrifice involved in 'abstinence'.

exchange in proportion to labour inputs. These proportions, Adam Smith suggests, will in practice be adjusted to allow for different degrees of hardship or skill involved. The exposition ends with the statement that in these conditions labour input is the only circumstance which can 'regulate the quantity of labour which it (a good) ought commonly to purchase, command, or exchange for' (Vol. I, p. 50). In this case labour input and labour commanded therefore give the same answer if used as measures of real value in terms of the pain cost of labour. This obviously fits in conveniently with the argument of Chapter V including the suggestion that labour input might affect labour commanded.[21]

Immediately Adam Smith goes on to demonstrate the difference between the determination of exchange value in a simple deer/ beaver society and one in which stock is used in production. The use of stock means, he argues, that goods will not exchange for each other or 'command labour', in proportion to the labour input. The profits of stock vary with the amount of stock. He explains further that the relative importance of stock to labour used in production will vary with different productions, so that the relative importance of profits compared to wages will vary. Moreover the variations of profits are in no way related to the inputs of managerial labour of the investor. Thus profits constitute a component 'altogether different from the wages of labour, and regulated by quite different principles' (Vol. I, pp. 50–1). Hence labour inputs cannot regulate exchange values if stock is used. The argument is then extended to deal with the case where all land has become private property so that rentlike profit appears as a component part of price,[22] so that –

> In every society the price of every commodity finally resolves itself into some one or other, or all of those three parts; and in every improved society, all three enter more or less, as com-

[21] See p. 115 above. See also above pp. 85–6 on Petty in relation to labour theories of value. Petty's remarks might possibly have suggested the labour theory to Adam Smith.

[22] The problem of reconciling Adam Smith's treatment of rent as a monopoly price, a residual and also a component part of price in various contexts in the *Wealth of Nations*, has I consider been solved by D. H. Buchanan in his masterly examination of the difficulties in his article 'The Historical Approach to Rent and Price Theory', *Economica*, 1929. I assume, in what follows, that Buchanan's explanation is generally accepted and do not therefore repeat it.

ponent parts, into the price of the far greater part of commodities (Vol. I, p. 52).

Adam Smith explains at some length how the relative magnitudes of these components of price will vary with the varying importance of labour, stock and land in their production. Thus he says that the relative importance of rent declines 'the more manufactured' a good is, e.g. in bread compared to corn. Even in improved societies there may be the same few commodities into whose prices no rent enters, or even no profit and no rent.

The rest of the chapter is concerned with the distribution aspect of the component parts of price: the demonstration that the total value of the national product must be equal to the sum of the totals of wages, profits and rent paid out in production. Since the prices or the exchange values of all commodities must resolve into their component parts, he concludes

that of all the commodities which compose the whole annual produce of the labour of every country, taken complexly, must resolve itself into the same three parts, and be parcelled out among the different inhabitants of the country, either as the wages of their labour, the profits of their stock, or the rent of their land. The whole of what is annually either collected or produced by the labour of every society, or what comes to the same thing, the whole price of it, is in this manner originally distributed among some of its different members. Wages, profit, and rent, are the three original sources of all revenue as well as of all exchangeable value. All other revenue is ultimately derived from some one or other of these (Vol. I, p. 54).

This proposition is not affected, Adam Smith points out, by the fact that in some cases one person supplies more than one factor and therefore receives an income which is composed of the separate rewards of the factors owned. Thus, the farmer who works his own land receives an income which is composed of wages for his labour, profits on his stock and rent from the land. He gives other types of examples. For instance –

A gardener who cultivates his own garden with his own hands, unites in his own person the three different characters of landlord, farmer, and labourer. His produce, therefore, should pay him the rent of the first, the profit of the second, and the wages of the third. The whole, however, is commonly considered as the earnings of his labour. Both rent and profit are, in this case, confounded with wages (p. 55).

Looking back over the arrangement of the chapter, it seems evident that the sole purpose of introducing the labour-input theory of value was to show its limited validity. The introduction of the three components of price is achieved simply by a statement that labour, stock and land are paid for by wages, profits and rents. This does not depend on the previous paragraphs on the labour-input theory. On the contrary the need to pay profits for stock and rent for land is immediately deliberately shown to limit the validity of the labour-input theorem. If Adam Smith had been really concerned only with identifying the component parts of price he could have done it without any reference to a labour-input theory of value. Nor are the subsequent paragraphs on distribution dependent on anything except the listing of the component parts of price. This argument supports the suggestion made at the beginning of this section that Adam Smith himself did not consider physical-input theories of value interesting, but considered it necessary to show that they were inadequate. If this is correct then the need to dispose of these theories could conveniently be satisfied by stating what the components parts of price were, and this would also serve as a preliminary to setting out the concepts of market and natural prices in Book I, Chapter VII.

It may perhaps be suggested that the actual arrangement of Chapter VI was intended *inter alia* to show that profits and rents were the results of exploitation. The famous passage stating that once stock was used 'the whole produce of labour does not always belong to the labourer. He must in most cases share it with the owner of the stock which employs him' (Vol. I, p. 51) is the more telling because it comes after the description of the beaver/deer society. The passage commenting on the emergence of rent as all land passes in private ownership is even more dramatic. Rent appears, of course, in this chapter simply as a monopoly or exploitation revenue from land:

> the landlords, like all other men, love to reap where they have never sowed, and demand a rent even for its natural produce. The wood of the forest, the grass of the field, and all the natural fruits of the earth, which, when land was in common, cost the

labourer only the trouble of gathering them, come, even to him, to have an additional price fixed upon them. He must then pay for the licence to gather them; and must give up to the land-lord a portion of what his labour either collects or produces. This portion, or, what comes to the same thing, the price of this portion, constitutes the rent of land, and in the price of greater part of commodities makes a third component part (Vol. I, p. 51).

The idea that Adam Smith deliberately framed these explanations in a way which incites interpretation in terms of the exploitation of the labourer seems to be consistent, neither with his emphasis on the productivity of capital throughout the *Wealth of Nations*, nor with his explanation that the three types of income exist even when one person supplies more than one factor. Can the freehold, working farmer, for instance, exploit himself as a worker in order to pay himself profits as a capitalist and rent as a landowner? I do not myself therefore think that Chapter VI was deliberately con-structed and inserted to demonstrate exploitation. There are how-ever plenty of well-known passages in the *Wealth of Nations* which show Adam Smith's antipathy to the rich, particularly the idle rich, and his sympathy with the workman. These attitudes are still clearer in the 'Early Draft of the Wealth of Nations' dis-covered by W. R. Scott. There can be little doubt that he dis-approved of gross inequality of wealth; the question however of what is meant by exploitation, and in particular what Adam Smith meant by it, is too complicated to discuss here, but some aspects of it are discussed in the last study in this book.[23]

*   *   *

Whatever the reason may be for the total neglect of profits and rent in the theory of natural price in the *Lectures*, it was obviously impossible for Adam Smith to continue to neglect them in the *Wealth of Nations* if it was to be regarded as an authoritative work. Other theories of value were already available. Versions of the Petty-Cantillon resource-input theory included land and labour, and recognised that there was a problem of how to deal with entrepreneurial profits but did not relate them to capital.

---

[23] See *Adam Smith, as Student and Professor*, op. cit., pp. 325–8, and see pp. 187 et seq. below on exploitation.

Steuart had included a lengthy analysis of profits in relation to his concept of 'real' value under varying conditions of competition but again not in relation to capital. The physiocratic development of the 'advances' theory of capital had emphasised the importance of capital in the productive process, and this clearly indicated the need to consider the question of the relation of capital to exchange value. The identification of the component parts of price in Chapter VI (Bk I) of the *Wealth of Nations* showed *inter alia* that Adam Smith was aware of the need to deal with profits of capital and with rent. In Chapter VII (Bk I) 'Of the Natural and Market Price of Commodities' he set out his re-statement of the natural price theory of the *Lectures* to allow for those additional components and to answer the third question about exchange value he had listed at the end of Chapter IV (Bk I).

Consistently with the chapter on the component parts of price, and consistently with the theory of natural price of the *Lectures*, Adam Smith defined the natural price of a commodity as follows: he says –

> When the price of any commodity is neither more nor less than what is sufficient to pay the rent of the land,[24] the wages of the labour and the profits of the stock employed in raising, preparing, and bringing it to market, according to their natural rates, the commodity is then sold for what may be called its natural price.
>
> The commodity is then sold precisely for what it is worth, or for what it really costs the person who brings it to market; for though in common language what is called the prime cost of any commodity does not comprehend the profit of the person who is to sell it again, yet if he sells it at a price which does not allow him the ordinary rate of profit in his neighbourhood, he is evidently a loser by the trade; . . . Unless they yield him this profit, therefore, they do not repay him what they may very properly be said to have really cost him (Vol. I, pp. 57–8).

The definition of the determinants of the natural prices of the factors of production is therefore crucial to the consistency of Adam Smith's theorem of the natural price of commodities. It is

[24] See Note 22, p. 118 above on the inclusion of rent as a component of natural price.

consistent with the importance of the natural prices of the factors of production in this connection that Adam Smith in fact opened Chapter VII with his definition of the determinants of natural prices. The difference between these definititions of the natural prices of factors and the natural price of commodities is not always, I think, sufficiently appreciated. For this reason it is worth quoting the definitions. He defined the natural prices of factors of production as '*the ordinary or average rate*' in every different employment at any particular time. In the case of wages and profits

> this rate is naturally regulated, as I shall show hereafter, partly by the general circumstances of the society, their riches or poverty, their advancing, stationary, or declining condition; and partly by the particular nature of each employment.

Similarly he says the '*ordinary or average rate*' of rent is regulated

> partly by the general circumstances of the society or neighbourhood in which the land is situated, and partly by the natural or improved fertility of the land.

The ordinary or average rates of wages, profit and rent are determined by the growth parameters of the society modified according to the particular circumstances of different employments, or the quality or fertility of the particular pieces of land. These ordinary or average rates are the rates which *actually exist* at any particular time. These ordinary or average rates Adam Smith explicitly explains are what he considers to be the natural rates relevant to the natural prices of commodities. Thus he says:

> These *ordinary or average* rates may be called the *natural* rates of wages, profit, and rent, at the time and place in which they commonly prevail.[25]

Thus the natural prices of commodities are simply the sum of the existing ordinary or average prices of the factors of production used in the production of each commodity. The natural price of a commodity is, therefore, always known and the natural prices of the factors of production are given to the price system for commodities by the macro-growth parameters of the economy. Being

[25] Vol. I, p. 57. My italics throughout.

without the full set-up of marginal productivity analysis, Adam Smith of course required some means of determining the natural prices of factors independently of the natural prices of commodities. These natural prices of factors were, however, determined by the macro-economic growth parameters of the system. They were not given by sociological, legal or institutional parameters, except in so far as the economic growth parameters themselves might turn out to be dependent in some way on institutional, legal or sociological factors as indeed Adam Smith considered them to be. Although the significance of Adam Smith's adoption of this idea can hardly be over-estimated, Steuart must, I think, be granted priority for excluding non-economic influences as determinants of factor prices.[26]

Adam Smith's natural price of a commodity was a supply price; it is important therefore to appreciate the care with which he worked out the influence of demand through the market price analysis. In order to analyse the relationship between market and natural prices of commodities Adam Smith introduced the new concept of *effectual demand*. Effectual demand is the quantity demanded of a good at its natural price, that is to say the price, in Adam Smith's words, which is 'sufficient to effectuate the bringing of the commodity to market'. This effectual demand is distinguished from the quantity that might be demanded at prices above or below the natural price. If the quantity brought to market was less than that coresponding to effectual demand then price would be bid up by those who would be prepared to pay more; similarly if the quantity brought to market was in excess of effectual demand price would fall owing to the competition of sellers (Vol. I, pp. 58–9). Although Adam Smith took note of some abnormal cases it is evident that he followed tradition in considering that the quantity demanded normally increased as price fell.

Adam Smith used his concept of effectual demand to show the relation between prices and resource-allocation. The quantity of every commodity brought to market would, he argued, naturally tend to be equal to the effectual demand for it. It is in the interest

[26] On Steuart on wages see p. 180 below. The physiocrats' position is perhaps somewhat obscure, but their reliance on subsistence-determined wages indicates that at least some of the prices of factors were not determined by pure economic elements.

of all suppliers that the quantity should never exceed this amount, and it is in the interest of all other people that it should never fall short of it. If at any time supply exceeded the effectual demand one or more of the factors would be paid at a rate below their natural rate. Whichever factor or factors were affected would tend to withdraw part of supply from this employment. So in this way the quantity brought to market would in Adam Smith's words 'soon be no more than sufficient to supply the effectual demand', and then the factor prices in that occupation would all rise again to their natural prices. The market and natural prices of the commodity would then again be equal. In the reverse case where too little was brought to market, one or more factor prices would rise above the natural rate in that particular occupation and there would be an incentive to increase supply until effectual demand was met and equilibrium restored (Vol. I, pp. 59–60). The price mechanism in the *Wealth of Nations*, as in the *Lectures*, allocated factors between uses by means of divergencies between market and natural prices of commodities which led to divergencies between market and natural prices of factors. Adam Smith concluded:

> The natural price, therefore, is as it were the central price, to which the prices of all commodities are continually gravitating. Different accidents may sometimes keep them suspended a good deal above it, and sometimes force them down even somewhat below it. But whatever may be the obstacles which may hinder them from settling in this center of repose and continuance, they are constantly tending towards it (Vol. I, p. 60).

Adam Smith concluded his analysis with a brief account of the circumstances which would produce differences between market and natural prices and affect the speed of adjustments. His list included, in addition to changes in demand, vagaries of harvest and the various restrictions on freedom of entry to different occupations, freedom of access to technical knowledge and inventions, privileges and so on and natural limitations on the supply of particular types of natural resources. The list in Chapter VII (Bk I) is not quite so complete as that in the *Lectures* but the subject was expanded in greater details in other parts of the *Wealth of Nations*.[27]

[27] See pp. 158–60 below.

Adam Smith's natural price of commodities was conceived in terms of the natural prices of factors in infinitely elastic supply to any industry at the current natural price, given time for re-allocations in a freely competitive market. As far as the supply of factors was concerned, therefore, the supply of a commodity was infinitely elastic in the long run at the natural price in the absence of restrictions. It seems to me evident that this natural price was regarded by Adam Smith as independent at any particular time of changes in the output of a commodity. The effects of the size of the market on the division of labour and therefore on technical co-efficients seems to have been regarded as a gradual historical process. He did not in his discussion of natural price suggest that a schedule of alternative natural prices related to quantity of output of an industry, or firm, existed at any particular moment. Under the conditions thus apparently assumed by Adam Smith (whether he realised their significance or not) the natural price for a commodity was therefore determined unambiguously by supply under conditions of constant costs. It should be emphasised however that, in the short run, both the prices of commodities and the prices of factors were directly determined by demand and supply, and could not be determined without taking both into account.

*   *   *

Enough has been said, I hope, to show that there is no difference in principle but only in elaboration between the theory of natural price in the *Lectures* and in the *Wealth of Nations*. This is consistent with the interpretations I have suggested of Chapters V and VI (Bk I).

Traditionally historians of economic theory have been apt to consider Adam Smith's theory of value in relation to Ricardo's or in relation to the development of marginal utility theories. I have of course done it before myself. Schumpeter more recently set the fashion of comparing Adam Smith's theory with that of the seventeenth-century theories as well. In this study I have tried to look at it to some extent in relation to the theories of Cantillon and of other eighteenth-century economists as well as those of the seventeenth century. This has shown the significance of:

(1) his deliberate rejection of physical input theories;
(2) the attempt to include capital along with labour and land in a theory of value;

(3) the introduction of macro-economic growth parameters to determine the natural prices of factors.

A system such as Adam Smith's which regarded the natural prices of commodities as dependent on the natural prices of factors, which were determined by some macro-economic parameters and thus given to the commodity price system, is less general than the system in which the natural prices of factors are imputed from the values of their products. How useful it is seems to me to depend on the nature of the assumptions which are made about the character of the economic system at any time. It is interesting in this connection that J. B. Say, who regarded himself as the populariser of Adam Smith in France, attempted to convert Adam Smith's system into one in which the values of factors were imputed from the values of their products as logically more satisfactory or more elegant. Say's theory of the relative productive contributions of factors of production which in principle is similar, of course, to that of the Austrian school, broke down because he was unable to isolate the individual productive contribution of factors, in other words because he had no marginal analysis available. A few of the pre-1870 attempts to resolve this problem with respect to labour and capital are considered in relation to Adam Smith's theories later in this book.

Addendum on the Just Price and Adam Smith's Natural Price
Earlier in this study it was pointed out that Adam Smith's natural price of commodities apparently turned out to be the same as the just price of commodities of the traditional Schoolmen. This is not surprising for they asked the same question – what is the lowest price which will maintain the supply of a commodity? The answers given are naturally the same – the price that equals the cost of producing it and bringing it to market. Adam Smith's explanation of the price mechanism could be seen as completing the analysis of just price; by demonstrating the resource-allocation function of divergences between market and natural prices it solved the difficulty, apparent in the schoolmen's discussions, of finding a way to reconcile both market and supply prices to the just price concept. In particular Adam Smith's reliance on competition to eliminate the divergences was wholly consistent with the acceptance by some of the later Schoolmen of the price ruling in a competitive market as the just price. The requirement of

competition by such Schoolmen was of course due, as with Adam Smith, to the need to prevent individuals, or groups, from obtaining and taking advantage of favourable bargaining positions to raise prices.

The Age of Religion and the Age of Enlightenment had reached the same conclusions about how the prices of commodities ought to be determined. The similarity however conceals important differences. The ultimate criteria in relation to which the question about prices was asked were not the same, nor were the assumptions underlying the answers. The difference between criteria is obvious. The traditional Schoolmen's criterion was that of commutative justice, and the basic object of defining the just price was in order to provide rules for individual conduct in selling and buying consistent with the Christian ethic, and therefore with spiritual welfare. The reason for adopting the competitive price as the criteria was that it was seen to be consistent with the rule that no Christian should take advantage of any type of relatively favourable bargaining positions, such as those provided by monopolistic, or monopsonistic, situations. Adam Smith's criterion was the maximisation of wealth per head; hence, as he had shown, it was necessary to prevent monopolistic, or monopsonistic, practices. The maximisation of wealth also had a distributive effect to which he attached importance, in that it enabled more people to enjoy 'the conveniency' of goods, for wealth meant plenty and plenty meant cheapness, so the greater the opulence the more goods the poorer classes could afford. This is made very clear in the passage quoted from the *Lectures* on p. 108 above.

It is obvious that Adam Smith attached great importance to this distributive effect. His explanation of the benefit of the division of labour both in the *Lectures* and in the *Wealth of Nations* emphasised the great superiority in living standards of even an unskilled labourer in a society based on the division of labour, compared to even the highest ranks of people in societies without division of labour. It is evident that he regarded this as in some way compensating for what he believed to be the effect of the division of labour in actually increasing the inequalities in the distribution of wealth between socio-economic classes, for like Hume he regarded great inequalities in the distribution of wealth as undesirable. The evidence for this statement will be found in the study of Adam Smith's treatment of wages in the last study in this book.

This reference to questions of distribution brings us to the difference between the assumptions underlying the criteria of the schoolmen and Adam Smith. The schoolmen's just price for commodities was based on the assumption that the costs to be covered by the price were themselves based on principles consistent with the principle of a just price – the labourer would receive the just reward for his labour and the merchant the just reward for his care and trouble etc. These just rewards were assumed to be established by law and custom. The just prices of commodities thus were assumed to be adjusted to and consistent with a just distribution of wealth in society. Just in this connection, however, in the schoolmen's world was associated with the maintenance of the particular status of the individual in a stable socio-economic hierarchy. (Presumably this required constant proportionate shares.)

Adam Smith's definition of the natural prices of factors on which the natural prices of commodities were based had no such implications of justice. In the *Lectures* the natural price of a man's labour was the price which will maintain supply in a particular occupation; in the *Wealth of Nations* the natural prices of all factors were ultimately determined by macro-economic parameters which influenced the relation between demand and supply. These are pragmatic not ethical concepts. Indeed Adam Smith used his natural price analysis to attack, as inconsistent with the maximisation of wealth, laws and customs some of which had usually been intended to help to safeguard the just prices for factors of production.

It is evident I think that Adam Smith was the conscious or unconscious heir in the direct line to the schoolmen with respect to the concept of the price mechanism and the natural prices of commodities. Indeed since Hutcheson, his teacher, made him familiar with Pufendorf's work, which set out the views of the Schoolmen, the line of affiliation of thought seems obvious. It is equally evident that with respect to the natural prices of factors there was no usable inheritance from this source in relation either to the problems to be solved, or the criterion of equity. The rationalisation of popular opposition to monopolistic practices into a justification of competition by the late schoolmen appeared, however, in a form even more appropriate to Adam Smith's analytical approach in some of the mercantilist writings of the seventeenth century. These identified the price of a competitive market with a 'natural' price suggesting that this was in some sense the right price because it conformed with natural laws.[28]

The difference in the relationships between Adam Smith's and the schoolmen's concepts of the natural and just prices of commodities and of factors respectively, has, it seems to me, been reflected in much subsequent thought on these matters both popular and analytical. Outside the Marxist and socialist literature there has been a fairly constant identification of the just price of commodities with Adam Smith's natural price of commodities in politico-economic or ethical discussion, particularly in relation to regulation of prices. Cost of production is commonly regarded as satisfying the criteria of both social justice and the maximisation of wealth through efficient resource-allocation, the latter more rigorously set out in marginalist welfare economics. There has been no such unanimity about the identity of the natural with the just prices of factors, or about criteria for the distribution of wealth. Indeed as the last study in this book shows, neither Adam Smith himself, nor those classical economists who were concerned with the matter, were convinced that the natural prices of factors led to a distribution of income satisfactory in terms of social justice. Admittedly it was argued under the influence of Malthusian doctrine that the natural price of labour might be raised by the labourers if they cultivated the virtue of prudence. Although this might be regarded as making increases in the natural wage rate appear to be a just reward for virtue, even this was regarded as implying that society had a duty to frame its institutions so as not to discourage the cultivation of the virtue and if possible to encourage it. The emphasis on 'wise institutions' particularly in connection with the poor laws is of course a feature of classical discussions on wage problems. However interpreted, this attitude involves dissatisfaction with the low levels to which a natural rate of wages might sink.

The normal ethical justification of the natural prices of factors established in competitive factor markets related not to the actual

[28] See pp. 53–4, 59 and 72 above.

levels of those prices, nor the distribution of income that followed from them, but was that they gave to owners of factors the opportunity to dispose of their own propertly to the best advantage. This was particularly eloquently argued with respect to labour by Adam Smith himself in the *Wealth of Nations* in the chapter 'Of Wages and Profits in the Different Employments of Labour and Stock' where he is considering the imperfections in the labour market created by governments. He declares

> The property which every man has in his own labour, as it is the original foundation of all other property, so it is most sacred and inviolable. The patrimony of a poor man lies in the strength and dexterity of his hands; and to hinder him from employing this strength and dexterity in what manner he thinks proper without injury to his neighbour, is a plain violation of this most sacred property (Vol. I, p. 123).

No attempt was made in the *Wealth of Nations* to show that this freedom would lead to a distribution of wealth consistent with Adam Smith's ideal of social justice or welfare whatever that is believed to be. It has led however to the view that the prices of factors in a fully competive market are *fair* as between individuals in the markets, rather in the sense in which *fair* is used in the concept of *fair play*, in contrast to the *unfairness* of imperfectly competitive markets. This idea of *fair* factor prices will be recognised as having apparently a family resemblance to the idea of some Schoolmen that prices in a competitive market were *just*. The ideas are not identical however, for the schoolmen applied the concept to commodity markets only and on the assumption that just prices for factors were established by law or custom. The idea of fairness of competitive factor prices has from time to time of course been regarded as implying that competition in factor markets necessarily leads to a distribution of wealth consistent with justice, or as even maximising welfare in some sense as well as wealth. The distinction between economic efficiency based on competition and welfare or social justice depending on the distribution of wealth was, however, painfully clear to Adam Smith and some economists in the classical tradition long before it was formally stated by Jevons in the warning

So far as is consistent with the inequality of wealth in every community, all commodities are distributed by exchange so as to produce the maximum of benefit.[29]

The bearing of the realisation of this problem on the attitudes of classical economists towards the growth of wealth is discussed a little in the last study in this book.

[29] *Theory of Political Economy*, 2nd edn, Ch. IV, p. 141.

IV Utility, the Paradox of Value and 'all that' and Classical Economics*

> Utility: The quality of being serviceable or beneficial to mankind. The utility of an object has generally been considered as proportioned to the necessity and real importance of these services and benefits.
>
> MALTHUS[1]

Since I wrote *Nassau Senior and Classical Economics* more than thirty years ago, I have altered in various ways my views both about the development of utility theory in the first half of the nineteenth century, and about the views and influence of Adam Smith. This is because I have learnt a little more about Adam Smith's predecessors and contemporaries and about the classical period itself. In this essay I have tried to set out what now seems to me to be a more correct interpretation of the history of utility theory from Adam Smith to Dupuit in certain respects.

(i) Adam Smith and Utility and 'all that'

According to the first paragraph of the section on economics of the Notes of Adam Smith's Lectures, Adam Smith used the paradox of value to demonstrate that cheapness 'is in fact the same thing with plenty', plenty being the same thing as 'opulence'.

---

* Some of the material used in this study was used in a summarised form in my paper 'The Predecessors of Jevons – the revolution that wasn't'. (*Manchester School*, March 1972, Special Jevons Centenary Number). That paper considered certain developments in utility theory for a rather different purpose to that of the present study. A few paragraphs from that paper have been incorporated in the study with only minor alterations. See notes 29 and 34 below. I am grateful to the editors of the *Manchester School* for permission to reprint them.

[1] *Definitions in Political Economy*, p. 234.

Following traditional explanations he pointed out that water was so cheap because it was so plentiful while diamonds were dear on account of their scarcity 'for their real use seems not yet to be discovered' (*Lectures*, p. 157). This particular account of the paradox is obviously elliptical as recorded in the *Lectures*, but a complete version in the traditional form is included later (ibid., pp. 176–7).

It will be noticed that Adam Smith here qualified the word 'use' by 'real' in the same way that Locke and Law had qualified their term 'intrinsic natural worth' to indicate the importance of the want, or wants, that could be satisfied by particular goods, this importance being assessed according to some absolute scale e.g. necessities, conveniences, luxuries.[2] Adam Smith could say therefore that goods could be demanded though they had no 'real' use; in this he conformed to the ordinary practice of the man in the street who may describe some expensive luxury as having 'no real use', or more simply as useless. He did however employ the word 'use' both in this sense, but without the prefix 'real', and also in a general neutral sense to mean 'those qualities (of goods) which are the ground of preference, and which give occasion to pleasure and pain, and are the cause of many insignificant demands' (*Lectures*, p. 159). It may be pointed out that the paradox of value as usually stated was simply a striking means of demonstrating the existence of the differences between valuations of the importance of wants satisfied by a commodity and its exchange value. Thus differences in the precise meaning attached to the word 'use' did not affect the significance of the difference between value in use and value in exchange, but merely indicated the nature of the particular scale of estimation used on various occasions.

The discussion of the nature of wants which followed immediately on from the opening paragraph resembled the seventeenth century discussions, such as those of Barbon and Locke, in emphasising that necessities account for only a small proportion of human wants, and their provision for only a small part of economic activities. It is the desire for variety and luxury on which the development of industry and trade depends. This discussion like Locke's maintains the distinction, it should be noticed,

----

[2] On Locke and Law see pp. 78–80 above.

between necessities, conveniences etc. as relevant to the question he is concerned with. Thus he sums up:

> Those qualities, which are the ground of preference, and which give occasion to pleasure and pain, are the cause of many insignificant demands, which we by no means stand in *need* of. The whole industry of human life is employed not in procuring the supply of our three humble necessities, food, clothes and lodging, but in procuring the conveniences of it according to the niceties and delicacy of our taste. To improve and multiply the materials which are the principal objects of our necessities, gives occasion to all the variety of the arts. (Ibid., pp. 159–60. My italics.)

The *Lectures* continue, it will be remembered, with a discussion of the ways in which wants are provided for, how opulence is increased by the division of labour, how the division of labour leads to exchange and, thence, Adam Smith reaches a discussion of exchange value and natural and market prices. He explained that market price was determined quite differently from natural price and depended on three factors, viz.:

> First, the demand or *need* for the commodity. There is no demand for a thing of *little use*; it is not a rational object of desire.
>
> Secondly, the abundance or scarcity of the commodity in proportion to the *need* of it. If the commodity be scarce, the price is raised, but if the quantity be more than is sufficient to supply the demand, the price falls. Thus it is that diamonds and other precious stones are dear, while iron, which is *much more useful* is so many times cheaper, though this depends principally on the last cause, viz.:
>
> Thirdly, the riches or poverty of those who demand. When there is not enough produced to serve everybody, the fortune of the bidders is the only regulation of the price. (pp. 176–7. My italics.)

The similarity of this explanation of market price to those of some seventeenth-century writers is obvious. Unless the notes of the *Lectures* omit some explanations, Adam Smith seems to have relied on the context to make clear the different senses in which he used the words I have put in italics. Thus *need* in the first quotation is obviously used in its ordinary sense and contrasted with the demands for goods which are not necessities, a distinction parallel to goods which have 'real use' and those which do not. In the first and fourth lines of the second quotation 'need' is used as synonymous with 'demand'. All very tiresome for Adam Smith's students, but who can seriously claim that they never use a word in different senses without explaining what they are doing? In the second passage *use* is also used in two senses. In referring to demand at the beginning he evidently means by *use* the capacity of a good to satisfy any sort of desire i.e. those qualities 'which give occasion to pleasure and pain' of the first passage. *Use* is evidently used here in the neutral sense of the modern economist's 'utility', without any implication of ranking of wants according to some accepted scale. A few lines further on, illustrating the influence of scarcity on exchange value by the paradox of value he introduces the words '*much more useful*', obviously meaning *useful* in relation to some absolute scale of grading *usefulness*. The introduction of the paradox of value in connection with market price helps to emphasise again the point made earlier in the *Lectures* that 'cheapness is the same thing with plenty'.

The terminology is exceedingly awkward, but the meaning seems to me to be clear in the light of ways in which these words were employed in the seventeenth and eighteenth centuries by, for instance, Locke, Law and Harris etc. and to this day in ordinary speech. Who does not remember those 'utility' goods in the last war? Considered in this way, Adam Smith was not inconsistent in the views he expressed as H. M. Robertson and W. L. Taylor stated in their article.[3] This interpretation is also consistent with what seems to me to be the correct interpretation of Adam Smith's references to utility and value in use in the *Wealth of Nations*.

In the *Wealth of Nations* Adam Smith refers to the paradox of value as such only once and for a quite different purpose from either of the occasions recorded in the *Lectures*. After he has shown how the division of labour leads to exchange and the use of money, he says that he is going to examine the question of 'the rules which men naturally observe in exchanging them (goods) for money or for one another'. These are the rules he explains which 'determine what may be called the relative or exchange-

[3] See their article 'Adam Smith's approach to the Theory of Value', *E.J.*, 1957

able value of goods'.[4] Before going further, however, he
endeavours to remove a possible source of confusion in the minds
of his readers which could arise because the word 'value' can be
used in two different senses. The wording of the famous passage
in which he gives the explanation of the two different meanings
is so important that I must quote it in full:

> The word Value, it is to be observed, has two different mean-
> ings, and sometimes expresses the utility of some particular
> object, and sometimes the power of purchasing other goods
> which the possession of that object conveys. The one may be
> called 'value in use'; the other, 'value in exchange'. The
> things which have the greatest value in use have frequently
> little or no value in exchange; and on the contrary, those which
> have the greatest value in exchange have frequently little or
> no value in use. Nothing is more useful than water: but it will
> purchase scarce anything; scarce anything can be had in
> exchange for it. A diamond, on the contrary, has scarce any
> value in use; but a very great quantity of other goods may
> frequently be had in exchange for it (p. 30).

It has been pointed out by critics of this passage that in the
third sentence Adam Smith states that things that have 'no value
in use' may have value in exchange. It is concluded that Adam
Smith had made an elementary mistake in denying the necessity
of utility to value.[5] The attribution of an error to Adam Smith
which is obviously inconsistent with the explanations of wants in
relation to demand in subsequent chapters of the *Wealth of
Nations* arises, it seems to me, from reading the *Wealth of Nations*
interpreting the terms 'value in use' or 'utility' in the general
neutral sense. If the passage is read equating 'value in use' to the
'real use' of the lecture notes, the apparent error disappears, for
in that sense of the word 'use' it is perfectly possible for goods to
have an exchange value though they have 'no use'. It is in this
sense it has been pointed out already that expensive luxuries are
described as useless in ordinary speech. This interpretation has
the advantage of being consistent with the way in which Adam
Smith uses the word 'utility' in another place in the *Wealth of*

---

[4] *Wealth of Nations*, Vol. I, p. 30.
[5] Robertson and Taylor, p. 184.

Nations.[6] In his explanation of the demands for the precious metals and gems he distinguishes between utility and beauty and prestige value as reasons for people wanting goods. He attributes the demand for the precious metals to their possession of all three qualities, but the demand for gems to their beauty and prestige value only for he repeats that they have 'no use but as ornaments' (Vol. I, pp. 172–3). Moreover it will be noticed that in one place at least in the *Wealth of Nations* where he wants a general term to indicate what modern economists call utility, he uses the word 'importance' (see p. 139 below).

Criticism of Adam Smith on this alleged ground that he did not understand that goods had to be capable of serving some want, providing some satisfaction, as a condition of being demanded at all cannot, as I think I have shown, be substantiated. Criticism might be made on the quite different basis that it is not useful in connection with value theory for economists to distinguish between categories of wants according to some recognised scale of importance, whether it be the customary necessities/luxuries scale or some other.[7] Whatever might be argued in support of such a viewpoint in relation to modern value theory, I do not think it justifiable in relation to the classical period. The paradox of value had been formulated much earlier as a result of observation of the striking differences between the 'exchange value' ranking of goods and the ranking of value of goods according to a scale of importance of wants recognised by ordinary people as well as by philosophers. Viewed historically the paradox of value focused attention of a long line of economists on the problem of the relation of utility to demand and price. Examples of this are discussed later in this study.

The passage on the paradox of value in the *Wealth of Nations* is sometimes criticised on the ground that it did not include an explanation of the contrast between the exchange values of water and diamonds in terms of 'scarcity'. It is suggested that the omission of this explanation indicates that Adam Smith was unfor-

[6] John Stuart Mill also interpreted Adam Smith's statement in the *Wealth of Nations* in the same way as I have. *Principles*, Bk III, Ch. 1, par. 2.

[7] Stigler's comment on Adam Smith's statement of the paradox of value that it deserves 'neither criticism nor quotation' seems to be due to this view. See 'The Development of Utility Theory' in Stigler's *Essays in the History of Economics*, pp. 68–9.

tunately not interested in scarcity in the *Wealth of Nations*. These comments surely can only be made as a result of not noticing Adam Smith's own reason for introducing the reference to the paradox. It is to illustrate the contrast between *value in use* and *value in exchange*, not as these commentators imply to explain the paradox. To explain it in this place in the *Wealth of Nations* would have anticipated the explanation of exchange value of succeeding chapters.

The more general criticism that Adam Smith neglects 'scarcity' in the *Wealth of Nations* can conveniently be considered briefly at the same time as the parallel criticism with respect to the treatment of wants. I can find no explanation for the former criticism except that Adam Smith does not use the actual word 'scarcity' often. This I would have thought was an improvement for the word is often used ambiguously by economists as well as by ordinary people. Let us consider the explanation of market price in the *Wealth of Nations* for this is relevant to both these criticisms. Here the concept of *'effectual demand'* is introduced and defined as the amount demanded at the natural price. This enables Adam Smith to discuss divergences of market price from natural price at the same time as he explains market price. He thus converts the usual statement that market price is determined by scarcity in relation to demand into the statement that market price is regulated by the proportion of the supply brought to market to the effectual demand. If supply is equal to *effectual demand*, market and natural prices will coincide; if supply is greater or less, market prices will be below or above natural price, respectively. The word 'scarcity' would be redundant. Nor does he neglect to point out the relation of wants to demand. He explains the effect on market price of a shortage of supply in relation to effectual demand in terms of the variations of people's willingness to pay more 'rather than want it [*sic* the good] altogether'. The extent to which market price will be driven up will depend on 'the greatness of the deficiency', and 'the wealth and wanton luxury' of the demanders. If the consumers are of equal wealth and luxury the increase in price will depend on whether 'the acquisition of the commodity happens to be of more or less importance to them' (Vol. I, pp. 58–9). He goes on to the case of market price falling below natural price and demand fluctuations.[8]

[8] See pp 148–9 below on Malthus's discussion of this paragraph in the

The rest of the specific discussions on the nature of wants and their relationship to demand is in Book I, Chapter XI, 'Of the Rent of Land', which contains the substance of the discussion in the *Lectures*. The limited nature of the demand for necessities, the desire for conveniences and luxuries are all included. It is here that Adam Smith makes his famous statement that 'the desire of food is limited in every man by the narrow capacity of the human stomach; but the desire of the conveniences and ornaments of building, dress, equippage, and household furniture seems to have no limit or certain boundary' (Vol. I, pp. 164–5). This chapter also includes the discussion already mentioned giving the reasons for the demand for the precious metals and gems (p. 138 above).

The reason for the position of these discussions seems perfectly clear. In the *Wealth of Nations* Adam Smith was concerned *inter alia* with the prices of the factors of production. The first passage referred to is included in his discussion of the source of demand for the products of land which helps to determine rent. The second passage is similarly part of the discussion of the demand for the products of mines which help to determine the rent of mines. (The importance of the variety of wants is also discussed in relation to the rate of profit in Book II, Chapter V.) The rearrangement is clearly due to an extension of the field of inquiry from the simple one-factor world to the complicated real world where there are three factors of production. Here the problem of explaining natural price becomes more complex and the question of the distribution of the product 'among the different ranks and conditions of men in society' emerges.[9]

The rearrangement does not mean that the reader who starts at the beginning of the *Wealth of Nations* is not made aware of the purpose of the *Inquiry into the Nature and Causes of the Wealth of Nations*, as an investigation of the causes of opulence

Wealth of Nations in connection with his own concept of 'intensity of demand'. Smith's actual definition of effectual demand is 'the demand of those who are willing to pay the natural price of the commodity' (*Wealth of Nations*, Vol. I, p. 50).

[9] See D. H. Buchanan, op. cit., in connection with rent, and pp. 220–2 below in connection with profits. See also Robbin's review of Schumpeter's *History of Economic Analysis*, Q.J.E., 1955, for a reply to the general criticism of the classical economists for the neglect of demand.

or the satisfaction of wants and the distribution of opulence among classes.[10] This is stated in the Introduction (pp. 1–2). The concern with the satisfaction of wants is emphasised again, at the beginning of Chapter IV 'Of The Origin and Use of Money', in the explanation of the emergence of exchange in order to facilitate the satisfaction of wants once the division of labour has been established. This is repeated again at the beginning of Chapter V 'Of the Real and Nominal Price of Commodities' which deals with the first question Adam Smith has listed for consideration in his analysis of the rules which govern exchange value. Finally the significance of the divergence of market price from natural price in relation to 'opulence' is a main theme of a great part of the whole discussion of policy.

I may perhaps have spent too long arguing that Adam Smith did not neglect the nature of wants, utility, demand and scarcity in the *Wealth of Nations*, and that his treatment there was not analytically inferior to that in his *Lectures* or in the works of his best-known predecessors. The reason is, as I have indicated earlier, that I used to hold the contrary view and this very much influenced the interpretation of the development of value theory in my *Senior and Classical Economics*. I do not think however that Adam Smith added anything new to formal utility analysis, though his elaboration of the extension of the analysis of market prices to factors of production must be regarded as a significant contribution to knowledge. Rather his contribution to pure theory of utility seems to me to have been what perhaps should be described as *passive*.

His retention of the distinction between value in use and value in exchange was emphasised by its introduction in the *Wealth of Nations* as a preliminary terminological clarification before examining the determinants of value in exchange. No student of the *Wealth of Nations* could miss it. The perceptive student could not fail to notice it as an indication that there was a problem involved in the relation of utility to exchange value. Consideration of this problem led *inter alia* to attempts to measure utility by later economists. The importance of the distinction was

---

[10] Messrs. Robertson and Taylor's article provides a most illuminating discussion of some of the effects of the difference in scope between the *Wealth of Nations* and the *Lectures* on the arrangement and relative prominence of certain topics including market price.

further emphasised by Adam Smith's broad definition of wealth in terms of the necessaries and conveniences of life and his emphasis on costs as the obstacles to acquisition of wealth; that cheapness is plenty and plenty is opulence, i.e. wealth, runs through the *Wealth of Nations* as through the *Lectures* – the theme which in Ricardo's terminology appeared in the contrast between value and riches.[11]

(ii) Ricardo, Say and Dupuit on the measure of utility

As everyone knows Ricardo opened the chapter 'On Value' in his *Principles* by quoting Adam Smith's distinction between value in use and value in exchange.[12] He concluded from this that value in use or utility neither measured nor determined value in exchange, although unless a commodity has some utility it could have no exchange value. Ricardo defines utility in the general sense of the power to contribute in any way to gratification, but ranks the importance of wants as usual, i.e. necessities and luxuries. He does not comment on, and seems not to have noticed the particular sense of 'real use' in which Adam Smith appears to employ the term in the *Wealth of Nations*. Other economists followed Ricardo usually without comment. Thus McCulloch in his 'Note on Value' in his edition of the *Wealth of Nations* defined utility in the same way as Ricardo, stressing the importance of the distinction between 'value in use' and 'value in exchange', pointing out that 'the utility of commodities' – i.e. 'the fitness for satisfying our wants' such as the capacity of bread to appease hunger, or water to quench thirst – is a totally different and distinct quality from their capacity of exchanging for other things. He pointed out that Adam Smith 'perceived this difference and has shown the importance of carefully distinguishing between utility, or as he called it value in use, and value in exchange'.[13] Longfield in his discussion of Adam Smith's distinction and Dupuit also employed the general definition of utility; so did

[11] On Ricardo's criticism of Adam Smith's measure of value in relation to his definition of wealth see pp. 115–16 above.

[12] Ricardo had noted with approval Adam Smith's distinction as early as 1810 or 1811. Ricardo's Notes on Bentham's 'Sur le Prix'. Note 24, p. 284, *Ricardo's Works*, Vol. III.

[13] *Notes and Dissertations*. Note II, 'Definitions, Sources and Regulating Principles of Value', pp. 816 and 818, McCulloch's edition of the *Wealth of Nations*, 1838.

Malthus.[14] Longfield and Senior did, however, notice that utility was normally used in ordinary speech in a more limited sense described by Senior as 'the quality of preventing pain or of indirectly producing pleasure, as a means'. They decided however that despite the inconvenience of departing from common usage it was necessary for economists to use it in the wider sense to include the direct provision of pleasure, for lack of a better term.[15]

The particular wording of the distinction between 'value in use' and 'value in exchange' in the *Wealth of Nations* did not prevent economists as different as Ricardo and Dupuit from regarding it as fundamental. Both considered that failure to appreciate its significance was the source of major errors in the work of J. B. Say. In fact one aspect or another of the treatment in the *Wealth of Nations* of utility and wants provided the acknowledged starting point of the considerable discussions of utility by economists of the classical period. It is with these that the rest of this study is concerned. It will be convenient to begin with Ricardo's and Dupuit's criticisms of Say's treatment of utility.

J. B. Say used the extended definition of utility, explaining that he used the word to mean the capacity of a good to satisfy any want whatever without any implication that utility was in any way proportioned to what he termed its *real utility 'utilité réelle'*. The just appreciation of *'real utility'* depended, he said, on the morals, knowledge, customs and institutions of a society, and was therefore, he considered, outside the field of political economy. Say's *real utility* seems thus to belong to the same family of concepts as Adam Smith's *real use* of the *Lectures* and value in use or *utility* in the *Wealth of Nations*. Following from his definition of utility, Say concluded it was the prior source of value, that price was the measure of value and therefore that price was the measure of utility. He justified this last conclusion as follows:

This price is the measure of the utility which it (the good) has,

---

[14] Longfield, *Lectures on Political Economy*, p. 25. All page references are to the L.S.E. reprint. Dupuit, *De L'Utilité et de sa Mésure*, collected papers ed. Bernardi, 1934, pp. 36–7. All page references are to this edition. Malthus's definition is quoted at the beginning of this essay. See p. 134 above. Malthus explained, it will be noticed, that utility was usually regarded as varying with the necessity etc. of the wants satisfied.

[15] Senior, *Political Economy*, p. 6. Longfield, ibid.

in the judgement of men, of the satisfaction which they will draw from its consumption; for they would not seek to consume this utility, if, for the price which they have to give for it, they could obtain a utility which would give them greater satisfaction.[16]

This analysis was based on Say's distinction between what he termed *natural riches* and *social riches*. The former included all satisfactions that did not have to be paid for: these included the satisfactions from free goods such as air, water, good health, but apparently in addition all satisfactions (utility) derived from goods which were not free, in excess of the utility sacrificed to obtain them. He argued that every such good contained a portion of utility provided free by nature, which was part of natural riches, and a portion that was created by labour and making land and capital work. Only the latter gave rise to any exchange value for it was only this part that had to be paid for; it emerged only in society and he therefore called it social riches; it was this utility which was measured by price. Economists he considered were only concerned with social riches for the free utility provided by natural riches did not enter into our appreciation of wealth. For this reason the distinction between value in use and value in exchange was pointless or at least irrelevant to economics.[17] He set out his point of view very clearly in one of his later letters to Ricardo.

C'est, permettez-moi de vous le dire, ce que ne peut enseigner la considération *de la valeur en utilité* (*value in use*) mots que me paraissent incompatibles, parce que l'idée de valeur ne peut être separée de celle de comparaison et d'échange.

Je persiste donc à croire que créer de l'utilité c'est créer de la richesse, mais que nous n'avons d'autre mesure de cette utilité créée, que le plus ou moins grande quantité d'un autre produit quelconque; quantité qui forme la *valeur échangeable* du premier, son *prix-courant*.

[16] *Traité d'Economie Politique* (all references are to the 1841 edition), p. 57 and note 1 and p. 58 and '*Epitome*', p. 606. The quotation is from the '*Epitome*'. My translation.

[17] *Traité*, op. cit., p. 315 and '*Epitome*', pp. 601 et seq. Although Say modified his wording in successive editions of his *Traité*, in attempts to clarify his explanation, he did not alter his theory.

L'utilité qui est naturellement dans une chose, et qui ne lui a pas été donnée, comme celle de l'eau, fait partie de nos *richesses naturelles*; mais n'ayant aucune valeur échangeable, elle ne peut être l'objet des recherches de la science economique. Et pourquoi l'eau n'a t'elle de valeur échangeable? Parce qu'elle n'est pas un subjet d'échange, parce que, pour en avoir, personne étant obligé d'en acquérir, elle n'est l'objet d'aucune demande.

Une grande utilité qui peut se donner à peu de frais rapproche la chose à laquelle elle est conferée, d'une *richesse naturelle*, d'une chose qui a son utilité par elle même et sans frais; mais en Economie politique, nous ne pouvons nous occuper que de la portion d'utilité qui a été donnée *avec les frais*.[18]

Say considered that he had resolved the problem of the relation of utility to value. Ricardo's disagreement as demonstrated in their correspondence from 1815 to 1822 turned precisely on Ricardo's conviction that the distinction between value in use and value in exchange was of fundamental importance. Thus in a letter to Say dated 18 August 1815 he writes that he does not think that Say has

mastered the difficulties which attach to the explanation of that difficult word. [value] Utility is certainly the foundation of value, but the degree of utility can never be the measure by which to estimate value. A commodity difficult of production will always be more valuable than one which is easily produced although all men should agree that the latter is more useful than the former. A commodity must be useful to have value but the difficulty of its production is the true measure of its value. For this reason Iron though more useful is of less value than gold.

Ricardo goes on to object to Say's definitions of riches on similar grounds.[19] The discussion was still continuing six years later,

[18] Letter from Say to Ricardo, 19 July 1821, *Works of David Ricardo*, Vol. IX, p. 32. See also Ricardo's letter to Say, 5 March 1822, also in Vol. IX.
[19] Ibid., Vol. VI, pp. 247–8. As Say very politely pointed out, Ricardo was wrong in stating that Say measured value by utility; it was the other way round. (Letter Say to Ricardo, 2 Dec. 1815, pp. 273–4.) This did not affect Ricardo's objection.

Ricardo explaining to Say that he has pointed out their differences of opinion about this in the third edition of his *Principles*.[20] The letter from Say to Ricardo, quoted already in illustration of Say's thesis, was in fact part of Say's reply to this letter of Ricardo's.

* * *

In 1844 in his paper 'De la mesure de l'utilité des Travaux Publics',[21] Dupuit also attributed the errors of Say's treatment of utility, including its measurement by exchange value, to Say's neglect of Adam Smith's distinction between value in use and value in exchange. He quoted McCulloch in support of his belief in the importance of the distinction.

No one perhaps in the period of classical economics explained this importance more clearly than Dupuit in his critique of the results of using Say's method of measuring the utility of roads and his analysis of the effects of a tax on wine. In the example of the roads Dupuit pointed out that if the total that had to be paid by society for its transport services fell owing to an improvement in efficiency, Say's method of measurement of utility led to the conclusion that the utility derived from those same services fell in proportion to fall in cost; a reduction in costs thus resulted in a decline in utility. This was obviously wrong; the price paid only showed that the utility derived from the transport was worth at least as much as the price. Hence Say's measure gave no indication of the total utility derived.

In the example of the tax on wine, Say only avoided saying that utility of the wine had increased to the consumer in proportion to the rise in price caused by the tax by introducing a distinction between 'real value', founded on utility as measured by the pre-tax price, and the value of the tax required by the government. In commenting on this dilemma Dupuit pointed out that it arose because Say's measure of value ignored the differing utilities of successive bottles of wine. After demonstrating by example the way in which utility declined with increases in quantity consumed, he argued that utility must be measured by adding together the utilities of the successive units as measured by the price that

---

[20] Ibid., Vol. VIII. Ricardo to Say, 8 May 1821, p. 379. *Principles*, Ch. XX.

[21] Included in the papers edn by Bernardi, op. cit.

would be paid for each successive unit.[22] He summed up with the following passage:

> Ainsi, tous les produits consommés ont une utilité différente, non-seulement pour chaque consommateur, mais pour chacun des besoins à la satisfaction desquels il les emploie: c'est ce que nous verrons d'ailleurs à chaque instant quand nous nous occuperons de la mesure de l'utilité publique. Mais avant, qu'on nous permette d'insister encore sur ces notions générales, qui servent de base à la méthode que nous proposerons tout à l'heure (p. 36).

It is at this stage of his argument that Dupuit brings in Adam Smith's distinction to support him; thus he continues:

> Et d'abord, nous éprouvons le besoin de repousser le reproche qu'on pourrait nous faire de distraire le mot utilité de sa définition scientifique, pour lui donner un sens tout à fait nouveau, et en faire sortir une méthode d'évaluation qui, au premier coup d'oeil, paraît assez compliquée. Il nous suffira de rappeler que la distinction que nous proposons se trouve dans le docteur Smith, qui reconnaît deux valeurs dans un objet; *sa valeur en usage*, qui est l'utilité telle que nous la comprenons, la valeur pour celui qui a besoin de consommer le produit; *sa valeur en échange*, qui est l'utilité de ce même produit pour celui qui a besoin de le vendre (p. 36).

To emphasise even more strongly that Adam Smith's great authority is on his side in the argument, he quotes McCulloch's famous note on Adam Smith's distinction (referred to already in this paper) and declares with triumph:

> Nous ne sommes donc pas les premiers qui ayons signalé l'importance de cette distinction, et l'exemple que nous avons cité, de la manière dont l'utilité des routes a été évaluée, prouve que MacCulloch ne s'est pas trompé en disant que, faute de cette distinction, on pouvait être conduit aux plus graves erreurs (p. 37).

In two subsequent papers, 'De l'influences des péages sur l'utilité des voies de communications' and 'De l'utilité et de sa mesure', Dupuit repeated and enlarged his views. The following

[22] Ibid., pp. 31–6.

quotation from the latter paper puts the matter particularly clearly:

L'erreur capitale de J.–B. Say n'est pas d'avoir méconnu la valeur en usage ou utilité, mais de l'avoir repoussée de la science, en y substituant la valeur en échange, qu'il a considerée comme sa mesure, et pouvant, par conséquent, la remplacer. Dans les citations que nous avons faites plus hautes, on aura, sans doute, remarqué cette phrase: *Tout le monde reconnaît que les choses ont quelquefois une valeur d'utilité fort différente de la valeur d'échange qui en elles.* Dans une autre citation: *Que la valeur ne s'élève pas au niveau de l'utilité, qu'elle ne s'élève qu'au niveau de l'utilité donnée par l'homme.* L'utilité et la valeur avaient donc, suivant J. B. Say deux niveaux différents; mais il ne voulait pas tenir compté de toute la hauteur dont le niveau d'utilité dépassait celui de la valeur (p. 173).

It was in these two later papers that he quoted from the Ricardo-Say correspondence to show that Ricardo too attached great importance to Adam Smith's distinction and considered Say was wrong to abandon it and thus confine economics to exchange value. Dupuit cited some of the passages from the correspondence already quoted in this study.[23] He also quoted Rossi in support of the importance of including utility not merely value in exchange in economics.[24]

(iii) Malthus and Longfield and the intensity of demand

Dupuit made reference to Malthus' concept of *intensity of demand*, or Longfield's use of it, in support of his own method of measuring utility, possibly because neither in fact explained its relation to utility. Whether this was because they themselves did not recognise the relation is perhaps an open question.

Malthus introduced the term intensity of demand to describe a person's willingness and ability to make a sacrifice in order to obtain something. It thus differed from Adam Smith's '*effectual demand*' and from the *extent of demand*, defined by Malthus as

---

[23] Dupuit, pp. 99–100 and 169–70. For the quotations from the Ricardo–Say correspondence see pp. 145–6 above.

[24] Dupuit, pp. 100–1 and pp. 170 and 172. R. W. Houghton's article 'A Note on the early History of Consumer's Surplus' (*Economica*, Feb. 1958) gives an interesting account of Dupuit's criticisms of Say.

the quantity demanded at a particular price. It was only demand in the sense of *intensity of demand*, Malthus argued, that could explain the determination of price by supply and demand. It was only the increased willingness of demanders to make a sacrifice when supply decreased that enabled prices to be raised. He pointed out that this had been indicated by Adam Smith in his explanation of the effect of supply being less than '*effectual demand*', in the sentence 'Rather than want it altogether, some of them will be willing to give more'. Malthus hoped that the use of the new term would prevent the sort of error that he considered Ricardo had made in his statement 'the demand for a commodity cannot be said to increase, if no additional quantity of it be purchased or consumed'.[25]

Malthus' intensity demand is of course the same as Dupuit's measure of utility 'le sacrifice maximum que chaque consommateur serait disposé à faire pour le se procurer'.[26] Longfield's use of Malthus' concept seems to indicate a greater appreciation of its importance than Malthus had himself.

In his second lecture on political economy, Longfield drew attention to Adam Smith's distinction between value in use and value in exchange. He approved of the distinction and pointed out that economists used the term value in use or utility in a more extended sense than that of ordinary speech. He continued that, though utility was necessary to exchange value, exchange value 'will not depend so much upon the extent of that utility as upon other circumstances'.[27]

Before leaving the subject he refers to the question of whether value is a measure of utility. Explaining that value

ought to be first considered; it is more elementary, it admits of greater certainty, and is subservient to the latter, but not in any respect dependent upon it.

Antithetical contrasts between value and utility are in general fallacious; and as we advance we shall see that perhaps for all practical purposes the best measure of utility is value, and that there is a sophism employed in the arguments used to prove that things of different utility may have different values, and that

[25] Malthus, *Principles*, pp. 65–9 and *Definitions*, p. 245; *Wealth of Nations*, Vol. I, p. 58.
[26] Dupuit, op. cit., p. 40.   [27] Longfield, op. cit., pp. 25–6.

things of equal value may have different degrees of utility. The proposition, to be of any importance, must be understood in a sense different from that in which it is proved. In fact the utility of any particular article to the possessors must vary according to their circumstances and situation, and exchanges serve the purpose of providing that the goods possessed by each individual shall in proportion to their value be of the greatest utility to him; that is, they shall contribute more to his happiness, and to the satisfaction of his wants and the gratification of his desires, than any other possessions of equal value. The same cause that prevents a person from giving any thing for that which has not some power of satisfying his wants or gratifying his wishes – that is, which has not some utility – will also prevent him from making any exchange, unless what he receives will conduce at least as much to his happiness as what he gives. When an exchange is made therefore it may be fairly presumed that each party to it has gained something, by receiving for the article he disposed of something which is, *relative to him*, of more utility.[28]

Presumably this passage was stimulated by the Say/Ricardo discussion. It is not an explicit statement of diminishing marginal utility; this is missing as in traditional discussions on the variability of wants. It displays, nevertheless, the process of maximising utility through exchange with much greater precision and insight than the usual vague descriptions. But the passage is remarkable for another reason. It will be noticed that the early part, beginning 'Antithetical contrasts between value and utility' and going as far as 'to different degrees of utility', follows Say's view closely. It includes the statement 'perhaps for all practical purposes the best measure of utility is value'. In the latter part of the passage, however, in referring to the goods possessed by each individual as a result of exchange, Longfield says that they will 'in proportion to their value be of the greatest utility to him; that is they shall contribute more to his happiness, and to the satisfaction of his wants and gratification of his desires, than any other possessions of equal value'. Further it will be noticed that the final sentence of the passage states that in exchange each person gains something 'by receiving for the article he disposed of something which is,

---

[28] Ibid., pp. 27–8.

relative to him, of more utility'. The exact meaning of this latter part of the passage seems to me uncertain. Taken by itself it appears wholly consistent with diminishing marginal utility and Dupuit's distinction between total and marginal utility which Dupuit had based on Adam Smith's distinction between value in use and value in exchange. It is however impossible, I think, to reconcile it with the earlier statement that value (in exchange) measures utility. Longfield appears to have tried to change horses in midstream without realising it, shifting from Say's approach intended to exclude total utility from economics to the Adam Smith/Ricardo/Dupuit approach which emphasised the importance of total utility. The apparent confusion exhibited in this passage I think partly explains Longfield's important development of Malthus' concept of intensity of demand.

It is not until Lecture VI that Longfield introduces the concept of intensity of demand. He reminds his audience that though the effect of utility on price is difficult to calculate, its effect is important for it is to utility 'that the demand is to be entirely attributed' (p. 110). He thinks however that it is necessary to explore further the nature of demand and its influence on price and value. For this purpose he introduces 'intensity of demand' though without referring to Malthus (p. 111). Developing Malthus' idea he observed that at any particular price there would be people whose intensity of demand would lead them to pay more for the good if they had to, and others whose intensity of demand was too low for them to be willing to purchase at this price:[29]

> the intensity of demand among different persons varies according to the sacrifices of other objects which they can conveniently afford to make; and yet all will make their purchases at the same rate, viz. at the market prices, and this rate is determined by the sum which will create an equality between the effectual demand and the supply.... Now if the price is attempted to be raised one degree beyond this sum, the demanders, who by the change will cease to be purchasers, must be those the intensity of whose demand was precisely measured by the former price. Before the change was made,

[29] This paragraph and the quotations and the following two paragraphs appeared in a slightly modified form in my paper 'The Predecessors of Jevons', pp. 25–6.

the demand, which was less intense, did not lead to a purchase, and after the change is made, the demand, which is more intense, will lead to a purchase still. Thus the market price is measured by that demand, which being of the least intensity, yet leads to actual purchases. . . . (p. 113)

He went on to elaborate an implication of this analysis:

the intensity of demand varies not only in different places, and among different individuals, but in many cases the same person may be said to have in himself several demands of different degrees of intensity (pp. 113–14).

This was illustrated by considering the effect of changes in the prices of provisions.

that portion which any person ceases to consume in consequence of a rise of prices, or that additional portion which he would consume if prices should fall, is that for which the intensity of the demand is less than the high price which prevents him from purchasing it, and is exactly equal to the low price which would induce him to consume it (p. 114).

Finally he combined these arguments to conclude:

that each individual contains as it were within himself a series of demands of successively increasing degrees of intensity; that the lowest degree of this series which at any time leads to a purchase, is exactly the same for both rich and poor and is that which regulates market price (p. 115).

Longfield observed that in the case of provisions the series of degrees of intensity will increase much faster as consumption decreases for rich men than for poor. He also noticed that in some cases people's intensity of demand was in excess of price because they would have been willing to pay more without altering their total consumption (pp. 113 and 115).

Longfield's exposition of diminishing degrees of intensity of demands provides an explanation of the downward slope of an individual's demand curve, as well as of the market demand curve. It has already been noticed that his degrees of intensity of demand coincide with Dupuit's 'maximum sacrifice' used by him as the measure of utility and the reflection of diminishing marginal utility. Longfield did not take the final step of showing the relation of the concept of intensity of demand to the concept of utility, although he had said that demand 'was to be entirely attributed' to utility. It seems to me then that Longfield introduced the degrees of intensity demand as a way round the difficulty of discovering the effect of utility on price because although he, like so many others, observed the phenomenon of diminishing utility, he was unable to draw conclusions from it in a way which demonstrated the precise influence of utility on exchange value.

It is probable that Longfield worked out his ideas without knowledge of Senior's statement of diminishing marginal utility.[30] Senior himself having provided the key did not appear to realise its implications. It appeared not in his discussion of utility in relation to value but in the discussion of the relation of limitation of supply to value! The actual formal statement was imbedded in a long discussion of the nature of wants along the traditional lines, as an explanation of the diversity of wants. It should probably be regarded as accidental that this explanation was cast in the form of a statement of the law of diminishing marginal utility.[31]

It is obvious, [he said] however, that our desires do not aim so much at quantity as at diversity. Not only are there limits to the pleasure which the commodities of any given class can afford, but the pleasure diminishes in a rapidly increasing ratio long before those limits are reached. Two articles of the same kind will seldom afford twice the pleasure of one, and still less will ten give five times the pleasure of two. In proportion, therefore, as any article is abundant, the number of those who are provided with it, and do not wish, or wish but little, to increase their provision, is likely to be great; and, so far as they are concerned, the additional supply loses all or nearly all its utility (p. 12).

The impression that Senior's statement of a law of diminishing

[30] Longfield's lectures were given in 1833 and published in 1834, two years before Senior's *Political Economy* which contained the lectures on value which Senior had given at Oxford 1826–27. There is no reason to suppose that Longfield was aware of the content of Senior's lectures before they were published in 1836. Senior himself makes no reference to Longfield in connection with utility and value.

[31] Senior, *Political Economy*. The discussion of utility is on pp. 6–7, Limitation of Supply, pp. 7–13.

utility was accidental is strengthened by the attention he devotes to the desire for distinction in the paragraphs succeeding that on variety. He declares that the desire for variety 'is weak compared with the desire for distinction' which 'may be pronounced to be the most powerful of human passions'. Following the usual form he cites diamonds as an example of goods with prestige value which would lose value if they became plentiful, and he leaves it at that with loose ends (pp. 12–13).

Senior like other classical economists made an attempt to explain the relation between utility and demand. Unfortunately he defined demand 'as expressing the utility of a commodity; or, what is the same – for we have seen that all utility is relative – the degree in which its possession is desired'.[32] Again the matter is not further explained.

There is less complete information about William Forster Lloyd's treatment of utility than about Senior's or Longfield's, for his lecture on utility is missing and we only have the one which followed it, called 'The Notion of Value, as distinguishable not only from Utility but also from Value in exchange'. This lecture delivered in 1833 at Oxford was published in 1834. It is full of interest however in relation to the history of utility theory and assuming that it was consistent with the missing lecture must give us an accurate idea of Lloyd's views on utility. One point may be disposed of quickly. Lloyd, while of course regarding utility as necessary to but distinct from value, abandoned the tradition that exchange between individuals was a necessary condition of value emerging. His introduction of Robinson Crusoe for the purpose of demonstrating this, was, as far as I know, the first use of that hero's activities as a tool of economic analysis.[33] Lloyd was specifically concerned with analysing the difference between the total utility an individual could derive from an object and the utility derived from successive units. He perceived that this was the basis of the explanation of the distinction between utility and

[32] Ibid., pp. 15–16. This definition of demand is repeated in an even less ambiguous form on p. 17. 'We have already stated that the utility of a commodity, in our extended sense of the term utility, or, in other words, the demand for it as an object of purchase or hire, is principally dependent on the obstacles which limit its supply.'

[33] All references are to the 1968 reprint of Lloyd's *Lectures on Population, Poor Laws, Value and Rent* in the *Reprints of Economic Classics* series, publ. Augustus Kelley.

value (in exchange) though, as he had shown, it was not necessary that there should be exchange between people for value to exist. Basing his argument on his study of Adam Smith, he argued that though utility had meaning only in relation to the satisfaction of wants, there must be scales of wants of varying importance for each person which could be satisfied by any one commodity. These scales related to what he regarded as absolute utility. The utility of any particular unit of a good to an individual however depended, he realised, on which want in the scale it would be used to satisfy, i.e. on the extent to which more important wants were already satisfied. It was the importance of the particular want of a person which would determine the value set on the particular unit of the commodity by comparison with the importance of the want which could not be satisfied as well. Lloyd demonstrated his argument by numerous examples. The following quotations will serve to illustrate the clarity of his analysis.[34] The first quotation comes near the beginning of the Lecture and demonstrates the principle by the example of food.

Let us suppose the case of an hungry man having one ounce, and only one ounce of food at his command. To him, this ounce is obviously of very great importance. Suppose him now to have two ounces. These are still of great importance; but the importance of the second is not equal to that of the single ounce. In other words, he would not suffer so much from parting with one of his two ounces, retaining one for himself, as he would suffer, when he had only one ounce, by parting with that one, and so retaining none. The importance of the third ounce is still less than that of the second; so likewise of a fourth, until at length, in the continual increase of the number of ounces, we come to a point, when 'through that infallible specific, eating', the appetite is entirely or nearly lost, and when, with respect to a single ounce, it is a matter of indifference whether it is parted with or retained. Thus while he is scantily supplied with food, he holds a given portion of it in great esteem – in other words, he sets a great value on it; when his supply is increased, his esteem for a given quantity is lessened, or, in other words, he sets a less value on it (pp. 11–12).

[34] This paragraph and the first quotation following it appeared, with a few verbal differences, in my paper 'The Predecessors of Jevons', pp. 22–3.

The second quotation refers to the margin of indifference:

> In its ultimate sense, then, the term (value) undoubtedly signifies a feeling of the mind, which shows itself always at the margin of separation between the satisfied and unsatisfied wants. One point, amongst others, in which it differs from utility, is, that it attaches only to an object in possession, while, with respect to the idea of utility, possession is a matter of indifference (p. 16).

Finally here is a good illustration of Lloyd's method of exposition.

> Perhaps the following may be a good rule for distinguishing between utility and value; . . . To obtain the idea of the utility of an object, imagine what would happen, what inconvenience would arise, from the loss, not of that object alone, but of the whole species to which that object belongs. . . . But value, as I have already mentioned, attaches to an object in possession, which, consequently cannot be unlimited in quantity. To obtain, therefore, the idea of value, imagine yourself deprived, not as before, of the whole of the species, but only of the possession of a certain definite quantity (pp. 18–19).

Unfortunately we do know what use Lloyd made of his analysis in subsequent lectures and, as far as we know, he did not pursue analytical economics after the end of his tenure of the Drummond Chair of Political Economy at Oxford. It is perhaps owing to the temporary tenures of the Drummond Chair and the Whately Chair at Dublin, held by Longfield, that so little attention appears to have been paid to the theoretical contributions of Lloyd and Longfield. They were concerned with economics only during their short tenures and do not seem to have joined in discussions with those of their contemporaries who considered themselves to be economists.

(iv) Conclusion

No attempt has been made in this study to provide a complete survey of the writers of the classical period who were interested in utility theory. Bentham has been omitted in particular, for his statement of the diminishing marginal utility of income was not used by him, or his contemporaries, in relation to the problem of the connection between the utility and value of a commodity.[35]

[35] See *Jeremy Bentham's Economic Works*, ed. Stark, Vol. I, p. 113. Dupuit did not refer to Bentham, or to his anticipator Bernouilli. He him-

Enough has been said however, I think, to show the concern of the classical economists with utility theory. It has also been shown that important discussions stemmed directly from consideration of what was known as Adam Smith's distinction, though it was much older, between value in use and value in exchange. It has been pointed out that great importance was attached to this distinction by some of the most distinguished writers on economics, including Dupuit as well as Ricardo.

It seems to me now that lack of interest in utility was not, as I used to think, a distinguishing feature of the classical period; nor do I now think that a sharp distinction between groups of economists of the period on this score is valid. The slow progress with utility theory appears to have been due simply to what was found to be the inherent difficulty of the subject, increased perhaps by a lack of communication between some of the contributors to the solution of the problem.

---

self recognised that the significance of his measure of utility was limited by differences of incomes, but he argued that consideration of this complication was outside the scope of political economy (op. cit., p. 178).

V *Market Structures and the Theory of Value in Classical Economics*

> In this world therefore every plain and simple doctrine as to the relations between cost of production, demand and value is necessarily false: and the greater the appearance of lucidity which is given to it by skilful exposition, the more mischievous it is. A man is likely to be a better economist if he trusts to his commonsense, and practical instincts, than if he professes to study the theory of value and is resolved to find it easy.
>
> MARSHALL, *Principles*, V.v. last two sentences of par. 2, p. 368, Ad. Var. ed.

(i) *Adam Smith and Ricardo on Monopoly*

The first systematic attempt to define the conditions under which the cost of production theory of value was valid appeared in 1825 in Samuel Bailey's *Critical Dissertation on the Nature, Measure and Causes of Value*. Bailey understood by the cost of production theory of value that, apart from temporary fluctuations, goods exchanged in proportion to their costs of production and that the latter were in no way affected by the demands for the goods or expressed in terms of prices – the natural price of a good was determined by its cost of production which was in no way affected by the demand for the good. (It will be convenient to call this version the pure cost of production theory to distinguish it from others whenever the context does not make it obvious.) Bailey's investigations led him into problems of market structures and supply functions with which both Adam Smith and Ricardo had been concerned.

Adam Smith's concern with monopoly and monopolistic practices derived from the importance he attached to their consequences in maintaining market prices above natural prices, thereby diminishing opulence. Monopolies he pointed out in the chapter 'Of the Natural and Market Price of Goods' might be due to accident or natural causes. They might however be due to privileges granted to particular individuals or groups or to efforts to preserve trade secrets etc. He distinguished further between monopolies, which he appeared to identify with one seller and 'a sort of enlarged monopolies' created by privilege or statute 'which restrain in particular employments, the competition to smaller numbers than would otherwise go into them'. In the former case there might be deliberate exploitation of the consumer by means of restriction of supply, in the latter the tendency to exploitation would be present 'though in a lesser degree'. Thus he says

> A monopoly granted either to an individual or to a trading company has the same effect as a secret in trade or manufactures. The monopolists, by keeping the market constantly under-stocked, by never fully supplying the effectual demand, sell their commodities much above the natural price, and raise their emoluments, whether they consist of wages or profit, greatly above the natural rate.

He goes on to explain that the natural price is 'the price of free competition' and 'is the lowest that can be taken, not upon every occasion indeed, but for any considerable time together' by sellers and 'continue their business'. The 'sort of enlarged monopolies' thus came in between monopoly proper and 'free competition'. They correspond to conditions of imperfect competition arising from barriers to entry.[1] In the chapter on Rent, however, the meaning of monopoly price is extended to include rent on the grounds that it is a price not in anyway proportionate to the costs of providing land, for there are no such costs. It is a price dependent only on what farmers can be induced to pay.[2]

This extension of the monopoly terminology derived from market-structure classification in terms of numbers of sellers to all

---

[1] *Wealth of Nations*, Vol. I, Bk I, Ch. VII, pp. 63–4. Professor Stigler does not refer to these passages in his article 'Perfect Competition, historically considered', *J.P.E.*, 1957 (reprinted in his *Essays on the History of Economics*).

[2] Ibid., Bk I, Ch. XI, pp. 146–7. On the relation of Adam Smith's concept of rent as a monopoly price to his inclusion of rent as a component of natural price see p. 118 above and Buchanan, op. cit.

cases where price was regarded as being determined by demand alone, or more generally not by cost of production alone, was ultimately rationalised for 'natural agents' by Bailey and Senior. They developed a classification of market structures based on conditions of entry. From this they were led to the conclusion that nearly all prices contained a monopoly element.

Ricardo in defining monopoly substituted *fixed* supply, irrespective of the number of sellers, for Adam Smith's restriction of the number of sellers. Thus Ricardo in Chapter XVII of the *Principles* (pp. 249–51) explains 'commodities are only at a monopoly price, when by no possible device their quantity can be augumented'. In these circumstances the price 'is the very highest' that consumers will pay for 'the competition is wholly on one side' – the buyers', and the price 'is nowhere regulated by the cost of production'. Monopoly will therefore exist not only in such cases as rare works of art and special wines but also in the case of 'corn and raw produce'. In the latter case, however, monopoly prices can *only exist permanently* 'when no more capital can be profitably employed on the land, and where, therefore, their produce cannot be increased'. This situation can, he adds, only arise when the price of corn is already at the highest price at which it can be sold and profits are no higher than in alternative employments. In the more frequently quoted passages in Chapter I 'On Value', Ricardo makes the same distinction between goods in *fixed* supply and those whose supply can be increased, and the ways in which their prices are determined. He does not introduce the word 'monopoly' at all in this Chapter, merely equating demand with 'scarcity' as the determinant of price of goods in fixed supply. It is here however that he introduces the phrase 'competition without restraint' with respect to the goods of which the supply can be increased indefinitely by additional labour (p. 12). Again there is no reference to number of sellers, nor is there any reference to barriers to entry, only to the elasticity of total supply.

The distinction between the relation of prices to costs, under monopoly and under competition respectively, is the same in the *Wealth of Nations* and in Ricardo's *Principles*, but the classification in terms of market structures differs. These conflicting and overlapping classifications providing the basis of more elaborate classifications by Bailey and, following him, Senior and John

Stuart Mill in their attempts to decide whether a pure cost of production theory of value provided a general theory of value or not.

(ii) Bailey and Senior on Barriers to Entry and J. S. Mill

Bailey approached the problem by considering whether Ricardo's distinction between monopoly and 'competition without restraint' was consistent with his statement that under the former price was determined by demand alone and under the latter by costs alone.[3] He accepted these relationships between demand and price and costs and price as tests of the existence of monopoly and 'competition without restraint' respectively. He proceeded to apply the tests to the cases of various conditions of supply by investigating them in terms of 'protection from competition' which was equivalent to 'barriers to entry'. The consequence was, as I shall attempt to show, that this barrier to entry classification ran also in terms of the influence of demand on price.

Bailey distinguished three main categories of goods according to the conditions under which they were supplied.[4]

1. *Monopoly.* Bailey modified Ricardo's definition of monopoly in terms of fixed supply to protection from competition 'by natural or adventitious circumstances'. He followed Adam Smith in distinguishing two cases: the single-seller case and the case where there are several sellers but a barrier to the entry of any more. This latter corresponded to Adam Smith's 'sort of enlarged monopoly', except that Bailey assumed that the maximum total supply of any one seller was fixed. Ricardo's explanation of monopoly price as determined by demand alone because the competition was among buyers only was, Bailey argued, correct only in the case of the single seller. For in the case of several sellers competition between sellers would force the seller to market all he possessed or could produce (collusion being ruled out by definition) so long as the average price yielded 'a higher profit than the ordinary employment of capital'. It was characteristic of this case that there was complete absence of freedom of entry; since this condition might be temporary or permanent so might the

---

[3] He noted of course that in the case of goods produced with the aid of land, Ricardo had in practice modified the statement about costs by introducing the word 'regulated'. (See on this p. 162 below.)

[4] Bailey, pp. 185-200. All page references are to the L.S.E. reprint.

influence of demand on price and therefore the existence of the monopoly. Bailey concluded that a temporary monopoly would exist when changes in supply took a long time; hence market price when it differed from natural price was a monopoly price. His examples included corn between harvests and labour both in general and of particular types (ibid., p. 188).

2. *Producers with special facilities.*   Bailey's second case was one in which entry to an industry was possible but not on equal terms for all producers. He described this as occurring when some producers have access to a superior grade of factor or of some production facility. He did not specify diminishing returns to additional applications of labour and capital to any one grade. The producers with access to a superior grade have, he said, a monopoly 'to a certain extent'. Price will therefore be determined as in the cases of monopoly already described, *except* that the actual or potential competition of higher-cost producers imposes an upper limit on price. This case included agriculture and the extractive industries and was thus of major importance. He noted that Ricardo was correct in saying in this case, not that value was *caused* but that it was *regulated* by the cost of production on the least fertile lands. Bailey argued that it could not be claimed that the cost of production of any unit of the commodity produced on the more fertile land (or more generally any intra-marginal unit, to use modern terms) determined or even regulated its value. Its value by definition of an intra-marginal unit exceeded its cost of production, the difference being rent. He agreed of course with Ricardo that rent did not enter into costs. Ricardo's error lay not, Bailey said, in his conclusion in this case which was the same as Bailey's, but in not realising that this case should be distinguished from the one in which 'competition operated without restraint' (ibid., pp. 193–8).

3. *Competition without restraint.*[5]   Bailey reached the conclusion that in this case all producers and potential producers must have equal access to equal facilities of production. It is in these circumstances only that price would contain no monopoly element and would therefore be *determined* by cost of production alone. It is the only case in which the pure cost of production theory is valid. It is reasonable to assume that Bailey regarded this case as that of constant costs for he does not refer to de-

[5] Ibid., pp. 198 et seq.

creasing costs.[6] It is to be noticed also that he does not specifically refer to the numbers of producers.

Ricardo's labour theory of value is seen by Bailey as an unsuccessful attempt to substitute physical inputs of labour for costs of production and Ricardo's qualifications to allow for differences in capital structure as demonstrating this. He dismissed Ricardo's treatment of different grades of labour as based on 'a mere assumption'.[7]

The principle of Bailey's classification system is clearly that of barriers to entry. The extent to which any producers are 'protected from competition' appears to be of equal significance in the classification as the actual competition in terms of the numbers of actual producers except in the case of the single monopolist.

Senior investigated the same general problem as Bailey in his analysis of 'the causes which limit supply' and their effect on price. Apart from the cases of absolutely fixed supply such as works of art, Senior treated cost of production as the fundamental obstacle to increases in supply. Consideration of this led him, like Bailey, into classification of market structures. But though, like Bailey, he adopted barriers to entry as his principle of classification, because he was considering it under the general problem of causes which limit supply, his conclusions were not framed in terms of the degree of the influence of demand.

Senior substituted the term 'equal competition' for Bailey's concept of 'competition without restraint'. His definition is somewhat bizarre, but as it brings out the importance of the idea of potential competition in the classification it is worth setting out. He distinguished between cost of production to the actual producer, or producers, and the cost of production (potential) to the purchaser or purchasers, if the latter instead of buying the commodity decided to produce it or arrange for someone else to do so. The former cost provided the minimum price, the latter the maximum. 'Equal competition' would exist only if the minimum and maximum would coincide. This could only occur if all persons (including the purchaser) could produce 'with equal advantage', i.e. constant costs, or in other words, no one was in

---

[6] R. M. Rauner describes Bailey's third case as 'the familiar Ricardian case of competition with constant costs'. *Samuel Bailey and the Classical theory of Value*, p. 69.

[7] Bailey, op. cit., pp. 215 et seq. and p. 212.

possession of special rights or had access to a superior productive facility or agent. Only when a purchaser was a potential producer or organiser of production on the same terms as existing producers would price be determined by cost of production; this potential competition would be sufficient to keep price down to the cost of production. Senior deliberately explains his definition in terms of purchasers and producers both in the singular and plural. It is thus clear that he considered that 'equal competition' or 'competition without restraint' could exist in a two-man world as long as the consumer *could* become a producer on equal terms as the existing producer. It will be noticed that this possible case would differ from the classic duopoly case in that one producer or potential producer would not be concerned with maximising profits. Thus according to Senior's principle of classification it is the existence of potential competition rather than the number of competitors that is the relevant consideration.

His definition of monopoly followed from his definition of 'equal competition' to cover all those cases in which there was not equal competition. These were those in which an 'appropriated natural agent' was used in production for in such cases the owner of the natural agent had an advantage in production. Natural agents were defined to include all 'those peculiar advantages of soil or situation', 'extraordinary talent of mind or body' and 'processes generally unknown, or protected by law from imitation'. Senior's choice of words is undoubtedly sometimes very odd![8]

Senior modified Bailey's classification. He divided Bailey's single-seller case without potential or actual competitors into two: the single seller with a fixed total supply, and the single seller with an exclusive right, such as a publisher's copyright, who was able to increase his output indefinitely at *constant* or *decreasing* costs. Ricardo's monopoly solution applied to the first of these cases only. In the second, however, Senior concluded that the advantage of falling costs with increasing output would lead the monopolist to maximise his profits through increasing sales by lowering his price *towards* cost of production. Costs therefore would influence the price charged but not regulate or determine it. He introduced a second case of *constant* or *decreasing* costs with *one* producer having special but not exclusive facilities e.g. a patent. Senior omitted to state whether other producers with less favour-

[8] Senior, pp. 101–3.

able facilities operated under increasing, decreasing or constant costs, possibly because he may have considered them as potential producers only. This case differed from Senior's other decreasing-cost case in that the costs of these potential competitors provided an upper limit to the price that the producer with special facilities could charge.[9]

Senior redefined Bailey's second case to exclude explicitly any producer being able to produce with constant or decreasing costs with any of the different grades of productive facilities.[10] He also specifically identified it with the use of any 'natural agent', i.e. land or any natural resource. He called this case 'qualified monopoly' or 'unequal competition'. His explanation of the determination of price under these conditions was of course the same as in Bailey's second case. Like Bailey he stated that rent was a monopoly price and did not enter into costs, and he referred to 'the great monopoly of land' in large print (p. 105).

The category of 'equal competition' already described completed Senior's classification, providing the constant costs case, and was the only case in which price was determined by cost of production only. Essentially it corresponded to Bailey's 'competition without restraint' case. It has already been pointed out, however (p. 146 above), that, owing to Senior's definition of freedom of entry on equal terms, this case could exist in a two-man world without reducing it to the classic duopoly case. This possibility is interesting as it emphasises the dependence of these classifications on barriers to entry instead of numbers of competitors.

[9] These are Senior's second, third and first cases, respectively, at the beginning of his discussion, pp. 103–5, but in his summary on pp. 111–15 he entirely alters the order in a most irritating way.

The incompleteness of Senior's discussion of decreasing costs is tantalising as he regards constant or decreasing costs characteristic of industry (ibid., p. 118). He does not commit himself in any way to the idea that decreasing costs tend to lead to monopoly. On the other hand he does note that taxes on decreasing-cost industries will increase prices by more than the tax and starts trying to work out the different effect with increasing cost industries but gets involved in unnecessary difficulties (ibid., pp. 120 et seq.). Senior did not include Bailey's case of *no* freedom of entry but more than one seller.

[10] Consideration of this exclusion in relation to his previous case might have led Senior to suggest that decreasing costs were in general incompatible even with 'unequal competition'. As so often he missed an opportunity.

Both Bailey and Senior concluded that the cases of 'competition without restraint' and 'equal competition', respectively, were rare and therefore that prices determined solely by cost of production were rare. The reason for this was that the prices of all commodities containing any material derived from the use of a natural agent that was not free necessarily included a monopoly element.[11] This conclusion illustrates incidentally very clearly that Bailey and Senior were concerned with market structures because of their concern with the relations between prices and costs of production. If they had been interested in market structures *per se* they might have noticed that 'competition without restraint' or 'equal competition' could exist among producers buying products derived from natural agents on identical terms e.g. in a commodity market.

The attempts made by Bailey and Senior to determine the relevance of the pure cost of production theory seem to me of considerable interest. Both had tried to show the analytical limitations of the theory and its practical irrelevance. Both had made it clear that Ricardo himself had had to modify his version of it in dealing with cases of increasing costs and both considered that, for the sake of analytical clarity, he ought to have abandoned it as his general theory of value. Moreover both Bailey and Senior had reached their conclusions by means of developing a classification of market structures based on barrier to entry. Thus by expanding the application of a principle set out in the *Wealth of Nations* they included land-using production as giving rise to unequal competition, in effect treating Adam Smith's fixity of supply of land approach as a special type of barrier to entry on equal terms. Whether or not one accepts their treatment of land in their classification, the conclusion that they reached is interesting: it is that monopolistic influences, or unequal competition, were so important that a general theory of value could not properly ignore them.

Inevitably to modern readers Bailey and Senior appear to have developed their analysis in a sort of upside-down fashion, and thereby to have entangled logically distinct problems. Their

[11] Bailey, pp. 198–232. Senior, pp. 111–14 on the 'equal competition' case. Senior stated that he must not be supposed to believe 'that any such commodities exist', of which the prices were solely determined by costs of production.

classification of market structures was quite unnecessary to show that the pure cost of production theory was only valid in cases of constant costs. Logically they could have classified market structures in terms of barriers to entry separately and then considered, as a separate question, the possibility that certain types of cost functions might create barriers to entry. It would all have been much more lucid and possibly also more fruitful. Economic theory however does not often, if ever, develop in the most logical way, for the nature of the questions that ought to be asked, in the interests of future progress in analysis, may only emerge at the end of an investigation and may not be those the investigators are interested in. Bailey and Senior started out to investigate the validity of the pure cost of production theory with the questions already entangled by Adam Smith's and Ricardo's theorem that under 'free' competition, or 'competition without restraint', price was determined by the cost of production alone.

John Stuart Mill's re-statement of the Ricardian theory of value did not help to separate the issues. He was influenced apparently by the efforts of Bailey and Senior to some extent, but only to some extent. This had, I think, possibly important consequences for the history of the theory of value. Like all other classical economists Mill started from the commonsense observation that anything having exchange value must be capable of satisfying a want and that there must be some difficulty in acquiring it.[12]

He accepted the need to distinguish between the constant-cost and the decreasing-cost case, but considered the constant-cost case as 'embracing the majority of all things bought and sold'. Thus he differed sharply from Bailey and Senior as to the importance of the constant-cost case. Monopoly he defined, like Ricardo, as the case of fixed supply, distinguishing the one seller case however as 'strict or absolute monopoly'. Although he admitted that the monopoly case included more things than works of art, special wines etc., and that temporary monopoly might occur, nevertheless he regarded monopoly as an exception though an important one.[13] Competition existed by presumption

[12] *Principles of Political Economy*, Bk III, Ch. II, para. 1.

[13] *Principles*, Bk III, Ch. II, paras. 1, 2 and 5, pp. 444–5 and 448–50. Ashley's edition to which all page references relate.

wherever monopoly did not, and he implied that competition must be 'free and active' to force market prices to equality with 'natural prices'.[14]

There is no disagreement between Mill and Senior over the determination of prices under strict monopoly conditions and constant costs. In the former case it is, Mill states, determined by demand and supply alone, except that costs of production provides a minimum price if the goods are produced. In the constant-cost case however 'demand and supply only determine the perturbations of value, during a period which cannot exceed the length of time necessary for altering the supply'; the natural price is the cost of production.[15] When he came to the increasing-cost case (Chapter V), he explained price determination in terms of the rent analysis showing how changes in demand affected the extent of cultivation and, therefore, that price will be 'determined' by the cost of the last unit produced. He did not, however, summarise this conclusion in the chapter which is largely devoted to arguing that rent is not a monopoly price and that differential rent cannot enter into the cost of production. There is no attempt to point out the difference in importance of demand in determining price in this case compared to the constant-cost case. In this he follows Ricardo rather than Senior or Bailey. Moreover in Chapter VI, 'Summary of the Theory of Value', Mill did not distinguish between the constant and increasing costs cases. In Section II he explained that 'the temporary or market values' of things are determined by demand and supply and he used the word *demand* only once more in Section V dealing with scarcity value, which he treated as synonymous with monopoly value. The non-monopoly cases of constant and increasing costs are not distinguished from each other. In Section IV he states that 'most things naturally exchange from one another in the ratio of their cost of production, or what may be called their "Cost Value"'. 'Cost Value' is explained in Section VII as synonymous with the

---

[14] Ibid., Ch. II, para. 1, p. 452. Mill limits his analysis of value to cases in which 'prices are determined by completion alone' for only in such cases can a law be established. This situation is described as one in which buyers and sellers act in a business-like way endeavouring to buy cheap and sell dear and inform themselves as to all relevant circumstances. Only in such markets, Mill says, will it be true that there can only be one price in the same market. Ibid., Ch. I, para. 5.

[15] Ibid., Ch. III, para. 2, p. 456.

natural value of a commodity and is explained as 'the cost value of the most costly portion'.

It might have been expected that Mill would have repeated his earliest recognition of the difference between the constant and increasing-costs cases in explaining how the most costly portion is determined as 'the most costly portion of the supply required'. He did not do so. The following ten sections of the Summary (VIII to XVII) deal with rent, the components of cost and the labour theory of value.[16] Whatever the reason for this method of exposition its effect was to make the theory of value look simple and monopoly unimportant. It also maintained the fixed and elastic supply distinction between monopoly and competition – so much simpler than the barriers to entry classification.

Bailey's and Senior's efforts to explain the varied relationships between demand, cost of production and value certainly had none of that 'appearance of lucidity' which Marshall stigmatised as often 'mischievous', nor did either of them advance 'a plain and simple doctrine'. In comparison J. S. Mill's treatment seems deliberately to evade the complex issues, in what might be described as a resolution 'to find it easy'.

(iii) Cournot and the Theory of the Firm

The Bailey/Senior classification involved consideration of the behaviour of the firm in the one-seller cases, while the inclusion of increasing-cost industries as creating a type of monopoly, and rent as a monopoly income, involved the supply schedules of the industry. This contrast between firm and industry is made particularly obvious by Senior's introduction of examples of single firms with decreasing costs. Hindsight enables one to realise that further progress required an entirely new venture, an attempt to develop a theory of the behaviour of firms.

In 1838 two years after the publication of Senior's *Political Economy*, Cournot took the first major steps in this hitherto unexplored field. Parts of Cournot's work are so widely recognised as an integral part of economic theory, that its historical significance, its relation to the work and problems of his contem-

---

[16] Sections I, III and VI have not been mentioned; none of these refer to demand. Section I explains the relative nature of the concept of value. Section III distinguishes between market and natural price. Section VI explains that monopoly value is a scarcity value.

poraries, is apt to be overlooked. His own explanation of why he wrote *The Mathematical Principles of the Theory of Wealth* however makes it clear that he intended to try to resolve some of the difficulties of contemporary economics 'which arise from the theory of wealth'. This meant the theory of exchange value for he considered that 'to form an intelligible theory we ought to absolutely identify the sense of the word *wealth* with that which is presented to us by the words *exchangeable values*'.[17] For this purpose he proposed to use mathematics explaining that he felt that people with mathematical training must feel the need 'of rendering determinate by symbols familiar to them, an analysis which is generally indeterminate and often obscure, in authors who have thought fit to confine themselves to the resources of ordinary language'.[18] The branch of mathematics that he considered to be appropriate for the purpose was of course the calculus. There is no indication of whether he knew Bailey's and Senior's works.

Cournot like his contemporaries started from the assumption that demand depended on price and that in general 'the cheaper the article is, the greater ordinarily is the demand for it' (p. 46). He did not, however, concern himself with the traditional question of whether price was *determined* by demand or by costs. He eliminated it by treating both demand and supply as functions of price. Nor does he start out by defining any particular degree of competition, 'competition without restraint' or 'equal competition', or even generally 'competition' in terms of a consequential equality of price with cost. His 'unlimited competition' emerges as a consequence of his analysis of the relationship between market structures and the equality or inequality of price with cost, while he starts from monopoly defined as the case of the single seller. Whether his key question 'how does a firm maximise its net revenue?' led him to his classification of market structures in terms of numbers of sellers only, or whether the order of ideas was the other way round, both question and classification were important innovations. The former must be regarded, I think, as providing the first step in the evolution of the theory of the firm, the latter as introducing a classification of market structures which deliberately abstracted from their causes.

---

[17] Cournot, *Researches into the Mathematical Principles of the Theory of Wealth*, p. 9. (I. Fisher's translation, 1897).
[18] Ibid., p. 5.

Cournot's analysis of monopoly price is too well known to need description here; it has passed into the general body of economic theory. One point however must be noticed. He stated the problem of the determination of the maximum net revenue of the monopolist in terms of the differential calculus. Hence he automatically stated the solution to be the equality of marginal revenue with marginal cost, for he showed that the monopolist would maximise his net returns when the increment to total receipts from an additional sale equalled the increment to total costs incurred thereby. Cournot did not give either increment a name or point out that the increment to total costs was the familiar Ricardian cost at the margin; nor did he point out that the increment to total revenue (marginal revenue) was a concept hitherto unlabelled in economic analysis.

He pursued his analysis from the case of no competition at all, the single seller, to that in which the number of sellers had increased so much that the output of each was 'inappreciable' in relation to the total and could be subtracted without affecting the price. This situation he described as 'unlimited competition', i.e. the situation reached when competition had reached its limit.[19] Price, he showed, would then be equal to the cost of the last unit produced instead of greater than that cost as in all cases of monopoly, duopoly etc. On this analysis the degree of competition was not affected by the existence of producers working with unequal facilities of production but only by their numbers,[20] and he did not distinguish between intensive and extensive cost margins.

Cournot pointed out that unless all firms were operating on rising marginal-cost curves the gross value of the product would be less than the total costs. On the other hand if firms had falling marginal-cost curves he concluded that 'nothing would limit the production of the article' and 'monopoly is not wholly extinct' or, put another way, 'competition is not so great but that the variation of the amount produced by each individual producer affects the total production of the article, and its price, to a perceptible extent'.[21]

Marshall was later to criticise Cournot for not realising that falling marginal costs would tend to lead to monopoly, and to cite his failure to do so as an illustration of the dangers of excessive

[19] Ibid., Ch. VIII, p. 90.   [20] Ibid., Ch. VI, pp. 86–7.
[21] Ibid., Ch. VIII, pp. 91–2.

reliance on mathematics. Nevertheless in 1838 it was rare to discuss decreasing costs in relation to price or monopoly at all. Indeed, except for Senior's two cases of decreasing costs, which were specifically monopoly or near-monopoly cases, I do not know of any earlier discussion. I think that it is inevitable that credit must be given to Senior and Cournot for drawing attention to a possible connection between decreasing costs and the existence of monopolistic elements in a market. One other point is relevant here. In completing his analysis of 'unlimited competition' Cournot had had to derive the supply curve of the industry from the cost curves of individual firms. He thus made explicit the need to consider the relations between them, a matter that had only been implicit in the work of other classical writers except in connection with agriculture and extractive industries.

Cournot did not define costs of production, but by implication they were the costs actually taken into account by firms in comparing their costs and receipts. They must be regarded therefore as including the prices that would be actually paid for factors of production, materials etc., irrespective of whether those prices were themselves determined under conditions of unlimited competition or not. His classification was not therefore geared to the discovery of the conditions under which *no* element of monopoly, qualified monopoly or unequal competition had any influence on prices. Whether or not it is appropriate to regard the presence of rent as indicating the presence of some degree of monopoly or unequal competition, this latter distinction was irrelevant to the Cournot classification. Looking around him Cournot was therefore able to say of his conclusion, that individual producers could not affect price under unlimited competition, that 'this hypothesis is the one realised, in a social economy, for a multitude of products, and, among them, for the most important products'. He went on to point out that this hypothesis 'introduces great simplification into the calculations'.[22]

Despite the fundamental theoretical differences between their definitions, Cournot was in seeming agreement with Ricardo and J. S. Mill that monopoly of any type was not of major practical importance in the real world. Adam Smith had of course taken the opposite view emphasising the actual existence of barriers restrict-

[22] Ibid., Ch. VIII, p. 90.

ing competition and the tendency always present to create new barriers. Bailey and Senior (later to be joined by Cairnes) pursuing one of the ideas implicit in Adam Smith's treatment, like him, regarded monoplistic influences as prevalent.

The reason for those various attitudes has been, I hope, made clear. It is tempting to speculate what the course of development in economic analysis might have been in the latter half of the nineteenth century, if John Stuart Mill had developed the Adam Smith, Bailey, Senior approach. Would perhaps the problems of the possible effects of the influence of various degrees of monopoly and unequal competition have received more attention, or would the analytical convenience of Cournot-type definitions and conclusions have determined the issue? Whatever might have happened, what did happen is well known. The spectacular developments in micro-economic analysis took place in relation to the analysis of resource-allocation under Cournot-type competition which it was realised, as Cournot had pointed out, introduced 'a great simplification into the calculations'.

It is tempting to go on and declare that concern about the possible prevalence of imperfect competition, as such, largely disappeared until the growth of restrictions on competition in the United States attracted the attention of J. B. Clarke to its practical importance at the end of the century. But simple statements of this type are almost always incorrect in connection with the history of economic analysis. Quite apart from the obvious exception to it of Pareto's work, another line of investigation, the development of the Marshallian theory of the firm during this period had much bearing on the problems of imperfect competition involved, and on the practical relevance of the Cournot-type concept of unlimited competition. I have already suggested that by the mid 1830s further progress on the analysis of price in relation to market structures, however classified and for whatever purpose, required a theory of the firm and that Cournot took the first steps towards its creation. That Marshall's own work in this field was at least partially stimulated by what he regarded as one of Cournot's mistakes, is a well-established tradition based on Marshall's letter to A. W. Flux in 1898. This contained the following passage: 'My confidence in Cournot as an *economist* was shaken when I found that his mathematics *re* I.R. led inevitably to things which do not exist and have no near relation to reality. One of the chief purposes of my Wanderjähre among factories was to discover how Cournot's premises were wrong. The chief outcome of my work in this direction, which occupied me a good deal between 1870 and 1890, is in the 'Representative Firm theory, . . . the supplementary cost analysis, . . . as well as the parts that directly relate to supply price for I.R.'[23]

(iv) Some General Conclusions

The words *competition* and *monopoly*, like so many others in the economists' vocabulary are, as they were in the classical period, words used in ordinary everyday speech. They are frequently used in ordinary speech like many others in several senses made clear sometimes by the context. Economists have also often proceeded in the same way, but sooner or later have found it necessary to try to provide definitions which seem appropriate to the particular problem in hand irrespective of common usage. This is only too well recognised as a fruitful cause of incorrect criticism of economists by each other, particularly of earlier by later economists for it is difficult to accustom oneself to the use of words in unfamiliar ways. Ricardo was neither the first nor the last economist whose definitional practices have resembled those of Humpty Dumpty in *Alice through the Looking Glass*. It will be remembered Humpty Dumpty declared to Alice's bewilderment, 'When *I* use a word it means just what I choose it to mean – neither more nor less.'[24]

Such difficulties are obvious and practical. There are more insidious dangers inherent in the necessity of selecting one out of several possible meanings for a word, for the exclusion of the other meanings may lead to problems which are implicit in them gradually disappearing from notice. Recent discussions of the evolution of the modern definition of perfect competition from the Cournot concept of 'unlimited competition' have suggested that this has led to neglect of the study of the actual competitive process.[25]

Unfortunately inter-personal interpretation of thought pro-

[23] Letter to A. W. Flux 7.3.1898 printed in *Memorials of Alfred Marshall*, pp. 406–7.
[24] *Alice through the Looking Glass*, Ch. VI.
[25] For an account of discussions of the problem see P. J. McNulty's interesting article 'Economic Theory and the Meaning of Competition'

cesses are difficult if not as impossible as inter-personal comparisons of utility, and particular interpretations of the historical development of ideas are often impossible to prove definitively. I would merely suggest therefore a rather different interpretation of the evolution of the definition of competition as follows.

The various definitions of competition and monoply of the classical period seem to me to have arisen partly from differences of the problems discussed by different writers and partly, perhaps, also from carelessness or ignorance. I have suggested that those differences may, indirectly, have had important indirect consequences in influencing the extent to which later economists assumed that the analysis of resource-allocation should be based on the assumption of the Cournot-type of unlimited competition. Later work in refining this definition has been of major importance in bringing about automatically a better appreciation of the limitations of the applicability of that analysis to the real world. The actual process of refinement of the definition has thus been of considerable value. It forms a parallel at more analytically competent level to the earlier attempts made in the late classical period described in this study.

Innumerable examples of the evolutionary process in the use of words in economics can be found, and another example has already been provided in the case of *utility*. To some extent the process is an essential part of learning, 'learning by using', in the development of economy theory, for it involves investigation of all the implications which may be inherent in the particular meaning given to a word. As it has already been suggested, the danger involved in this learning-by-using process is that excessive concentration on the refining of a definition by this process is apt to lead to the neglect of questions implied in other possible definitions. That the danger is real has been amply illustrated in this study. The remedy is not, it seems to me, to try to abandon the valuable process of learning by using. This would lead to attempts to make excessively complex definitions before appreciation of the implications of the problems involved had been discovered, or it would lead to refusal to abandon unsuitable or ambiguous definitions in the course of analysis. Rather it seems to me much of

Q.J.E., 1968. For an account of the refinement of the definition of competition since Cournot see Stigler's article 'Perfect Competition, Historically Considered', op. cit.

the danger would be eliminated if there was a greater willingness to accept that there may be fundamentally different meanings in which an ordinary word is used according to differing contexts. Then either different definitions may be developed parallel with each other, probably resulting in the development of qualifying terminology, or the consequence of discarding altogether one meaning may be fully considered. In essence, the problem is to make the process a conscious one.

VI *Aspects of Wages and Profit Theory from Cantillon to John Stuart Mill*

with an
Addendum on Adam Smith's Explanation of the Falling
Rate of Profit

> It is not because one man keeps a coach while his neighbour
> walks a-foot, that the one is rich and the other poor; but
> because the one is rich he keeps a coach, and because the
> other is poor he walks a-foot.
>
> ADAM SMITH[1]

(i) Wage Theory before Cantillon

It must be explained that this study is not intended to provide a
coherent and complete account of the development of wage
theory from Cantillon to Senior. On the contrary, it is concerned
with certain contrasts between a number of theories of wages in
which I have become interested. What I have tried to do has been
to identify some of the assumptions made and questions actually
asked by the economists whose theories are included. I have
avoided assessing the 'correctness' of theories in terms of the questions asked and assumptions made by later economists.

After what has been said in earlier studies in this book it is not
necessary to explain why I think it important to consider Cantillon's and Adam Smith's treatments of wages within the context of
other eighteenth-century opinions. The next few pages contain a
very brief account of what seem to me the most relevant of these
opinions.

Discussions of wages from the late seventeenth century up to
the publication of the *Wealth of Nations* centred on two general
issues: the relation of wages to subsistence, and whether high or
low wages were desirable. Statements about the relation of wages

---

[1] *Wealth of Nations*, Vol. I, Bk I, Ch. VIII, pp. 77–8.

to subsistence were numerous and often vague. Among the clearest were those which claimed that increases in the price of necessities, and in particular taxes on necessities, would result in compensating increases in money wages. Locke had stated this with extreme clarity. He argued that as the labourer and handicraftsman 'just live from hand to mouth' if the prices of their purchases were increased by taxes 'either his wages must rise with the price of things to make him live; or else not being able to maintain himself and his family by his labour, he comes to the parish' (Locke, pp. 91–2). Similar views were expressed by Davenant for instance in 1699, by William Pulteney in 1732 and Sir Matthew Decker in 1743, and of course it will be remembered by Turgot with the qualification *in the long-run equilibrium situation.*[2]

The precise time at which Cantillon's rationale of the subsistence theory of wages became available to British economists is a matter of conjecture. It appeared, however, in 1757 both in Joseph Harris's *Essay on Money and Coins* and in Postlethwayt's *Great Britain's True System* and it is probably safe to assert that it was not known in England before the end of the 1740's or even later.[3]

Instances of the opposite opinion to the subsistence thesis both at the end of the seventeenth century and just before the publication of the *Wealth of Nations* can also be cited. For example John Houghton in 1683, William Temple in 1770, Sir James Steuart in 1770 and of course Hume in 1752.[4]

Precise definitions of what constituted the necessary subsistence

[2] Davenant, *Essays on the Probable Methods of making a People Gainers in the Balance of Trade* (1700 ed., p. 45); Pulteney, *Case of the Revival of the Salt Duty*, p. 56; Decker, *Serious Considerations on the Several High Duties which the Nation . . . labours under*, p. 15. Letter from Turgot to Hume, March 25, 1767 printed in Turgot's *Reflections on the Formation and Distribution of Riches.* (Reprints of Economic Classics, pp. 106–8.)

[3] Postlethwayt included much of the later part of Cantillon's *Essai* in *A Dissertation on the Plan, Use, and Importance of the Universal Dictionary of Trade and Commerce* in 1749, but this does not necessarily mean that the earlier part of the *Essai* became available at that time. See Higgs, 'The Life and work of Richard Cantillon', op. cit., pp. 383 et seq.

[4] Houghton, *Collection of Letters*, p. 184; *An Essay on Trade and Commerce*, pp. 59–60. Steuart, op. cit., Vol. II, pp. 690–1; Hume, *Essays on Economics*, 'Of Taxes', ed. Rotwein, p. 83. (This edition also contains Turgot's letter referred to in n. 2 above.)

of the labourer are naturally not available. Certainly some writers regarded the level of comfort implied by subsistence as varying from place to place. It seems to have been considered to be higher in England than in France. Want of definition however has never prevented discussion.[5]

Examples can be found of believers in the desirability of high wages. They are not common, Bishop Berkeley and Hume being the most often quoted. The similarity between Hume's views and those expressed by Adam Smith in the *Wealth of Nations* justifies a short quotation from Hume's essay, 'On Commerce'.

> Every person, if possible, ought to enjoy the fruits of his labour, in a full possession of all the necessaries, and many of the conveniences of life. No one can doubt that such an equality is most suitable to human nature, and diminishes much less from the *happiness* of the rich than it adds to that of the poor (op. cit., p. 15).

Hume's generous sentiments were naturally not shared by those who attached major importance to the export trade and believed that high wages weakened the competitive position of exporters. This ground for objection to high wages was greatly strengthened by the belief, which seems to have been common in the late seventeenth century and through the eighteenth century in Britain, that the individual labourer's supply-curve of work was sharply backward-sloping. Evidence of the belief in 'the sloth and idleness of the labouring classes and their addiction to drink is repetitive and depressing. These characteristics it was believed led the labourer to confine his exertions to the minimum necessary to provide him and his family with a miserable subsistence plus enough to enable him to drink away the time thus saved from work. Thus Petty wrote in his *Political Arithmetic:*

> It is observed by Clothiers, and others, who employ great numbers of poor people, that when Corn is extremely plentiful, that the Labour of the poor is proportionately dear: And scarce to be had at all (so licentious are they who labour only to eat, or rather to drink) (Hull's ed., Vol. I, p. 274).

[5] See on this point E. S. Furniss, p. 177 and in general Ch. VII on his interpretation of theories of wages of this period. On Cantillon's views see pp. 181 et seq. below.

Among the well-known writers who expressed similar views are Manley and John Houghton, Child and Pollexfen, for instance, in the late seventeenth century. Gee, Tucker, Defoe, Arthur Young, William Temple are but a few names chosen almost at random from among the holders of this view in the eighteenth century, either as a result of their own observations or reports or hearsay.[6] Adam Smith himself in his lectures stated categorically that in 'the commercial parts of England' the work of half a week was sufficient to maintain a tradesman, and that 'through want of education they have no amusement for the other, but riot and debauchery. So it may very justly be said that the people who clothe the world are in rags themselves' (*Lectures*, pp. 256–7). Adam Smith had of course changed his mind about this by the time he wrote *The Wealth of Nations*; the remarkable *volte face* is discussed later. Sir James Steuart held what was still a common view in 1770 however, and it is in his *Political Oeconomy* that perhaps the most elaborate analysis of the implications for policy of the backward-sloping supply-curve is to be found. Belief in the practical importance of the backward-sloping supply-curve led directly to the conclusion that high real wage-rates reduced the national output and undermined Britain's competitive position in foreign markets. Additional output it was thought would be obtained if the terms on which labourers obtained their subsistence were worsened, so that they would have to work harder and longer to maintain themselves. This led on to consideration of ways of reducing the local wage-rate indirectly by taxation or by policies directed to raising the prices of necessities. Various possibilities are set out with great care by Steuart, in his *Political Oeconomy* (pp. 400–4 and pp. 690–7).

Like most of those of his contemporaries who did not believe that wages were determined by subsistence, Steuart was chiefly interested in actual market rates. His summary statement of his version of their determination by demand and supply is notable in that it explicitly related wage-rates to the value of the product of labour. Thus he says, 'the rate of wages is in proportion to the value of the work performed, relatively to the person who employs the workmen, and not in proportion to the price of subsistence.'[7]

---

[6] See Furniss, Ch. VI, for a detailed account.
[7] Ibid., p. 400.

(*ii*) *Cantillon*

In the setting of late seventeenth-century and eighteenth-century discussions on wages, Cantillon's belief that wages of unskilled labour were determined by subsistence levels is in no way remarkable. What is remarkable is that he set out to explain why subsistence levels determined unskilled wages and the means by which the supply of labour was adjusted to demand at the subsistence wage. Again unlike most of his contemporaries he realised that it was relevant to explain how it was that subsistence levels might be above physiological subsistence and still determine wages. An account of his treatment of wages has already been given earlier in this book; and it is only necessary to draw attention to those aspects of his treatment of wages particularly relevant to the questions to be considered here:

First: The discussion of wages was necessary for Cantillon's analysis of value which required a scale of valuation for different types of labour, skilled and unskilled, that could be translated into land by means of his *par* between labour and land.

Second: He set out systematically the economic and sociological influences which determined the differentials between skilled labour of various types and unskilled labour. He assumed that these influences were stable and therefore the differentials also. These assumptions were probably based on data included in his missing *Supplement*. He considered that *the supply of labour adjusted* to demand so as to maintain these differentials. Cantillon does not appear to have considered that temporary changes in the differentials were as important in bringing about adjustment as changes in the amount of employment available.

Third: He accepted that men would breed 'like mice in a barn' if sufficient subsistence was available at the accepted level. This accepted level was regarded as being determined in some way by custom and possibly by the outlook of landlords. He analysed the interconnection between the accepted standard of subsistence, the size of the population and the politico-social character of societies as reflected in the structure of land ownership. In consequence an economic theory of the determination of the general level of wages was redundant, for the subsistence level was determined by the character of society.

Fourth: Since the 'given' standard of living determined the amount of land required to maintain a family, the *maximum* possible population was also determined.

Fifth: The actual population was, however, determined by the character of the landowners' demands which determined the composition and size of aggregate demand for labour.

Sixth: Although the subsistence level was not an economically determined variable, it had profound effect on intrinsic values for it determined the *par* between labour and land.

Seventh: Wage rates were at appropriate levels to provide subsistence for each family on the scale required to maintain the supply of each type of labour constant.

The key price, the price of labour, required for Cantillon's theory of intrinsic value was that given by the external socio/political parameter determining the subsistence level, wages of men being so related to this to enable them to maintain a supply of replacements just sufficient to maintain constant supplies. The population could be increased or decreased with changes in aggregate demand flowing from changes in the landowners' tastes etc., by changing the allocation of different quantities of land for food production. Cantillon clearly appreciated that since the key price of labour was given, the economic questions to be discussed included the volume of employment.

Looking at Cantillon's analysis from another angle, it is evident that what he was trying to do was to explain how certain economic variables in an esentially static society were determined. His way into the problem seems to have been suggested by Petty's work combined with tradition and probably confirmed by his own empirical investigations lost with the *Supplement*. The approach depended on the supply of labour with a *given* wage being adjusted by a mixture of customary, prudential as well as positive checks. He seems to have had much more faith than either Adam Smith or Malthus in human commonsense.[8] It will

---

[8] Jevons correctly credited Cantillon with an anticipation of Malthusian population theory, but Cantillon does not really make it clear how an increase (as distinct from a decrease) of population would be stimulated except by pre-planned allocation of more land for providing subsistence by the Landlords. He does not, I think, anywhere set out the effect of an increase in aggregate demand for labour pushing wages above customary subsistence and, thereby, increasing survival and the demand for subsistence so as to increase the allocation of land for its production. (See Jevons's essay on Cantillon in the R.E.S. edition of the *Essai*.)

be noticed that Mandeville's problem of aggregate demand was dealt with very subtly by Cantillon's theory of the influence of landowners in determining the size and composition of the aggregate demand for labour. The detailed discussion of wages was necessary as a part of his theory of value; this meant that he was not asking the question what determines the wage-rate for its own sake; he was examining the functioning of the price mechanism in a system in which a major variable was fixed by influences outside the price mechanism.

(iii) Adam Smith

According to the notes of Adam Smith's Glasgow *Lectures* his discussion of the price of labour formed an integral part of his analysis of the price mechanism. It is extremely brief. He opened it by stating 'when men are induced to a certain species of industry, rather than any other, they must make as much by the employment as will maintain them while they are employed' (pp. 173–4). He then goes on to explain why in certain occupations more than this is required in order to cover cost of training, risks etc. He concludes the discussion with the following summary statement:

A man then has the natural price of his labour, when it is sufficient to maintain him during the time of labour, to defray the expense of education, and to compensate the risk of not living long enough, and of not succeeding in the business. When a man has this, there is sufficient encouragement to the labourer, and the commodity will be cultivated in proportion to the demand (ibid., p. 176).

He then goes on to discuss the market prices of goods and labour and to show their relation to the price mechanism. These references to wages in the *Lectures* are confusing, whether because Adam Smith had not made up his mind or because he failed to make himself clear to at least one member of his audience is anybody's guess. In discussing the influence on market prices of the incomes of purchasers he says 'The prices of corn and beer are regulated by what all the world can give, and on this account the wages of the day-labourer have a great influence upon the price of corn'. (Perhaps on the price of beer too?) But the very next sentence is 'When the price of corn rises, wages rise also, and

vice versa' (ibid., p. 177). On the next page there is another passage which seems to imply the same theory; it suggests that if
wages are high and corn prices low for some time wages in that
area will be reduced as a result of an inflow of labour. On the
other hand wages do not increase if corn prices increase 'because
the labourers have no other way to turn themselves' (p. 178). It
will be noticed that this last statement seems to be the opposite
of the one quoted from the preceding page!

The only other discussion of wage problems in the *Lectures* is
the passage already quoted (p. 180 above) in which Adam Smith
accepts as a fact the labourer's backward-sloping supply-curve of
work. More charitable in outlook than some of his contemporaries, he attributes the phenomenon to the lack of education of
labourers' children rather than to any innate depravity of the
working classes. The passage comes indeed in the *lectures* in
the section dealing with the need for the public provision of
education, in the section 'Of the Influence of Commerce on
Manners'.

The backward-sloping supply-curve of work is of course inconsistent with the eighteenth-century subsistence theories of wages
which were based on a normal week's work. It is possible therefore to regard Adam Smith's belief in it as an indication that the
passages on the natural rate of wages should not be interpreted
in terms of a subsistence theory. In view of the obscurities of some
references to wages in the lecture notes, I do not find this a very
convincing argument myself and I remain uncertain what his
theory of wages was at this time.

The treatment of wages in the *Lectures* considered from the
point of view of a theory of wages evidently provided nothing
novel and is far less complete as it has come down to us than
Cantillon's, or even Joseph Harris's version of Cantillon's. This
does not seem surprising to me, for it is evident that when lectur-
ing at Glasgow he was not concerned with explaining the natural
price of labour, except in relation to the distinction between market and natural prices of commodities in connection with resource
allocation. On the other hand, as has been pointed out in the
third study in this book, he was concerned with social aspects
of the distribution of wealth. He claimed that as a result of the
division of labour even the unskilled labourer had more of the
conveniences of life than 'the chief of a savage nation'. Neverthe-

less, though he thought the real incomes of all classes were higher when society was based on the division of labour, he pointed out that the relative distribution of wealth did not correspond with the relative amounts of work done:

> though there is a division of labour, there is no equal division, for there are a good many who work none at all. The division of opulence is not according to the work. The opulence of the merchant is greater than that of his clerks, though he works less; and they again have six times more than an equal number of artisans, who are more employed. The artisan who works at his ease within doors has far more than the poor labourer who trudges up and down without intermission. Thus, he who as it were bears the burden of society, has the fewest advantages (pp. 162–3).

In the 'Early Draft of the Wealth of Nations' the suggestion of disapproval of the inequality between the distribution of work and wealth of the *Lectures* is far more explicit. He referred to the rent 'which goes to support the slothful landlord' as 'all earned by the industry of the peasant'. For the 'monied' man he seems to have only shocked abhorrence. He is described as indulging himself 'in every sort of ignoble and sordid sensuality' on the interest of his capital lent to the industrious merchant and tradesmen. While the wretched labourer is described as one

> who has the soil and the seasons to struggle with, and who, while he affords the materials for supplying the luxury of all other members of the common wealth, and bears, as it were, upon his shoulders, the whole fabric of human society, seems himself to be pressed down below ground by the weight, and to be buried out of sight in the foundations of the building.[9]

Nevertheless despite this situation, which Adam Smith stigmatised in this draft as 'so much oppressive inequality', this poor labourer is 'commonly possessed' of more abundance than the most aristocratic savage owing to the division of labour. The introduction of the qualification 'commonly' suggests perhaps that a doubt has crept in since the time of the *Lectures*. In the *Wealth of Nations* the qualification became more important. Although the reference to 'oppressive inequality' is omitted, it is now only stated that the

---

[9] *Adam Smith, Student and Professor*, op. cit., pp. 325–8.

increase of wealth is so great as a result of the division of labour 'that all are *often* abundantly supplied' and that the workmen

> even of the lowest and poorest order, *if he is frugal and indus-trious, may* enjoy a greater share of the necessaries and con-veniences of life than it is possible for any savage to acquire.[10]

The obvious interpretation of this passage is that it cannot be assumed that the poorest classes will automatically benefit in terms even of increased real income; in the chapter 'Of the Wages of Labour' this question of whether the labourer always benefits from the increased wealth of the community reappears as a central problem. Adam Smith's well-known belief that the divi-sion of labour may lead to such monotonous work that the labourer's intellectual faculties and social qualities will deteriorate gave rise to a disadvantage of a different type, but one for which he believed a remedy could be provided by the state inter-vention in education. It evidently seemed to him, as it has ever since, to be a simpler problem than the other.

In the *Wealth of Nations* there is another contrast with his *Lectures.* Adam Smith is at great pains to present the labour-ing classes in a favourable light and to disprove the existence of the backward-sloping supply-curve of work. The last part of the chapter on wages is indeed devoted to demonstrating that the traditional arguments against high wage-rates are fallacious. All this makes the discussion of wages not only more interesting than in the *lectures*, but even more interesting than Cantillon's dis-cussion. All three discussions had this in common, however, that a theory of wages was seen to be essential to the analysis of the price mechanism. This aspect of the *Wealth of Nations* treatment of wages must now be considered though it involves repetition.

In the *Wealth of Nations* the natural price of a commodity was defined as the sum of the natural prices of the factors of pro-duction multiplied by the quantities used, but the natural prices of the factors were defined very carefully in a quite different way. They were the 'ordinary or average rate' actually prevailing for each particular factor in each occupation and place. Thus

> There is in every society or neighbourhood an ordinary or average rate both of wages and profit in every different em-

[10] *Wealth of Nations*, Introduction, p. 2. My Italics.

ployment of labour and stock. This rate is naturally regulated, as I shall show hereafter, partly by the general circumstances of the society, their riches or poverty, their advancing, stationary or declining condition; and partly by the particular nature of each employment.

There is likewise in every society or neighbourhood an ordinary or average rate of rent, which is regulated too, as I shall show hereafter, partly by the general circumstances of the society or neighbourhood in which the land is situated, and partly by the natural or improved fertility of the land.

These ordinary or average rates may be called the natural rates of wages, profit and rent, at the time and place in which they commonly prevail (Vol. I, p. 57).

The natural prices of factors were thus always known; they were not prices that would only be reached in some stationary state which might emerge in the distant future. This was of course essential to Adam Smith's theory of value for the prices of commodities could not fluctuate closely about, or be equal to, their natural prices if factor prices were not at their natural rates at the same time. The market price of factors might diverge from their natural prices in particular occupations as a result of changes in conditions of supply or demand in those occupations. Such divergences would only be temporary however, except in cases of artificial or natural obstacles to factor mobility (Vol. I, pp. 61 et seq. and pp. 123–4 above).

The general approach to the explanation of how the natural prices of factors were determined had already been indicated in terms of 'produce less deductions' in the chapter 'of the Component Parts of Price' (Bk I, Ch. VI). Adam Smith had concluded that in the primitive one-factor society labour received the whole, i.e. gross, product of labour which comprised the whole product of society. In advanced societies however, with other scarce factors besides labour, the whole product was attributed to labour working *with the assistance* of the other factors, capital and land. The product of labour was still therefore identified with the gross product and the productivity of labour was measured by it.[11] As it is stated in Chapter VIII, 'Of the Wages of Labour',

In that original state of things, which precedes both the appro-
___
[11] This identification of the product of labour with gross output was in

priation of land and the accumulation of stock, the whole produce of labour belongs to the labourer. He has neither landlord nor master to share with him.

Had this state continued, the wages of labour would have augmented with all the improvements in its productive powers, to which the division of labour gives occasion (Vol. I, p. 66).

Although Adam Smith made it clear that the other two factors were necessary to production and in particular that increases in the amount of capital used increased the total product, he always wrote of this as increasing the productivity of labour. Hence he formulates his problem in terms of *gross product* (he refers to net product occasionally in case of rent): if labour dies not receive the whole gross product of labour, how is its share determined? He does not ask what is the net product of labour, does the labourer receive it? Since then the natural price of labour is not determined by an *obvious* relation to its productivity, any explanation of the natural price of labour must eschew productivity as the sole or direct determinant, and must explain the natural price of labour as apparently divorced from the productivity of labour.

Adam Smith could have answered the question by adopting either Cantillon's customary subsistence-level theory, or the common assumption that wages were in fact at some sort of physiological subsistence level. He rejected both these solutions regarding neither as consistent with the facts. He pointed out that in Great Britain wages were above the level required to enable a labourer to bring up a family.

In order to satisfy ourselves upon this point [he said] it will not be necessary to enter into any tedious or doubtful calculation of what may be the lowest sum upon which it may be possible to do this. There are many plain symptoms that the wages of labour are no-where in this country regulated by the lowest

---

the *ordinary* tradition of the eighteenth century in England. Although Cantillon, following Petty, bracketed land with labour as the source of the gross product, this remained unusual. Thus it was common to regard the employment of labour in utilising natural resources as the source of wealth, and the gross produce as attributable to this labour. Capital was not regarded as a separate productive resource. On this see Furniss, Ch. II.

rate which is consistent with common humanity (Bk I, Ch. VIII, p. 75).[12]

These symptoms he did in fact describe at considerable length. He argued that not only had real wages risen over a long period, but that they were highly variable over time and by no means changed in the same direction as the price of goods consumed by labourers. Moreover they differed between neighbouring districts and changed at different rates at different times and places. It was impossible to relate them consistently either to physiological minimums or to any other types of subsistence standard. He finally dismissed the idea that wages are determined by standards of living as 'a strange misapprehension'. Referring to the difference in standards of living of labourers in Scotland and England he says:

> This difference, however, in the mode of their subsistence is not the cause, but the effect, of the difference in their wages; though, by a strange misapprehension, I have frequently heard it represented as the cause. It is not because one man keeps a coach while his neighbour walks a-foot, that the one is rich and the other poor; but because the one is rich he keeps a coach, and because the other is poor he walks a-foot (Bk I, Ch. VIII, pp. 77–8).

The significance of Adam Smith's rejection of all the versions of the subsistence theory of wages has not received the attention it deserves. He himself obviously attached great importance to it and his emphasis on it is evidence of the strength of the contemporary influence of subsistence theories. Without this rejection the discussion of the effects on the incomes of labourers of increases in wealth through the division of labour would have been pointless. But in consequence of it he had to find a theory of wages which would explain the standard of living and also examine the range of problems introduced if wages were not a given parameter of the economic system – in particular, wages might adjust to the level of employment instead of vice versa. The only alternatives

[12] It is obvious that the phrase 'consistent with common humanity' has no humanitarian meaning in the modern sense of the word, but merely means physiologically consistent with the survival of human beings at a rate to maintain the supply of labour constant. (See pp. 191–2 below.)

to the subsistence theories current were simple supply and demand explanations.

Although Adam Smith rejected subsistence theories of wages, he did not reject Cantillon's thesis that the total supply of labour was affected by the availability of subsistence. 'Every species of animals [he said] naturally multiplies in proportion to the means of their subsistence, and no species can ever multiply beyond it' (Vol. I, p. 81). His theory of wages would have to take this factor into account also. It led in effect to a modification of the *Lectures'* original simple statement as to the influence of the division of labour on the incomes of labourers.

Looking at the circumstances under which wages were actually determined to find some lead into the problem, Adam Smith observed that the institutional features of the labour market were heavily weighted in favour of the purchasers of labour. The market was not one of atomistic perfect competition in which neither buyer nor seller was able to influence the outcome. On the contrary, the market was seen to be one with monopsonistic features as well as having the special characteristic that the price could be influenced by deliberate temporary withdrawals of demand; the employers Adam Smith observed could afford to wait, the resourceless labourers could not. Wages were the result of a bargain between men and masters in a market in which each side tries to combine, the former to raise and the latter to lower the wage. Having thus disposed of any idea of a normally competitive market, Adam Smith describes the disadvantageous position of the labourers.

It is not, however, difficult to foresee which of the two parties, must, upon all ordinary occasions, have the advantage in dispute, and force the other into compliance with their terms. The masters, being fewer in number, can combine much more easily; and the law, besides, authorises, or at least does not prohibit their combinations, while it prohibits those of the workmen. . . . In all such disputes the master can hold out much longer. A landlord, a farmer, a master manufacturer, a merchant, though they did not employ a single workman, could generally live a year or two upon the stocks which they have already acquired. Many workmen could not subsist a week, few could subsist a month, and scarce any a year without employment. In the long run the workman may be as necessary to his master as his master is to him, but the necessity is not so immediate (Vol. I, p. 68).

He goes on with a blast of contempt for anyone who is so ignorant as to believe that employers do not normally combine together:

> We rarely hear, it has been said, of the combination of masters, though frequently of those of workmen. But whoever imagines, upon this account, that masters rarely combine, is as ignorant of the world as of the subject. Masters are always and everywhere in a sort of tacit, but constant and uniform combination, not to raise the wages of labour above their actual rate. To violate this combination is everywhere a most unpopular action, and a sort of reproach to a master among his neighbours and equals.[13]

These masters' combinations Adam Smith asserts are not talked of because 'it is the usual, and one might say, the natural state of things which nobody ever hears of'. Further special very secret agreements are sometimes made to depress wages below their current rate. Combinations among workmen are sometimes intended to resist such downward pressures, sometimes to push wages up, but as Adam Smith concludes the workmen as desperate men usually resort to 'clamour' and sometimes 'violence and outrage'. They usually gain nothing from these 'tumultuous combinations' and the ringleaders are punished. So much for the normal state of the labour market, in such a situation an explanation was needed of the failure of the employers to keep wages down to subsistence. It will be remembered that in completing his account of the struggle in the labour market Adam Smith explained 'that there is, however, a certain rate below which it seems impossible to reduce, for any considerable time, the ordinary wages even of the lowest species of labour' (Vol. I, p. 69). This lowest rate was the physiological subsistence level and no rate of wages could be maintained below this '*for any considerable time*' (my italics) because of course the supply of labour would presently fall and

---

[13] One is reminded of Marshall's account of firms not lowering prices in order to avoid social obloquy. *Principles*, Bk V, Ch. V, para. 6.

demand, unless it had decreased in the meantime, would push wages up again.[14]

The introduction of this argument at this stage is perhaps confusing for it anticipates the elucidation of the nature of demand which occurs in the next few paragraphs. I think Adam Smith introduced it here to clarify the aspect of the problem with which he was most concerned: why in a market so weighted in favour of the employers, did the rate of wages ever, even perhaps generally, exceed the physiological subsistence level?

Adam Smith proceeded, I think perfectly logically, to look for circumstances which undermine the favourable bargaining position of employers in the labour market. Once the question was framed in this way, the answer was obviously suggested by his own use of demand and supply analysis to explain short-term variation in wages, and in market prices of commodities, in the preceding chapter on market and natural prices of commodities.

Adam Smith described the favourable circumstances which give labour an advantage and enables it to push wages above subsistence:

> When in any country the demand for those who live by wages; labourers, journeymen, servants of every kind, is continually increasing; when every year furnishes employment for a greater number than had been employed the year before, the workmen have no occasion to combine in order to raise wages. The scarcity of hands occasions a competition among masters, who bid against one another, in order to get workmen, and thus voluntarily break through the natural combination of masters not to raise wages (Vol. I, p. 70).

The explanation of the demand for labour, in terms of a simple exposition of the *advance* concept of capital, had already been given in Chapter VI, 'Of the Component Parts of Price'. This concept, already briefly introduced by Cantillon and by Adam Smith himself in the Glasgow lectures, had been so fully developed by the Physiocrats that its relevance could not be overlooked. Hence Adam Smith was led to introduce the wages fund in the well-known paragraph:

> The demand for those who live by wages, it is evident, cannot

[14] See p. 189 above on the meaning of 'consistent with common humanity'.

increase but in proportion to the increase of the funds which are destined for the payment of wages. These funds are of two kinds; first, the revenue which is over and above what is necessary for the maintenance; and, secondly, the stock which is over and above what is necessary for the employment of their masters (Vol. I, pp. 70–1).

With the introduction of the Wages Fund Adam Smith had found his answer to his question as to the circumstances under which all labour would benefit in the form of increased real wages with the increase of wealth. As long as the *process* of increase continued the wages of labour would rise, for it required continued net accumulation of capital which automatically increased the aggregate demand for labour, via 'the funds which are destined for the employment of labour'. Moreover he made it clear that the faster the rate of growth of wealth the higher would real wages be. It was in rapidly developing countries such as those of North America that wages would be highest. The description of the progressive state leaves me in no doubt that Adam Smith believed that an increasing aggregate demand for labour would raise the demand for all types of labour, and that there would be for all practical purposes no unemployment. The distribution of wealth might become still more unequal, though this is not mentioned in the *Wealth of Nations*, but at least as long as wealth continued to increase even the poorest class of labourer would be better off. The importance of this idea to the post-Ricardian economists will be illustrated later.

Adam Smith is frequently criticised for failure to explain how the size and growth of the wage fund was determined. I propose to put forward what seems to me a plausible account of what Adam Smith thought about this. This involves me in a discussion of Adam Smith's theory of accumulation and profits. This is not really a digression, for a subsidiary theme of this study is the influence on discussions of wages of the various views as to the function relating the supply of saving to the rate of profits. It is customary I think, at least in textbooks, and I myself held this view until very recently, to state that Adam Smith gave an incomplete and somewhat confused account of this relationship.

The crucial fact about Adam Smith's theory of saving, it seems to me, is that net saving is entirely independent of the rate

of profit except at the one particular rate of profit at which net
saving is zero. This is the rate that prevails in the stationary
state. It is described as follows in Book I, Ch. IX, 'Of the
Profits of Stock':

> The lowest ordinary rate of profit must always be something
> more than what is sufficient to compensate the occasional
> losses to which every employment of stock is exposed. It is this
> surplus only which is neat or clear profit (Vol. I, pp. 97–8).

Adam Smith explains that any interest a borrower can pay is
in proportion to this clear profit only. He points out that in a
very wealthy country approaching stationariness the rate of neat
profit would be so low that only the very richest people could
afford to live on interest as this would fall with the falling rate of
profit. (In the rest of the discussion I shall ignore interest and,
also, when referring to profit mean 'neat' profit only). It must be
remarked in passing that Adam Smith also treats the dis-
saving of the declining state as independent of the rate of profit.

The way in which Adam Smith may have reached these conclusions requires some description. A view prevalent in the
seventeenth century was that the rate of interest was crucial to
the question of whether people hoarded or invested their savings,
and investment as distinct from saving seems to have been regarded as something like a continuous positive function of the rate
of interest. On the other hand it was generally believed that the
rates of profit and interest declined as the volume of capital
increased and that this was a long-term trend in a society with
growing wealth. This was regarded as a straightforward statement
of fact. Accumulation continued although the rate of profit continued to fall. This seems to have been a common view also
during the eighteenth century. Saving appears to have been regarded as dependent on the habits and outlook of society, on its
thriftiness arising from an attitude of mind and on the desire of
certain sections to better themselves. The contrast between the
landed gentry and the middle classes in this respect was commented on by David Hume for instance.[15]

It is well known that Adam Smith denied that net hoarding

[15] See pp. 46 et seq. above and Tucker, Ch. III. Tucker also notes,
p. 72, that Adam Smith did *not* consider that saving declined with the
rate of profits unless the stationary state was reached, and that the latter
was an abnormal state.

occurred in countries in which law and order were established: 'What is annually saved is as regularly consumed as what is annually spent, and nearly in the same time too; but it is consumed up by a different set of people' (Vol. I, p. 320). Thus he denied the practical relevance of those circumstances in which it had been recognised that net investment, as distinct from net saving, was directly stimulated by the rate of interest or profit. What remained to Adam Smith of the earlier conclusions was that saving was not stimulated by the rate of profit, and that as the quantity of capital increased the rate of profit fell. Adam Smith examined and accepted the evidence for these propositions. He concluded that saving would tend to increase with the ability to save and depended on habits and outlook of society rather than on the rate of profit. All this is set out as everyone knows in Book I, Ch. IX, 'Of the Profits of Stock', and in Book II, Ch. III, 'Of the Accumulation of Capital'. The following passage from the former illustrates his views particularly clearly in their relation to wages.

As riches, improvement, and population have increased, interest has declined. The wages of labour do not sink with the profits of stock. The demand for labour increases with the increase of stock whatever be its profits; and after these are diminished, stock may not only continue to increase, but to increase much faster than before. It is with industrious nations who are advancing in the acquisition of riches, as with industrious individuals. A great stock though with small profits generally increases faster than a small stock with great profits. Money, says the proverb, makes money. When you have got a little, it is often easy to get more. The great difficulty is to get that little (Vol. I, p. 94).

This general absence of dependence of the decision to save on the rate of profit did not of course diminish people's wish to choose the most profitable investments available. Nor did it affect Adam Smith's belief, already mentioned, that there was some minimum rate of profit at which people would decide that it was not worth while investing more and therefore net investment and net saving would cease. In this Adam Smith seems to have held views typical of his period.

The general absence of a relation between the rate of profit and decisions to save did not affect Adam Smith's belief, as already mentioned, that there was some minimum rate of profit at which net investment and saving would cease. The same argument appears to have been used to explain a declining state. The decision to dis-save was regarded as the consequence of sociological or political factors *not* of the rate of profit which, Adam Smith argued, would rise as dis-saving took place.[16]

It follows, I think, from this approach that provided that an increase in the aggregate demand for labour (at any particular time) derived from an increment in accumulation is related in a predetermined proportion to that increment in accumulation, the increase in the wages fund would be independent of the expected profitability of employing labour (above the minimum rate of profit required or net accumulation). In other words the elasticity of aggregate demand for labour at any particular time would be unity. Adam Smith seems to imply this.

The obscurity in the *Wealth of Nations* as to the relationship between the funds 'destined for the payment of wages' and the composition of capital and changes in that composition are well known.[17] Put another way Adam Smith did not integrate properly the 'advances' theory of capital, used as the basis of the wage fund theory, with the discussion of capital composition in Book II which itself was more descriptive than analytical. He seems to have been aware that there must be some connection; for instance he refers to the effect of labour saving inventions on the demand for labour in Book II, Ch. II, pp. 270–1. He even points out that the proportion of wages to materials and tools required to be accumulated beforehand will fall as the scale of operation increases. He

[16] Adam Smith stresses the lag in adjustment of the supply of labour to change in demand, and in his description of the stationary state implies that after capital accumulation ceased there would be a considerable interval before wages fell to subsistence level. He does not however seem to notice that the fall in wages would itself tend to raise the rate of profit above the no-net-saving minimum and thus tend to stimulate for a time a renewal of net saving.

[17] A recent discussion of some problems within the general field is contained in an interesting article by S. Hollander, 'The role of fixed technical co-efficients in the Evolution of the Wages Fund Controversy', *O.E.P.*, 1968. It seems to me that Mr Hollander introduces some extra difficulty into a difficult subject by thinking in terms of comparative static analysis. In Adam Smith's 'progressive' state the supply of labour increased continuously but not so fast as the wages fund.

described the different capital structures of different industries at length in Book II, Ch. I. He did not seem to think that anything had been left unexplained.

Once, however, we accept that Adam Smith assumed unitary elasticity of aggregate demand for labour at any particular time as consistent with his theory of the rate of profits in relation to investment, a number of apparently odd passages and arguments become clear. For instance he often refers to so much labour being 'wanted' without any reference to the profitability of employing it, giving the impression that there is a definite amount of capital that has to be invested in wage payments. This indeed is just precisely what he seems to have meant in the passage quoted on p. 195 above – 'the demand for labour increases with the increase in stock whatever be its profits'. Such statements follow logically from the view of Adam Smith's theory of saving an investment that I have suggested. It must be remembered however that if the rate of profit falls to the minimum level, net saving and investment will be discontinued.

This basic assumption of unit-elasticity of aggregate demand for labour leads to other conclusions as to the relationship between wages and productivity that seem to belong to the world of *Alice Through the Looking Glass* to orthodox economists, but not I think always to trade unionists. For instance Adam Smith explained that increases of capital caused high wages by increasing the wages fund, but also tended to increase the productivity of labour so that a smaller quantity of labour produced a greater output. This occurred because the use of more capital facilitated the division of labour and the invention and use of machinery. The increase of wage-rates was not due however to the increased productivity of labour, but to the increase in the wages fund. Increases of wages rates and increased productivity were two independent consequences of the increase in capital (Vol. I, p. 88).

Again Adam Smith claimed that increased wages resulting from an increase in the wage fund might increase the productivity of labour by increasing the willingness to work and the physical ability to work. He explained

The wages of labour are the ecouragement of industry, which, like every other human quality, improves in proportion to the encouragement it receives. A plentiful subsistence increases the bodily strength of the labourer, and the comfortable hope of bettering his condition, and of ending his days perhaps in ease and plenty, animates him to exert that strength to the utmost (Vol. I, p. 83).

Here then is a statement of the thesis of the efficiency of high wages, but it is evident from the context that these high wages were initially the result of the increase of the wages fund. The increase in productivity that occurred had no bearing on the question of *why* those high wages were paid. Obviously this passage directly contradicts the opinion that the labourers' supply-curve of work was backward-sloping, that he himself, had accepted when he lectured at Glasgow.[18]

The passage just quoted follows directly on Adam Smith's argument that high or rising wages are the necessary accompaniment of a progressive state, and his description of that state as 'cheerful and hearty state for all members of society'. It formed part of his attempt to disprove the existence of the backward-sloping characteristic of the supply-curve of work as at all common, and with it the thesis that dear food increases, and cheap food decreases, the supply of work. He put forward fatigue as an explanation of voluntary short-time, supporting this by what he believed to be evidence of the shortening of the working lives of highly-paid piece-workers through 'excessive application'. He also found reasons for the apparent shortages of labour in times of cheap food in terms of voluntary movement of labourers in and out of the wage-labour market (vice versa in times of dear food). He also referred to evidence found by his own researches (Vol. I, pp. 83–7).

It is perhaps idle to speculate as to how Adam Smith would have fitted the backward-sloping supply-curve into the analysis of wages in the *Wealth of Nations*. It seems to me it would have been difficult unless treated as a temporary phenomenon arising from inadequate public provision of education.

Before leaving this subject it should be noticed that Adam Smith must be regarded as establishing for good or ill, the belief in the normal-shaped supply-curve of work assumed by nineteenth-century economists.

*   *   *

There are plenty of problems associated with the wage fund left

[18] See p. 180 above.

unnoticed or unsolved by Adam Smith. Some problems, however, which seem later to have caused much trouble had in fact been dealt with by him, or were created later by imposing particular interpretations on his exposition.

For instance, a problem associated with the later literature on the wage fund is whether it is a fund in money or a fund in goods. Adam Smith I think made his views on this perfectly clear and it seems to me that later difficulties arose with the later tendency to think in terms of wage goods as distinct from all other consumption goods. Adam Smith seems to have envisaged the process thus. Individuals' decisions to save and invest involved decisions not to use directly themselves some of their revenue or stock but to transfer it to other people. In this way they decided what proportion would be used by other people, expressing this decision by trying to buy labour for money. The labourers receiving the money would then have claims for the appropriate proportion of the goods not consumed by the savers. The whole process is set out in the following passage which occurs near the end of the chapter on wages.

> The money price of labour is necessarily regulated by two circumstances; the demand for labour, and the price of the necessaries and conveniences of life. *The demand for labour according as it happens to be increasing, stationary or declining, or to require an increasing, stationary or declining* population, *determines the quantity of the necessaries and convenience of the life which must be given to the labourer; and the money price of labour is determined by what must be given to the labourer for purchasing this quantity.* Though the money price of labour, therefore, is sometimes high when the price of provisions is low, it would be still higher, the demand continuing the same, if the price of provisions was high.
>
> It is because the demand for labour increases in years of sudden and extraordinary plenty, and diminishes in those of sudden and extraordinary scarcity, that the money price of labour sometimes rises in the one, and sinks in the other.
>
> In a year of sudden and extraordinary plenty, there are funds in the hands of many of the employers of industry, sufficient to employ a greater number of industrious people than had been employed the year before (Vol. I, p. 87, my italics).

An example of a difficulty largely created by the imposition of a particular interpretation on Adam Smith's treatment is provided by assumptions made about prior accumulation of the fund in one period for use in another. Prior accumulation, it is argued, leads to the completely unrealistic assumption of discrete production periods.

Certainly the passage just quoted states clearly that harvest fluctuations may affect the demand for labour, implying evidently that the 'funds' are partly dependent on the annual supply of food, thus indicating an annual period. Adam Smith does not, I think, pay much more attention to this particular type of period. He is however explicit on the necessity of accumulation as prior to investment; this is basic to his theory of capital. It is stated unambiguously not only in the chapter on the division of labour and the component parts of price but also in the introduction to Book II, 'Of the Nature, Accumulation and Employment of Stock'. Thus:

> As the accumulation of stock must, in the nature of things, be previous to the division of labour, so labour can be more and more subdivided in proportion only as stock is previously more and more accumulated. The quantity of materials which the same number of people can work up, increases in a great proportion as labour comes to be more and more subdivided; . . . As the division of labour advances, therefore, in order to give constant employment to an equal number of workmen, an equal stock of provisions, and a greater stock of materials and tools than what would have been necessary in a ruder state of things, must be accumulated beforehand (Vol. I, p. 259).

Certainly prior accumulation is required for the weaver must be tided through the period of production and sale. But there is no suggestion of a uniform production period for all industry. Nassau Senior was to point out later that though Adam Smith laid himself open to the interpretation that the whole of the stock required had to be accumulated before any project commenced, this was not necessary either to Adam Smith's theory, or in fact. If the materials, tools and provisions required for a particular project were produced *pari passu* with the project, prior accumulation of a sufficient supply to start the operation only was necessary.[19] Classical economists did, however, frequently write in terms of uniform annual periods and James Mill set out a formal justification of this:

> A year is assumed, in political economy, as the period which includes a revolving circle of production and consumption. No period does so exactly. Some articles are produced and consumed in a period much less than a year. In others, the circle is greater than a year. It is necessary, for the ends of discourse, that some period should be assumed as including this circle. The period of a year is the most convenient. It corresponds with one great class of productions, those derived from the cultivation of the ground. And it is easy, when we have obtained forms of expression . . to modify them in practice to the case of those commodities, the circle of whose production and consumption is either greater or less than the standard to which our general propositions are conformed.[20]

The procedure led to difficulties from time to time for the 'modifications' that James Mill mentioned so glibly were not usually made and not always easy to make. As far as the *Wealth of Nations* is concerned, however, the idea of a production period in relation to prior accumulation does not seem to me to be the major difficulty or obscurity, for it appears as varying with the project in hand while harvest fluctuations tended to produce random fluctuations in the aggregate demand for labour.

*   *   *

Adam Smith's account of wages in progressive, stationary and declining states raises a question of a different type. This relates to his views on the flexibility of wages and unemployment. It appears from the text that he did not associate any general unemployment or under-employment with the progressive state. In a stationary state the tendency of population to increase, would prevent wages remaining for long above 'the lowest rate which is consistent with humanity', i.e. sufficient to maintain the population constant for any length of time. Nevertheless though there would be apparently no continuous unemployment, it seems that the

---

[19] Senior, pp. 78–9.

[20] James Mill, *Elements of Political Economy*, Ch. IV, section II, 1st edn, 1825 (p. 326, *James Mill's Selected Economic Writings*, ed. Winch).

stationary state would be in a position of under-employment equilibrium, for labourers would not be able to obtain as much work as they wanted at the current wage-rate. Thus Adam Smith said that in China the artificers 'are continually running about the streets with the tools of their respective trades, offering their services, and as it were begging employment'.

Adam Smith's account of the standard of living in China leaves no doubt as to the meaning of wages 'consistent with common humanity'. 'The poverty of the lower ranks of people in China far surpasses that of the most beggarly nations in Europe.' They are glad to consume garbage from European ships and carrion from the canals, while the destruction of unwanted infants is customary. Nevertheless in a declining state the natural rate of wages would be lower still for the competition for employment would reduce them 'to the most miserable and scanty subsistence'. Moreover even at those rates *Many would not be able to find employment* . . . but would either starve, or be driven to seek a subsistence either by begging, or by the perpetration perhaps of the greatest enormities'[21] (pp. 74–5, my italics). This deplorable situation would continue until the population was reduced by starvation or disaster to a number that could easily be maintained by such revenue and stock as remained. It is not surprising that Adam Smith commented

> it is in the progressive state . . . that the condition of the labouring poor, of the great body of the people, seems to be the happiest and the most comfortable. It is hard in the stationary and miserable in the declining state. The progressive state is in reality the cheerful and hearty state to all the different orders of society. The stationary is dull; the declining melancholy.[22]

The implied under-employment of the stationary state, and the admitted unemployment of the declining state raised questions which Adam Smith did not discuss. The total wage fund was dependent, he makes clear, on the stationariness or decline in the quantity of capital. What he does not explain is why it was not distributed by competition from the labourers at such lower rates

[21] *Wealth of Nations*, Vol. I, Bk I, Ch. VIII, pp. 73–5. My italics.
[22] Ibid., Vol. I, p. 83. Adam Smith does not explain whether a new stationary state would come into existence at any point.

of wages per hour, or per job, that it would have eliminated under-employment or unemployment respectively.

It seems to me reasonable to assume that Adam Smith did not realise the significance of his description of under-employment in the stationary state, and that he tacitly assumed that wages would not fall fast enough in the declining state to ensure full employment with a declining wage fund. It does not seem to me possible to argue that he had introduced some tacit assumption of wage-rates being given by some sort of subsistence level below that required to maintain the supply of labour constant. Such an interpretation is not inconsistent with the main paragraph on the declining state (Vol. I, pp. 74–5) but it is not necessary to it, and it is difficult to make it consistent with the summing-up statement in the next paragraph, viz.: 'the scanty maintenance of the labouring poor . . . is the natural symptom that things are at a stand, and their starving condition that they are fast going backward'. A starving condition can hardly be called subsistence. Moreover, such an interpretation is inconsistent with Adam Smith's explicit rejection of the theory that the standard of living determines the wage-rate, already mentioned, which is based on the analysis of the demand for labour formulated in terms of a wage fund. It is of course notorious that Homer all too often nods, and the *Wealth of Nations* is no more free of inconsistencies than other major (or minor) works on economics. Nevertheless it seems to me to serve no purpose to seek to impute inconsistencies when other interpretations are available.[23]

It is not, I think, surprising that Adam Smith did not comment on this problem. He was interested in progressive states not in stationary or declining ones. Moreover it is evident that he atributes these two latter conditions to the institutions of societies. China is stationary because it had 'acquired that full complement of riches which the nature of its laws and institutions permits it to acquire'. While the declining condition of Bengal and other parts of the East Indies is attributed to the bad government of

---

[23] It would be possible to find a short-term explanation of the under-employment in the stationary, and the unemployment in the declining state in terms of an inappropriate composition of capital, inadequate quantities of tools and materials for instance to increase employment. There is however, I think, no suggestion in the *Wealth of Nations* that such a situation would arise.

the East India Company.[24] It is to be noticed however that it is in Adam Smith's two cases of apparently sticky wage-rates, the stationary and declining states, that unemployment is discussed.

* * *

Adam Smith considered that he had shown that the standard of living was the result, not the cause, of the level of the natural rate of wages. The essence of his argument may be summarised as follows: the supply of labour is a function of the subsistence available to the labourer in the form of wages. Although in the long run the elasticity of the function is infinity the adjustment of the supply to changes in wages was lagged. Hence, if the demand for labour changed more or less continuously in one direction the appropriate adjustments in the supply of labour lagged continuously behind and the ordinary, average or natural rate of wages would be continuously above or below subsistence. If demand ceased to change and remained unchanged for long enough, the adjustments in supply would eventually be completed and wages would equal subsistence. The lag in adjustment is of course essential to explain deviation of actual price from supply price if the supply curve is infinitely elastic. To establish a theory of wages independent of standards of living, it was necessary to show that such deviations were more significant in the labour market than the familiar temporary fluctuations of market prices about natural prices in commodity markets. For this it was necessary to show either that the lag was so long that the long-run supply price of labour was an uninteresting limiting case only, or that the demand for labour had a tendency to change continuously over long periods in one direction. The latter alternative required the demand for labour to be linked to some potentially dynamic element in the system. The dynamic element in the *Wealth of Nations* was of course the growth or decline etc. of capital, and the wage fund provided the link between the natural, average or ordinary rate of wages and growth or decline etc. of the economy. (The apparent assumption of unit elasticity of aggregate demand for labour at any time strengthened the link.) Adam Smith's optimism about wages depended on his belief that continuous net capital accumulation and investment was to be expected in any well-governed state with suitable institutions and

[24] Vol. I, Bk I, Ch. VIII, pp. 73–5 and Ch. IX, pp. 96–7.

policies. Absence of net accumulation of capital, and *a fortiori* capital consumption were, he believed, unlikely in the absence of unsuitable institutions and policies or actual bad government. It is important to stress this for Adam Smith emphasised the dependence of the supply of labour on wages; he clearly believed that neither customs nor institutions would limit the excessive fertility of humanity. Thus he stated:

> The liberal reward of labour, by enabling them to provide better for their children, and consequently to bring up a greater number, naturally tends to widen and extend those limits [*sic* 'to multiplication']. It deserves to be remarked too, that it necessarily does this as nearly as possible in the proportion which the demand for labour requires. If this demand is continually increasing, the reward of labour most necessarily encourage in such a manner the marriage and multiplication of labourers, as may enable them to supply that continually increasing demand by a continually increasing population.

He goes on to explain the reverse process of decrease in supply and concludes 'It is in this manner that the demand for men, like that for any other commodity, necessarily regulates the production of men' (Vol. I, pp. 81–2).

I have commented earlier that the significance of Adam Smith's contribution to wage theory is insufficiently recognised. This seems to me not to be due primarily to obvious deficiencies of sections of his analysis, such as for instance the theory of investment, nor even to the subsequent history and rejection of the wage fund theory. Rather the obstacles to proper evaluation of the treatment of wages in the *Wealth of Nations* seems to me to arise because he formulated some of his main questions in ways alien to modern economists, while some of his assumptions though relevant to the eighteenth-century world have since been discarded. For instance, it has been noted that there appears to be a divorce between the productivity of labour and wages in the *Wealth of Nations*. It is easy for modern readers to forget that Adam Smith used the term productivity of labour in a different sense to that of more recent wage theory. We too often forget that the problem which led him into wage theory initially was 'why does labour not receive the whole product of labour' – treating the product of labour as the gross product of labour assisted by other factors. For Adam Smith therefore the question to be answered was 'why are wages *not* determined by the productivity of labour?' Again, modern economists do not start from the presumption that it is necessary to explain how, on economic grounds, the natural rate of wages can be above some given subsistence level and why high wage-rates are not frustrated by backward-sloping supply-curves of work. The object of the lengthy account of Adam Smith's treatment of wages has been to try to set it out in relation to the questions he himself asked and the assumptions he himself made. This may remove some of the obstacles to understanding the significance of the questions he tried to answer in relation to views on wages common when he wrote the *Wealth of Nations*.

(iv) Ricardo

Adam Smith had shown that the theory that population bred up to subsistence level did not necessitate the conclusion that wages were determined by the subsistence level. Ricardo did not reverse Adam Smith's argument by denying the existence of lags in the response of the labour supply to wage changes. His reinstatement of the subsistence theory of wages was caused by his combination of the law of diminishing returns in agriculture with Malthus's population theory; it was reinforced by his own interpretation of Say's law.[25] Ricardo's system contained built-in tendencies towards a stationary state – the treatment of population increases stimulated by increases of capital as the inevitable and only cause of the fall in the rate of profits in a world of diminishing returns in agriculture. This reversed yet another important conclusion of Adam Smith's analysis that increases in population retarded the fall in the rate of profit by reducing the upward pressure on wage-rates caused by increases in capital. Ricardo's reintroduction of the subsistence parameter as the determinant of the natural rate of wages transformed the wage-fund analysis into a theory of the short-run market-price type, as well as into a mechanism showing

[25] For without diminishing returns and subsistence wages he could not explain the phenomena of falling rates of profit in a way which was consistent with *his* interpretation of Say's Law. (See Ricardo's *Principles*, Ch. XXI.) R. L. Meek's Essay 'The Decline of Ricardian Economics in England' in *Economics and Ideology and other Essays* contains suggestive comments relevant to this point.

the forces reducing wages to a level determined by the subsistence parameter. In consequence it can be said I think that the Ricardian system does not provide an economic theory of the determination of the natural level of wages, but only a theory of the adaptation of the economic system to a given natural wage level.

Although population theories figured so prominently in both Adam Smith's and Ricardo's discussions of wages, it is important to remember that the population theories used differed. The Malthusian theory incorporated by Ricardo introduced the idea of prudential checks restricting population. Not only would these reduce the need for the painful positive checks, but they would also retard the response of the labour supply to increases in wages, thus helping to postpone pressure on the food supply and reduction of the rate of profit. They might also enable a 'psychological' subsistence standard to be substituted for a 'physiological' one. Though these developments would not prevent the establishment of a stationary state, they would ensure that the working class standard of living would be relatively high in that state. It is this hope that inspired the famous sentences in Ricardo's Chapter V, 'On Wages':

> The friends of humanity cannot but wish that in all countries the labouring classes should have a state for comforts and enjoyments, and that they should be stimulated by all legal means in their exertions to procure them. There cannot be a better security against a superabundant population.[26]

Malthus and Ricardo between them made it clear that fundamentally the progress of the working classes depended on themselves, on their prudence in propagation. Not merely this, it was clear that continued progress of society, postponement of stationariness, depended on the prudence of the working classes. In the *Wealth of Nations* however the working classes were pawns in the march of progress, 'The liberal reward of labour, therefore, [Adam Smith said] as it is the effect of increasing wealth, so it is the cause of increasing population. To complain of it is to lament over the necessary effect and cause of the greatest public prosperity.[27] Adam Smith did not believe that habit, custom or deliberate attempts at prudence would succeed in restraining propagation; man was incapable of controlling his own fertility.

[26] *Principles*, p. 100.   [27] Vol. I, p. 83.

Progress depended not on 'prudence' but on the openings for investment and the habit of accumulation. These were not adversely affected by increases in population. It has already been emphasised that this reinforced Adam Smith's optimistic view as to the continuation of the profitability of accumulation. This was based on his analysis of the probable indefinite continuation of openings for investment set out in the chapter 'Of the Different Employments of Capital'[28] (Bk II, Ch. V). His treatment of increases in the wage fund as a dynamic process was the consequence.

This brings out a contrast between Ricardo's and Adam Smith's treatment of wages pointed out by Taussig in his *Wages and Capital*.[29] Ricardo's method of reasoning about the payment of wages from capital in the framework of food production periods treated the wage fund as rigidly fixed for discrete production periods. James Mill was of course over-optimistic in claiming that it was easy to make any adjustments to the fixed production-period method of analysis required in order to make it conform to reality. He did not notice that it might involve nothing less than changing from a comparative static to a dynamic analysis. Those of the post-Ricardian classical economists who retained the wage-fund analysis seem to have retained this comparative static, instead of the dynamic, treatment of it.

(v) *Senior and Longfield*

It is well known that in the ten years after Ricardo's death interest in his analysis of the stationary state had greatly diminished. It was no longer regarded as relevant to contemporary conditions. One reflection of the change was scepticism as to the probability of population increases frustrating wage increases unless institutions (such as an ill-conceived poor law) encouraged population growth. In these circumstances discussions of wage theory acquired a new interest and importance, for wages above some subsistence level ceased to be regarded as inevitably temporary phenomena. Senior, it will be remembered, was one of those who believed that Malthus greatly underestimated the desire of people to improve their conditions and the strength of that desire as a curb on population growth in the absence of 'unwise' institutions.

[28] See on this the 'Addendum on Adam Smith's Explanation of the Falling Rate of Profit', pp. 220–3 below.   [29] pp. 178–81, L.S.E. reprint.

This change in outlook is reflected in Senior's work on wage theory and also in Longfield's. Neither was concerned with the effect of a supply function of labour based on population theory, indeed neither paid much attention to the supply function.[30]

The chief point of interest in Senior's theory is the treatment throughout of wages as a residual instead of profit. This was a revolutionary change. It was not a necessary consequence of dropping Ricardo's subsistence theory of wages. Adam Smith too had rejected a subsistence theory, but Adam Smith had treated profits as a residual. Adam Smith's views of net accumulation as independent of the rate of profits above a threshold minimum made it difficult for him to do otherwise.

The deliberate reversal of traditional procedure seems to me to reflect a shift in interest. In the Ricardian analysis capital had of course been recognised as the positive growth factor and Ricardo was deeply concerned with the effect of falling profit rates on the supply of capital. Nevertheless the subsistence theory of wages in conjunction with the law of diminishing returns was an inherent anti-growth element which must ultimately prevail. Once the anti-growth syndrome was broken up by rejection of the subsistence theory of wages (whether psychological or physiological subsistence was postulated) the law of diminishing returns in agriculture became relatively unimportant as an anti-growth influence. Continued growth became a serious possibility for which continuous capital accumulation was the essential condition. Senior himself stressed the supreme importance of capital as the basis of increased productivity.[31]

The essentials of this theory can be summarised. In the absence of rent and 'improper taxation' the produce is divided between labour and capital. Then 'the facts which decide in what proportions the capitalist and labourer share the common fund appear to be two: first, *the general rate of profit in the country on the advance of capital for a given period; and*, secondly, *the period which, in each particular case, has elapsed between the advance of capital and the receipt of the profit.*[32]

---

[30] Senior's discussion on population in his *Political Economy* is entirely separate from his discussion on wages and the latter does not refer to the former!

[31] See for instance Senior *Political Economy*, pp. 67–81.

[32] Ibid., pp. 185–6. Senior's italics.

His later statement in wage-fund terms added nothing whatever. This involved him in replacing the simple division of the final product by a division of labourers between the production of goods for the profit receivers and production of goods for the wage fund. (The actual real wage-rate would be affected, he pointed out, by the productivity of labour in producing wage goods.) The division of the labour force is of course determined by the rate of profit and the period of advance of capital.[33]

While Adam Smith was essentially optimistic as to the strength of the desire to save and invest, the classical economists of the nineteenth century including Ricardo himself were frequently pessimistic. Ricardo argued the motive of farmers and manufacturers for accumulation 'will diminish with every diminution of profit'.[34] While James Mill took pains to demonstrate the weakness of all motive for accumulation concluding 'that more than moderate effects can rarely flow from the motives to accumulation.'[35] Senior indeed was chiefly remembered by later economists for his analysis of the sacrifices involved in saving; he claimed that the sacrifice of abstinence from present enjoyment 'or to seek distant rather than immediate results, are among the most painful exertions of the human will.'[36]

Senior's conclusion that profit was the reward for the sacrifice of abstinence just as wages were the reward for labour, obviously helped to justify profit and to dispose of suggestions of exploitation. Nevertheless the fact that he was so concerned with this problem, taken in conjunction with stress on the importance of capital as a growth factor, suggests anxiety about political attacks on profits and that the supply of capital might dry up. Senior's treatment of wages as the residual at the no-rent margin, *after* the essential return to capital had been provided, can be interpreted as recognition of the importance of ensuring that the growth factor received sufficient reward to maintain growth.

*   *   *

Senior was by no means alone among the post-Ricardian classical economists in his fear of a decline in the rate of profits and consequent checks to accumulation and growth.

[33] Ibid., pp. 198–9.
[35] *Elements*, op. cit., pp. 234–7.

[34] *Principles*, Ch. VI, p. 122.
[36] Op. cit., p. 59.

In the chapter on wages in the *Wealth of Nations* the following passage occurs with reference to high or rising wages:

Is this improvement in the circumstances of the lower ranks of the people to be regarded as an advantage or as an inconveniency to the society? The answer seems at first sight abundantly plain. Servants, labourers and workmen of different kinds, make up the far greater part of any great political society. But what improves the circumstances of the greater part can never be regarded as an inconveniency to the whole. No society can surely be flourishing and happy, of which the far greater part of its members are poor and miserable. It is but equity besides, that they who feed, cloath and lodge the whole body of the people, should have such a share of the produce of their own labour, as to be themselves tolerably well fed, cloathed and lodged (Vol. I, p. 80).

Neither Ricardo nor Senior nor any of the other leading economists of the classical period would have disagreed with the sentiment; they were all concerned in varying degrees about poverty and distress. Nevertheless I do not believe that any of them would have written it with such carefree buoyancy. There would always have been the *caveat* 'as long as it is not at the expense of profits', for if it were it would simply lead to the death of the goose that laid the golden eggs. This fear was I believe genuine.

The underlying situation with regard to the supply of capital may have changed. Capital may have been plentiful in relation to openings for investment when Adam Smith wrote. He himself seemed to believe that the economy of Great Britain was progressive with capital and wealth increasing, a falling rate of profit and increasing real wages and population, but he had no fear of the rate of profit falling so low as to stop net investment. Were the economists of the first half of the nineteenth century faced with a fundamentally different situation? Was there in some sense a shortage of capital compared to Adam Smith's time? Or was net accumulation actually decreasing?

Whatever the facts about net accumulation may have been, politico-economic changes had taken place since the eighteenth century which undoubtedly influenced attitudes. The hostility shown by Adam Smith in the *Wealth of Nations* to the manufacturing as well as the mercantile capitalists is notorious. They were always trying to get the better of everyone else, to take advantage of others' weakness. Their interest in contrast to the landed interests was opposed to those of the community. Ricardo had of course changed all that even though Malthus and many others either disagreed or took a modified view. The manufacturers' interests had become identified with those of the community and with this anxiety naturally developed about capital and profits. Again whereas Adam Smith had been convinced that labour was inherently in a weak position in the market, it seems to me that the heirs to Ricardo thought the reverse. Times had changed, the social and economic conditions of production were changing, labour was comparatively speaking more congregated in towns, trade unions were more to the fore. Certainly political fear of the growing power of labour had increased. This fear is as evident in the work of McCulloch as in that of Senior, although McCulloch was sympathetic to the principle of the organisation of labour in trade unions and Senior was deeply opposed to it.[37] After all the French Revolution had occurred after the *Wealth of Nations* was written and the output of revolutionary and socialist literature was significant.

Such fears must have been at least partly responsible, it seems to me, for the emphasis on the limitational aspect of the Ricardian treatment of the wage fund by those economists, such as McCulloch and John Stuart Mill. who continued to use the concept. The contrast between their attitudes and that of Adam Smith is striking. To Adam Smith the formulation of his theory of the funds 'destined for the payment of wages' had evidently brought the keenest satisfaction. It enabled him to show that wages could rise *and* stay indefinitely above subsistence; it provided hope for the labouring classes. Moreover it showed how the natural monopsonistic advantages of the masters in the labour market was destroyed or diminished. From the time of Ricardo onwards the wages fund acquired a different connotation. It became the limiting factor which demonstrated that average real wages could not be increased at any particular time except by a decrease in employment. Since the wages fund itself would not

[37] For a most illuminating account of McCulloch's attitude see D. P. O'Brien's *J. R. McCulloch, a Study in Classical Economics*, Ch. XIV; on Senior's attitude see my *Nassau Senior and Classical Economics*, pp. 277 et seq.

increase so fast if profits fell, as net saving was dependent on the profit rate, it provided a defence of existing profits. Senior's derivation of the wages fund as a residual after provision for profits had been made fits in with these opinions, and with anxieties about the rate of profits and the supply of capital. The importance of the limitational aspect of the wage fund is perhaps most clearly shown in John Stuart Mill's final exposition of the wage-fund theory. Nothing could be done, he showed, to alleviate the situation of the working classes unless capital was increased, so any immediate advantage gained at the expense of capital accumulation would be to their future detriment. Indeed it seems to me that the importance that Mill attached to the family of limitational conclusions drawn from the wage-fund theory is the explanation of his retention of it in the editions of the *Principles* published after he had admitted the validity of the criticisms of it. I am sure that he remained convinced that the conclusions were correct although he was unable to find another way of proving them, and they were important in relation to his hopes for the improvement of the conditions of the working classes.

All these anxieties seem to me to have been reinforced by the decline in the influence of Ricardo's model after his death. For as this influence dwindled so of course did belief in the correctness of his theory of distribution. In that theory the suggestion of exploitation of labour in the labour theory of value had been by-passed by the subsistence theory of wages, based on Malthusian population theory, and the conflict of interest between landowners and community attracted attention rather than that between employers and employed. The decline of the influence of Ricardo's model thus created an immense analytical void. Its very existence invited political concentration on the numerous passages in the *Wealth of Nations* and in Ricardo's statement of the labour theory of value which considered in isolation implied, or could be interpreted to imply, the exploitation of labour.[38]

Thus even if there were no economic basis as such for anxiety about capital accumulation, politically based pressures on profit

[38] Malthus it will be remembered called Adam Smith's language 'exceptionable' in that he represented 'profits as a deduction from the produce of labour' and referred to Landlords 'invidiously' as 'loving to reap where they have not sown'. *Principles of Political Economy*, 2nd edn, p. 76. See also Meek, op. cit.

might jeopardise it and with it growth. The need to fill the analytical void was felt perhaps even more strongly by Montifort Longfield in Ireland than by Senior in England. Longfield set out his reasons for dealing with distribution in the Preface to his *Lectures on Political Economy* published in 1834.

> The distribution of wealth among the different orders of society [he says] appears not to have attracted much attention, although it is the most important subject in *Political Economy*.

Fame is indeed a vanity; Ricardo's preoccupation with the problem is passed over though his analysis as developed by McCulloch is criticised in subsequent lectures. Adam Smith's 'notions on this point' were described as 'very vague and undefined'.[39]

Longfield explained that he had

> accordingly endeavoured to place the subject of profits in a juster light, and to show that the only order in which a correct analysis of the sources of revenue can be carried on is – 1st Rent, 2nd Profits, 3rd Wages. From this analysis I think that some important consequence can be drawn. It can be proved how impossible it is to *regulate wages generally*, either by combinations of workmen, or by legislative enactments. Such regulations are frequently shewn to be impolitic or impracticable, on account of the numerous evasions to which they would give rise; but the argument can be carried farther, and it can be shown that such regulations must be ineffectual even if all parties were on all occasions sincerely anxious to comply with them. The case would be found analogous to a law limiting the price of provisions in times of scarcity. The spirit of such a law could not be obeyed, for it would require that all who were willing to give the legal price for provisions should be able to procure them, and the deficient supply would render that impossible.[40]

Here the issue is baldly stated. The concern, the purpose, of the inquiry is to show that intervention by unions or state in the labour market is impossible, much stronger than impolitic. The reason given in effect is that total demand would need to be

39 Longfield, op. cit., Preface, pp. v–vi.
40 Ibid., pp. vii–viii. Longfield's italics.

controlled and it is implied that this is impossible. Longfield's anxiety about the labour movement and its consequences for progress are clearly stated in the peroration to the last lecture in this series on p. 237.

> Undoubtedly, a dense population is in many respects highly favourable to the diffusion of knowledge and civilization, but it does not necessarily lead to such results. Freedom and security are equally essential; and the intellectual moral, and religious education of the people are not less necessary. If these are carefully protected and promoted by our institutions, and if no artificial stimulus is given to the increase of population, we have every reason to hope, that with the progress of society, population and wealth will increase together, and that more human beings will be supported in greater comfort than heretofore. At least our trust in the wisdom and goodness of the Supreme Being, would lead us to expect with confidence that it will be so. For experience and reason alike prove that there is a certain degree of poverty among the inhabitants of a country, which is incompatible with obedience to the laws, with an intellectual or moral education, and is adverse to the propagation of true religion.

Could any sentiment be more appropriate, or should we say more acceptable, to the Establishment in the Ireland of the 1830s? The optimistic religiosity of the passage just quoted comes at the end of a careful and lengthy discussion on profit and wage theory in three lectures (VIII, IX and X). In these it becomes clear that, like Senior, Longfield had a profound conviction in the power of technological progress and human restraint to offset the effect of the law of diminishing returns in agriculture. Failure to understand what he called 'the driest and least interesting part of Political Economy' might threaten continuation of progress. He believed evidently that this was a serious danger.[41]

As everyone knows, Longfield developed a 'discounted productivity of labour' theory of wages. He started his analysis by determining the rate of profit. It will be remembered that he set out a primitive marginal productivity theory of profit in conjunction with a theory of a continuous supply schedule of capital as a function of the rate of profit. The latter was based on a careful

[41] Ibid., p. 242.

discussion of the issues involved in decisions to save. He seems to have treated this savings function as always relevant, not merely as a long run influence. The wages of labour then, as in Senior's theory, depended on the proportion of the total product taken by profits and the productivity of labour in the production of goods for use by labour, i.e. with the resources left available after satisfying the requirements of the profit receivers. But Longfield introduced an entirely new causal explanation of the process, for though the significance of capital was that it provided the necessary advances to labour to enable it to be productive, the rate of profit was seen as the discount rate which reduced the gross output of labour to its present value in terms of labour productivity.[42] This present value formed labour's share which was thus derived from the productivity of labour. The share of capital also was seen as *directly* related to its productive contribution and the conditions under which capital became available to make that contribution. The analysis was not limited to the stationary state.

Why should Longfield have suddenly evolved this important concept and approach? It can, I think be explained on purely analytical grounds, in terms of Longfield's starting point from Say's theorem that the value of factors must be derived from the value of their productive contributions. This led him directly to the marginal productivity analysis of capital's contribution, a point that Say failed to reach. The attempt to combine this with an 'advances' theory of capital led almost automatically to a discounted productivity theory of wages. His new components were the character of his supply function for capital and the rudimentary marginal productivity analysis. With these he showed how the shares of profits and wages were determined without any implications of exploitation of labour. His analysis naturally ignored the wage fund concept; it was unnecessary for his purpose. 'Unwise institutions' appeared in his analysis as the element which would jeopardise the natural tendency of men to improve their position by restraint in propagation. The inherent tendencies of economic motivation would he believed lead automatically to progress without limit of period, despite diminishing returns in agriculture.

Longfield appeared to be convinced that the results thus achieved would be the best possible because progress would be

42 Ibid., Lectures VIII, IX and X.

realised in a system in which all elements would precisely adjust to each other. Any intervention to fix prices was doomed to failure and in any case would upset the adjustment of supply and demand.

In Longfield's system all the prices given by non-economic parameters had disappeared; all prices were flexible and explained in terms of economic influences and thus all quantities were related to prices. The aggregates had disappeared from the theory of distribution and hence the need to try to determine labour's share in terms of the wage fund. Longfield can formally be given the title of the first of the Victorian economists, or perhaps the first of the neo-classics.

(vi) Growth and Wage Theory

Adam Smith's introduction of the idea that continuous growth was not only possible but necessary in order to avoid the dullness and misery of a stationary state altered attitudes. Previously interest in growth had been as it were optional. Increases in wealth might be desirable to increase national power, or they might be desired for their own sake – the way to Eldorado. But growth might not even be a subject of major concern. It did not for instance play a prominent part in Cantillon's *Essai*. This was much more concerned with showing how resources were allocated, and income distributed, in a stationary society with a given aggregate demand dependent on the character of the landownership system. He made no suggestion that such a stationary state was unpleasant; he merely pointed out that the size of landownership units would affect the size of the population and the proportion of luxuries to necessities produced. Even the Physiocrats though analysing conditions of growth with great care appeared to regard a stationary society, properly based on free markets and competition, as satisfactory.

After Adam Smith however the position appeared to be quite different. Some of his successors by dropping his theory of population and rejecting the Ricardian stagnation thesis seem to have become enthusiasts for growth for its own sake. McCulloch, Senior and possibly also Longfield provide examples. Growth was no longer seen by them as necessary to avoid disaster perhaps, but it was necessary to improve standards of living for the working classes by raising wages. The implication, that could be derived from the *Wealth of Nations*, that the faster the growth the better for this purpose was adopted seemingly without question. It easily became identified with the maintenance of high rates of profit; this is particularly clear in the case of McCulloch. Certainly Senior and McCulloch were well aware of and, concerned about social costs of growth.[43] They devoted attention to the problems of workers in dying industries, the conditions of the growing industrial towns, the fluctuations in employment, conditions of work in mines and factories, public health and so on. They accepted Adam Smith's conclusion as to the necessity of education. They were prepared for government intervention to remedy some of these ills where they thought it practicable, accepting implicitly that the rate of growth might be slowed down thereby, but not in fact considering the possibility that there might be some optimum rate of growth in terms of socio-economic welfare.

Ricardo and John Stuart Mill both, however, were concerned with the idea, not of an optimum rate of growth for both were convinced that growth must ultimately cease, but of an optimum position for the cessation of growth. Ricardo pointed out that in a country in which all the land was occupied continued capital accumulation would become undesirable, for it would lead to ever-increasing pressure of population on food supples. This could go on until practically all resources were swallowed up in supporting a large population at a miserable subsistence level. Much better, he suggested, for capital accumulation to cease before this, while there was still a reasonable quantity of resources available for purposes more interesting than grubbing a miserable subsistence from the soil.[44] John Stuart Mill went much further than this. He himself rejected indefinite growth as a worth-while criterion in any case. But he realised that acceptance of cessation of growth before it was inevitable involved a change in the outlook of society with regard to the desirability of ever more material wealth. It also required deliberate encouragement to changes which would lead to a more even distribution of wealth. This could not be achieved by labour trying to make the aggregate wage bill exceed the wage fund; this

[43] On McCulloch on growth see D. O'Brien, Ch. XII, and on social policy, Chs XIII and XIV. On Senior see my *Nassau Senior*, Part II, Ch. I.

[44] *Principles*, op. cit., Ch. V, p. 99.

was doomed to fail. Rather, attempts must be made to alter the character of the labour supply and its rate of growth by improved education; experiments must be tried with new ways of organising production through co-operatives and lastly of course he made various suggestions for tax reform. Without such changes, suggestions to restrict growth would appear as intended to put an end to increases in wages. These things are set out in Mill's famous chapter 'On the probable Futurity of the Labouring Classes' in his *Principles*. It is in the preceding chapter, 'Of the Stationary State', that he mounts his attack on the goal of ever more wealth. Its topical relevance in the year 1973 tempts me to quote from it at some length. The mere increase of production and accumulation are in themselves, he says,

> of little importance, so long as either the increase of population or anything else prevents the mass of the people from reaping any part of the benefit of them. I know not why it should be a matter for congratulation that persons who are already richer than any one needs to be, should have doubled their means of consuming things which give little or no pleasure except as representative of wealth. . . . It is only in the backward countries of the world that increased production is still an important object; in those most advanced, what is economically needed is a better distribution, of which one indispensable means is a stricter restraint of population.[45]

and further on

> A population may be too crowded, though all be amply provided with food and raiment. It is not good for man to be kept perforce at all times in the presence of his species. . . . Nor is there much satisfaction in contemplating the world with nothing left to the spontaneous activity of nature; with every rood of land brought into cultivation, which is capable of growing food for human beings; every flowery waste or natural pasture ploughed up, all quadrupeds or birds which are not domesticated for man's use exterminated as his rivals for food, every hedgerow or superfluous tree rooted out, and scarcely a place left where a wild shrub or flower could grow without

[45] *Principles*, op. cit., Bk IV, Ch. VI, p. 749.

being eradicated as a weed in the name of improved agriculture.[46]

Addendum on Adam Smith's Explanation of a Falling Rate of Profit

Adam Smith is sometimes regarded as holding a stagnation thesis based on the tendency of the rate of profit to fall. There is, however, a distinction to be made between explaining the circumstances under which the rate of profit will fall so low that stagnation will result, and believing that such circumstances are likely to occur. Adam Smith's full explanation of the circumstances leading to stagnation needs to be considered together with his comments on the improbability of these circumstances occurring except in conjunction with particularly restrictive types of institutions. This leads to the conclusion that he did not regard stagnation as either inevitable or even probable. He dealt with two problems, the opportunities for investment and the effect of the increase of capital on wages.

Like his contemporaries Adam Smith believed that the rate of profit tended to fall as capital accumulated. Thus he declared at the beginning of Chapter XI, 'Of the Profits of Stock':

The increase of stock, which raises wages, tends to lower profit. When the stocks of many rich merchants are turned into the same trade, their mutual competition naturally tends to lower its profit; and where there is a like increase of stock in all the different trades carried on in the same society, the same competition must produce the same effect in them all (Vol. I, p. 89).

It is with Adam Smith's explanation of the second reason, to which Ricardo objected so much,[47] that this note is mainly concerned. It has to be pieced together from different sections of the *Wealth of Nations*. It turns on two assumptions. The first is that

[46] Ibid, p. 750. Marshall's development of Mill's general theme (though not of nature conservancy) in his paper 'The Future of the Working Classes' read in 1873, is well worth reading. It contains an implication that there is a problem of an optimum rate of growth in terms of socio-economic welfare. (See *Memorials of Alfred Marshall*, pp. 101 et seq.)

[47] Ricardo, *Principles*, Ch. XXI. Adam Smith reversed the argument for the case of decreases in stock in the declining state (*Wealth of Nations*, Vol. I, p. 95).

the demand for individual goods is satiable; it is only in relation
to the desire for variety and display that demand can be regarded
as insatiable. Thus in one of the most famous passages of the
Wealth of Nations in Book I, Chapter XI, Adam Smith says:

> The desire of food is limited in every man by the narrow capa-
> city of the human stomach; but the desire of the conveniences
> and ornaments of building, dress, equipage, and household
> furniture, seems to have no limit or certain boundary (Vol I,
> p. 165).

Further the demand for any particular good is limited at any
particular price. Thus the prices at which individual goods can be
sold will fall as output increased and with it the profitability of
producing them.

Adam Smith's second assumption was that the capacity to produce a variety of goods in any *one* country was restricted, so that
it was impossible to maintain the rate of profits by exploiting the
desire for variety indefinitely within an individual country; production would not create its own demand. Thus in his discussion
of the various ways in which capital can be employed in Book II,
Chapter V, 'Of the Different Employment of Capitals', he states:

> When the produce of any particular branch of industry exceeds
> what the demand of the country requires, the surplus must be
> sent abroad, and exchanged for something for which there is a
> demand at home. Without such exportation, a part of the pro-
> ductive labour of the country must cease, and the value of its
> annual produce diminish. The land and labour of Great Britain
> produces generally more corn, woollens, and hardware, than
> the demand of the home market requires. The surplus part of
> them, therefore, must be sent abroad, and exchanged for some-
> thing for which there is a demand at home. It is only by means
> of such exportation, that this surplus can acquire a value suffi-
> cient to compensate for the labour and expense of producing
> it (Vol. I, p. 352).

This has been ribaldly called the 'pots and pans' argument.

The opportunity of foreign trade thus played an important
part in retarding declines in the rate of growth and to this Adam
Smith clearly attached great importance, for he pointed out

> The extent of the home-trade and of the capital which can be

employed in it, is necessarily limited by the value of the surplus produce of all those distant places within the country which
have occasion to exchange their respective productions with
one another. That of the foreign trade of consumption, by the
value of the surplus produce of the whole country and of what
can be purchased with it (Vol. I, p. 353).

But the carrying trade provided a last possible outlet when the
capital stock of any country had become so large 'that it cannot
be all employed in supplying the consumption, and supporting
the productive labour' of that country, for it was limited only
'by the value of the surplus produce' of the whole world and 'is
capable of absorbing the greatest capitals' (Vol. I, p. 353). This
was consistent with Adam Smith's original explanation that
exchange stimulated production by affording markets for surplus
produce; the emphasis on the importance of the variety of goods
as a stimulus to production may well have been borrowed from
Hume.[48] The opening up of new markets by inventions or foreign
trade and the carrying trade were the main ways of avoiding the
decline in the rates of profits and cessation of accumulation and
growth. Hence it was only countries without such opportunities,
or whose form of government discouraged inventions and trade
and investment, that faced serious dangers of a cessation of
growth. China, the only example of a stationary state which Adam
Smith was able to think of, might have been richer, he thought,
with different laws and institutions and if it had had more
interest in foreign commerce.[49]

Undoubtedly Adam Smith was optimistic about the opportunities of investment. Moreover though the other influence on the
rate of profit, wages, was recognised as lowering the rate of profit
as wages rose while capital was increasing, there was a moderat-
ing factor. Increases in wage-rates stimulated increases in the
population and therefore in the size of the labour force, thus
slowing down the increase in wage-rates. Further increases in
capital helped to increase the productivity of labour by making
possible the increased use of machinery and development of the

[48] See Hume's 'Essay on Commerce', pp. 10, 13–14 (Rotwein's edition).
Oddly enough Tucker does not refer to this discussion in Bk II, Ch. V
of the *Wealth of Nations* in his account of Adam Smith's theory of the
falling rate of profit (Tucker, Ch. IV).
[49] See p. 203 above.

division of labour, and increases in wages in themselves tended to increase both the capacity of labour to work and the incentive to work. Thus whereas Ricardo's thesis showed increases of the supply of labour in conjunction with diminishing returns in agriculture as the cause of the ultimate fall of the profit rate, Adam Smith's thesis showed increases in the supply of labour as helping to retard that fall.

Index